Towards an Integrated Environmental Permit in China

Xiheng Chen

Towards an Integrated Environmental Permit in China

A Legal Study Based on EU Regulatory Experiences

Springer

Xiheng Chen
School of Law
Foshan University
Guangdong, China

ISBN 978-981-97-5187-7 ISBN 978-981-97-5188-4 (eBook)
https://doi.org/10.1007/978-981-97-5188-4

This Springer imprint is published by the registered company Springer Nature Singapore Pte Ltd.
The registered company address is: 152 Beach Road, #21-01/04 Gateway East, Singapore 189721, Singapore

Preface

Industrial production processes account for a considerable share of the overall pollution in China, as well as in Europe, due to their emissions into the air, water, and land. Different approaches to controlling emissions into the air, water, or soil separately bear the risk of being ineffective to combat the pollution as a whole: when pollution is eliminated in one media, there is a risk that the pollution will increase in another media. In order to combat the hydra-headed ogre of pollution, the legal framework that attempts to implement integrated pollution prevention and control using the permit instrument was adopted in 1996 at the EU level and in 2020 in China. At the EU level, the idea of applying an integrated environmental permit was introduced in 1996 by the Integrated Pollution Prevention Control Directive (IPPCD), later transformed into the Industrial Emissions Directive (IED) in 2010. In China, on 9 December 2020, the State Council took an important step towards an integrated environmental permit system: it adopted an Administrative Regulation that establishes one permit system that regulates industrial emissions into various environmental media.

Compared to the EU regulatory efforts towards integration that have lasted for over two and a half decades, China's exploration is still at the embryonic stage. In this sense, the establishment of the emissions permit system at the EU level can be used as a helpful reference to understand how the design of the emissions permit system adopted in China may be improved for implementing an integrated approach. This book aims to examine to what extent the regulatory design of the emissions permit system in China, considering the EU regulatory experiences towards integration and seen from the perspective of the specific Chinese situation, provides possibilities for or barriers to the implementation of integrated pollution prevention and control.

In order to answer the main research question, the research in this book is divided into four steps. This first step is to identify the core elements of a regulatory framework for establishing an integrated environmental permit system on the basis of a doctrinal study, in particular a literature review, so as to provide a conceptual framework for analyzing regulatory attempts to create an integrated environmental permit system in the EU and China, respectively, and, subsequently, for the comparative analysis between these two systems (Chap. 2). Second, while keeping the focus on the core elements of an integrated environmental permit system as identified in Chap. 2, Chap. 3 provides an in-depth legal examination of the IED in order to understand how the emissions permit system of the IED that attempts to implement an integrated environmental permit has been developed in terms of its regulatory design and relevant case law. With the same focus, but moving to address the Chinese jurisdiction, the third step examines how the emissions permit system has been developed in China to implement an integrated environmental permit in terms of its regulatory design (Chap. 4). Following the above analysis, Chap. 5 will undertake a comparative analysis between the EU and Chinese regulatory approaches to establishing an integrated environmental permit and then discuss what sort of regulatory possibilities for or barriers to implementing an integrated permit system appearing in the EU may also be followed in China. After this discussion, the answer to the main research question will be given.

The book was based on my doctoral work which would have not been finished without the generous support of Guangzhou government. I am extremely grateful to Prof. Marjan Peeters and Prof. Zhiping Li, my Ph.D. supervisors. They gave me endless trust and inspiring comments during my writing. Many professors, colleagues, and friends encouraged and guided me to be a good researcher. It is not possible to mention all of them. But I still want to thank some of them: Prof. Zhanwen Que, Prof. Bo Miao, Prof. Huizhen Chen, Dr. Ancui liu, and Dr. Xiaoya Cheng.

Guangdong, China Xiheng Chen

Contents

Abbreviations

BAT	Best Available Techniques
BAT-AELs	Best Available Technique-associated Emission Levels
BATNEEC	Best Available Technology Not Entailing Excessive Costs
BREFs	BAT Reference Documents
CO_2	Carbon Dioxide
COD	Chemical Oxygen Demand
EAP	Environmental Action Program
EC	European Community
EIA	Environmental Impact Assessment
ENGO	Environmental Non-governmental Organization
ETS	Emissions Trading System
EU	European Union
GHG	Greenhouse Gas
HFCs	Hydrofluorocarbons
IED	Industrial Emissions Directive
IEF	Information Exchange Forum
IPPC	Integrated Pollution Prevention and Control
IPPCD	Integrated Pollution Prevention and Control Directive
MWth	Megawatt of Thermal Input
NEC	National Emission Reduction Commitments
NGO	Non-governmental Organization
NOx	Nitrogen Oxides
ODS	Ozone-depleting Substances
OECD	Organisation for Economic Co-operation and Development
SO_2	Sulphur Dioxide
SOx	Sulphur Oxides
TEC	Treaty Establishing the European Community
TEU	Treaty on European Union
TFEU	Treaty on the Functioning of the European Union
TWG	Technical Working Group

UK	The United Kingdom
USA	The United States of America
WFD	Water Framework Directive

Chapter 1
Introduction

Abstract In order to combat the hydra-headed ogre of pollution, the legal framework that attempts to implement integrated pollution prevention and control using the permit instrument was adopted in 1996 at the EU level and in 2020 in China. By setting forth the research background, research questions and introducing the research methodology and research structure of this book, this chapter initiates the exploration of 'to what extent the regulatory design of the emissions permit system in China, considering the EU regulatory experiences in relation to integration and seen from the perspective of the specific Chinese situation, provides possibilities for or barriers to the implementation of integrated pollution prevention and control' in later chapters.

> *This is a fable about the hydra-headed ogre of pollution (the Hydra). [...] The Hydra became quite bold in its attacks in the air, water and land, showing different heads at different places. [...] As the saga unfolded, it became apparent that the felling of one head of the Hydra often resulted in the appearance of another. [...] Instead of being eliminated or neutralized (by chemical or physical processes that changed it into a non-pollutant), a pollutant was simply transferred from one medium to another. Pollution controllers failed to realize that each head (of pollution) arose from its source (the Hydra's body or wastes) and that the whole Hydra constituted the real enemy.*[1]

1.1 Introduction

This research addresses how to combat the hydra-headed ogre of pollution caused by industry.[2] At its core, there are at least two strategies for regulators to combat pollution in the different media of the environment. The first strategy is to take

---

[1] Lakshman Guruswamy, 'Integrating Thoughtways: Re-opening of the Environmental Mind' (1989) Wis. L. Rev. 463, 463.

[2] As the quote above already shows, this allegory is borrowed from Lakshman Guruswamy (1989), 463 (In Greek mythology, the Hydra is a monster with multiple heads: these symbolize, in Guruswamy's allegory, the different forms of pollution in the different environmental media, see 'Hydra', https://www.britannica.com/topic/Hydra-Greek-mythology, accessed on 6 May 2022.

X. Chen, *Towards an Integrated Environmental Permit in China*,
https://doi.org/10.1007/978-981-97-5188-4_1

separate actions to reduce pollution in each environmental media—air, water, and land. However, this strategy has the risk of being ineffective to combat pollution as a whole: when pollution is eliminated in one media, there is a risk that pollution will increase in another media. Literature has addressed certain pollution transfers that have occurred in practice due to addressing specific media separately, which is presented below:

- '[T]he provisions of the Clean Air Act directed at reducing sulfur dioxide require the use of "scrubbers" in smoke stacks. Huge quantities of lime, limestone solution, and water are sprayed on exhaust gases as they flow up power plant smokestacks. Sulfur dioxide in the gas reacts with the spray and forms a solution from which sulfur dioxide is later removed, strained, and disposed of in the form of sludge.'[3] The creation of large quantities of sludge resulted in water or solid waste disposal problems, which could then cause greater overall damage to the environment.[4]
- While the Montreal Protocol on Substances that Deplete the Ozone Layer successfully phased out ozone-depleting substances (ODS), it led to a shift towards hydrofluorocarbons (HFCs) which are potent greenhouse gases that can be hundreds to thousands of times more potent than carbon dioxide (CO_2) in contributing to climate change.[5] Hence, while addressing emissions that damage the ozone layer, the replacing gases contributed to another environmental problem, climate change, for which new regulatory approaches need to be established.[6]

It can be seen that, when applying a separate approach, new environmental problems can be generated that substitute the old ones. If these new problems are not sufficiently recognized and addressed, the initial approach to targeting one environmental problem is not sufficiently effective given the increase of another environmental problem.

Driven by the ineffectiveness of separate actions against pollution to each media, regulators have explored another strategy, namely integrated pollution prevention and control. In this research, the legal framework that attempts to implement integrated

---

[3] Lakshman Guruswamy, 'Integration & Biocomplexity' (2000) 27 Ecology L. Q. 1191, 1208.

[4] Lakshman Guruswamy, 'The Case for Integrated Pollution Control' (1991) 54(4) Law and Contemporary Problems 41, 44–45. This example is derived from environmental law practice in the USA.

[5] See Jonathan B. Wiener, 'Precaution and Climate Change', in: Cinnamon P. Carlarne, Kevin R. Gray and Richard G. Tarasofsky (eds), *The Oxford Handbook of International Climate Change Law* (Oxford 2016), 171 and 174–175; Also see 'Recent International Developments under the Montreal Protocol', available at https://www.epa.gov/ozone-layer-protection/recent-international-developments-under-montreal-protocol, accessed on 18 December 2019.

[6] The Kigali Amendment to the Montreal Protocol, which entered into force on 1 January 2019, called for the phasing-out of hydrofluorocarbons (HFCs). See 'The Montreal Protocol Evolves to Fight Climate Change', available at https://www.unido.org/our-focus-safeguarding-environment-implementation-multilateral-environmental-agreements-montreal-protocol/montreal-protocol-evolves-fight-climate-change, accessed on 16 January 2022. See also for a discussion: Mark W. Roberts, 'Finishing the job: The Montreal Protocol moves to phase down hydrofluorocarbons' (2017) 26(3) RECIEL 220.

pollution prevention and control using a permit instrument in the EU and the mainland of the People's Republic of China[7] (hereafter referred to as China) is examined. The aim of this chapter is to introduce the research background, the research question, the research methodology and the research structure.

1.2 Research Background

The idea of an integrated permit system was introduced into legislation already in 1996 at EU level, and in China—twenty-four years later—in 2020 to control pollution resulting from the operation of industrial installations. In the EU, permit regimes for industrial installations represent the 'backbone' of environmental law in all Member States.[8] At the EU level, the idea of applying an integrated environmental permit was introduced in 1996 with the Integrated Pollution Prevention Control Directive (IPPCD),[9] which was later transformed into the Industrial Emissions Directive (IED) in 2010.[10] Recital 3 of the IED states: 'different approaches to controlling emissions into air, water or soil separately may encourage the shifting of pollution from one environmental medium to another'.[11] Consequently, the IPPCD and later the IED laid down rules on integrated prevention and control of pollution caused by industries, in order to achieve a high level of protection of the environment taken as a whole.[12] This objective, 'a high level of protection of the environment taken as a whole', states that a high environmental goal will be combined with an integrated approach. Several studies have been carried out to examine to what extent the IPPCD and later the IED implement integrated pollution prevention and control. Among these studies, most emphasis in the legal literature has been put on the extent to which the concept of the so-called best available techniques (BAT)—a concept prescribed by the

[7] In this book, the research is limited to the mainland of China, and it does not include the specific regulatory approaches in Taiwan, Hong Kong and Macao.

[8] Eberhard Bohne and Doris Dietze, 'Pollution prevention and control in Europe revisited' (2004) 13 European Energy and Environmental Law Review 198, 199. See also for a discussion: Geert Van Hoorick, 'Environmental permits: origins and nature and recent tendencies' in Michael Faure (eds), *Elgar Encyclopedia of Environmental Law* (Elgar 2020), 231–232.

[9] Council Directive 96/61/EC of 24 September 1996 concerning integrated pollution prevention and control (1996) OJ L 257/26 (IPPCD). This Directive was later codified in 2008: Directive 2008/1/EC of the European Parliament and of the Council of 15 January 2008 concerning integrated pollution prevention and control (Codified version) (2008) OJ L 24/8. In addition to the special note, the IPPCD in this chapter refers to Directive 96/61/EC.

[10] Directive 2010/75/EU of the European Parliament and of the Council of 24 November 2010 on industrial emissions (integrated pollution prevention and control) (2010) OJ L 334/159 (IED).

[11] Almost the same recital was also provided in the IPPCD: 'different approaches to controlling emissions into the air, water or soil separately may encourage the shifting of pollution between the various environmental media rather than protecting the environment as a whole'. See IPPCD recital 7.

[12] IPPCD art 1 and IED art 1.

IPPCD and later the IED[13]—can facilitate the implementation of integrated pollution prevention and control. In light of this, the literature has discussed several issues, such as re-regulation or de-regulation,[14] centralization or decentralization,[15] generic or case-specific decision-making,[16] and soft law or hard law.[17] These discussions in the literature are relevant for addressing the question—which is subject of this research—of how to deal with the incommensurability of environmental goods to implement integration.[18] The reports on the implementation of the IED and the development of relevant case law provide further insights into this question.[19]

In China, efforts have been made since 2016 to establish an integrated emissions permit. In 2016, the State Council of China issued the Implementation Plan for the Permit System for Controlling Emissions, aiming to establish an integrated emissions permit as a core instrument to control industrial pollution.[20] Since this Implementation Plan was adopted, a trial approach to establishing one emissions permit system was undertaken. A set of policies to undertake this implementation plan were issued by the environmental ministry.[21] In addition, on 10 January 2018, a trial legislation with binding force was adopted by the environmental ministry: Administrative Measures on Emission Permitting (for Trial Implementation).[22] The aim of these efforts was for the State Council of China to gain experience adopting an administrative regulation on emissions permits. On 9 December 2020, the State Council took an important step towards an integrated environmental permit system: it adopted an Administrative Regulation that establishes one permit system for industries that regulates emissions into various environmental media.[23] However, literature

[13] See a further discussion in Chap. 3.

[14] Marc Pallemaerts, 'The Proposed IPPC Directive: Re-regulation or De-regulation?' (1996) 5(6) European Energy and Environmental Law Review 174.

[15] Michael G. Faure and Jürgen C. Lefevere, 'The Draft Directive on Integrated Pollution Prevention and Control: An Economic Perspective' (1996) 5(4) European Energy and Environmental Law Review 112.

[16] Eberhard Bohne and Doris Dietze (2004).

[17] Charalampos Koutalakis, Aron Buzogany and Tanja A. Börzel, 'When soft regulation is not enough: The integrated pollution prevention and control directive of the European Union' (2010) 4(3) Regulation & Governance 329.

[18] For a discussion of the options to deal with the incommensurability of environmental goods to implement integration, see Sect. 2.3.1.3 of Chap. 2.

[19] See a further discussion in Chap. 3.

[20] State Council, Implementation Plan for the Permit System for Controlling Emissions (in Chinese: 控制污染物排放许可制实施方案的通知 国办发〔2016〕81号), 10 November 2016.

[21] For information about the policies to deliver on the Implementation Plan for the Permit System for Controlling Emissions, see 'Resouces' (in Chinese: 文件库), http://www.mee.gov.cn/wjk/?keyword=控制污染物排放许可制实施方案, accessed on 15 October 2020.

[22] Ministry of Environmental Protection (abolished on 17 March 2018), Administrative Measures on Emissions Permitting (for Trial Implementation) (in Chinese: 排污许可管理办法(试行)), 10 January 2018 (no longer in force).

[23] State Council, Administrative Regulation on Emissions Permitting (in Chinese: 排污许可管理条例), 9 December 2020. See a further discussion in Chap. 4.

on China's effort to implement integrated prevention and control of industrial pollution through a permit system is in general scarce. The following highlights some of the main sources of literature. First, already in 2006, Li and Cai criticized that the previously existing sectoral emission permits led to administrative inefficiency and thus called for one permit to regulate industrial emissions of air pollutants, water pollutants and noise.[24] During the period of the trial approach to establish one emissions permit system, Li and Chen examined the organizational foundation and barriers for implementing an integrated emissions permit system in China, mainly focusing on the institutional coordination between the stage of granting permits and the inspection stage.[25] At the same time, Xie advocated a legal framework that underpins the implementation of best available techniques in the process of establishing emissions permits and strengthens the coordination between emissions permits and other environmental regulatory instruments, but why and how such a legal framework should be established is not addressed in further detail in his study.[26] The Administrative Regulation on Emissions Permitting has not caused much discussion by scholars since its adoption in late 2020. Two publications can be highlighted.[27] Liu and Wang criticized that the Administrative Regulation on Emissions Permitting does not provide for a clear scope of emissions permitting; fails to establish an effective coordination mechanism with other environmental regulatory instruments and, furthermore, they worried that the Administrative Regulation on Emissions Permitting may not be fully implemented by the relevant enterprises and governments.[28] Shi and Yang also criticized that the emissions permit system prescribed by the Administrative Regulation on Emissions Permitting does not effectively coordinate with other environmental regulatory instruments, and they pointed out that it fails to provide for clear rules on the relationship between the implementation of emissions permitting and the achievement of environmental quality standards.[29] None of these studies directly address the issue of preventing the transfer of pollution from one

---

[24] Qijia Li and Wencan Cai, 'The Integration and Expansion of an Emission Permit System in China' (in Chinese: 论我国排污许可证制度的整合与拓展) (2006) 00 Environmental and Resources Law Review 171.

[25] Zhiping Li and Xiheng Chen, 'On the Institutional Foundation and Barriers for Implementing an Integrated Emission Permit System' (in Chinese: 综合排污许可制度运行的体制基础及困境分析) (2019) 01 Journal of Political Science and Law 104.

[26] Wei Xie, 'Research on the Implementation of China's Pollutant Discharge Permit' (in Chinese: 论我国排污许可证的执行) (2018) 33(6) Legal Forum 105, 111–112.

[27] In addition to the two literature sources highlighted in this chapter, some other literature sources, which do not focus on analyzing the Administrative Regulation on Emissions Permitting, but do mention this legislation and make some comments about it, will also be addressed in this book; see Chap. 4.

[28] Ning Liu and Jin Wang, 'The Regulation on the Administration of Pollutant Discharge Permits: Characteristics, Challenges and Responses' (in Chinese: 《排污许可管理条例》的特点、挑战与应对) (2021) 49(9) Environmental Protection 13.

[29] Xueying Shi and Bowen Yang, 'Research on Legislative Coordination and Normative Co-Governance Structure of China's Emission Permit Management System' (in Chinese: 我国排污许可管理制度的立法协同与规范共治结构研究) (2021) 42(05) Journal of Dalian University of Technology (Social Sciences) 78.

environmental sector to another. Hence, the developments in relation to establishing and implementing an integrated emissions permit system in China deserves further analysis.

Compared to the EU regulatory efforts towards integration that have been ongoing for over two and a half decades, China's exploration is still at the embryonic stage. In this sense, the establishment of the emissions permit system at the EU level can be used as a helpful reference to understand how the design of emissions permit system adopted in China may be improved with respect to implementing an integrated approach.

1.3 Research Questions

As mentioned above, since 2016 China has been exploring the reform of its emissions permit system aiming to implement integrated pollution prevention and control. In view of this, in 2020 China adopted the Administrative Regulation on Emissions Permitting that establishes one permit procedure covering different environmental media. However, it must be examined *to what extent the regulatory design of the emissions permit system in China provides possibilities for or barriers to the implementation of integrated pollution prevention and control.* In order to analyze opportunities and limits of the emissions permit system for implementing integration in China, a comparative legal analysis with the EU emissions permit system for integration, as established by the IPPCD and later the IED will be undertaken in this book. Hence, the main research question this book will attempt to answer is: *to what extent does the regulatory design of the emissions permit system in China, considering the EU regulatory experiences in relation to integration and seen from the perspective of the specific Chinese situation, provide possibilities for or barriers to the implementation of integrated pollution prevention and control?*

In order to answer the main research question, the following sub-questions will be explored using four steps:

The first step is to answer the question: *what theoretical insights have been developed regarding the integrated environmental permit in environmental law literature?* Here, the existing literature will be reviewed to understand how the idea of integrated pollution prevention and control can be achieved using the permit instrument. Based on this, the core elements of a regulatory framework for establishing an integrated environmental permit system will be identified (Chap. 2). This will provide a conceptual framework for analyzing regulatory attempts to develop an integrated environmental permit system in the EU and China respectively, and, subsequently, to support the comparative analysis between these two systems.

Second, while keeping the focus on the core elements of an integrated environmental permit system as identified in Chap. 2, Chap. 3 will address the question: *considering the aim to implement an integrated environmental permit, how has the EU emissions permit system been developed in terms of its regulatory design and in light of relevant case law?* (Chap. 3).

With the same focus, but moving to address the Chinese jurisdiction, the third step examines *how the emissions permit system has been developed in China to implement an integrated environmental permit in terms of its regulatory design.*[30] (Chap. 4).

Fourth, a comparative analysis will be carried out, aiming to answer the question: *to what extent does the regulatory design of the emissions permit system in China have similarities and differences with the EU emissions permit system?* Based on the comparative analysis, an answer to the main research question of *to what extent the regulatory design of the emissions permit system in China, considering the EU regulatory experiences in relation to integration and seen from the perspective of the specific Chinese situation, provides possibilities for or barriers to the implementation of integrated pollution prevention and control* can be given (Chap. 5).

1.4 Research Methodology

This section introduces the methodology applied in this research, namely doctrinal methodology and comparative law methodology.

In general, 'most studies addressing "comparative" environmental law [...] focus on legal and institutional responses to problems that virtually all states are believed to face'.[31] The starting point of this research is also to identify the legal response to a typical environmental problem, that is how to control industrial pollution in an integrated way. As mentioned in Sect. 1.1 of this chapter, the problem of pollution shifting from one environmental medium to another is related to separate approaches to pollution prevention and control. In order to respond to this problem, first in the EU and now also in China, a permit system was chosen to implement the integrated prevention and control of industrial pollution. In order to carry out this comparative study, the legal doctrinal method is used, consisting of a review of the relevant literature, legislative documents and case law. By doing so, the aim is 'to describe the existing law [...] in a way that is as neutral and consistent as possible...'.[32]

However, comparative law requires a conceptual framework in order to discover the similarities and differences between the legal systems involved in the comparative studies. This research develops a conceptual framework for an integrated environmental permit on the basis of a doctrinal study, particularly a literature review (Chap. 2). This conceptual framework provides a common basis to identify key elements for a structured investigation of the emissions permit system adopted in the EU and China, respectively, so that these two systems can be compared.

---

[30] There is no case law yet that is relevant to an integrated approach, which means that this research will focus on the regulatory design of the emissions permit in China.

[31] Jorge E. Viñuales, 'Comparative Environmental Law: Structuring a Field' in Emma Lees and Jorge E. Viñuales (eds), *The Oxford Handbook of Comparative Environmental Law* (Oxford University Press 2019), 17.

[32] Jan Smits, 'What is Legal Doctrine? On the Aims and Methods of Legal-Dogmatic Research' in Rob van Gestel, Hans-W Micklitz and Edward Rubin (eds), *Rethinking Legal Scholarship* (Cambridge University Press 2017), 213–214.

As will be seen in Chap. 2, most of the literature focuses on elaborating how integrated pollution control might be achieved. Hence, a functional perspective for analyzing regulatory attempts to develop an integrated environmental permit system is provided by the conceptual framework, established on the basis of a doctrinal study in Chap. 2. A comparative analysis from a functional perspective requires an interpretation of the laws as responses to the problems,[33] and identifying rules in different legal systems that can be interpreted as performing equivalent functions, while acknowledging that functions are always system-specific.[34] In this regard, a functional perspective would provide for a solution that makes the seemingly incomparable legal systems of the EU and China, a federal centralized system and a domestic system, comparable. In this vein, Chaps. 3 And 4 respectively interpret how the EU and China's emissions permit systems attempt to implement integrated pollution prevention and control from a functional perspective, as provided by the conceptual framework in Chap. 2. Thereafter, a comparative analysis is undertaken on the basis of the concept framework as developed in Chap. 2, examining to what extent the regulatory design of the emissions permit system in China has similarities and differences with the EU emissions permit system, taking into account the specific EU and Chinese situations. The results of this comparison will then be discussed to identify what sort of regulatory possibilities for or barriers to implementing an integrated environmental permit system, as exists in the EU, may also be undertaken in China. Based on that discussion, the answer to the main research question can be given.

1.5 Research Structure

In accordance with the research questions set out in Sect. 1.2 above, the structure of this book is the following:

- Chapter 2 will develop the conceptual framework for examining the EU and Chinese regulatory approaches to an integrated environmental permit system on the basis of a doctrinal study, in particular a literature review; this conceptual framework will provide key elements for a structured examination of the regulatory design of an integrated environmental permit in specific jurisdictions;
- on the basis of the conceptual framework, Chaps. 3 and 4 will respectively provide an in-depth study of the IED and the Administrative Regulation on Emissions Permitting, to understand how the emissions permit system in the EU and China have been developed to implement integrated pollution and prevention control;

---

[33] Ralf Michaels, 'The Functional Method of Comparative Law' in Mathias Reimann and Reinhard Zimmermann (eds), *The Oxford Handbook of Comparative Law (2nd ed)* (Oxford University Press 2019), 386–387.

[34] Ibid, 387.

- following the above analysis, Chap. 5 will undertake a comparative analysis between the EU and Chinese regulatory approaches to establishing an integrated environmental permit and then discuss what sort of regulatory possibilities for or barriers to implementing an integrated permit system appearing in the EU may also be followed in China. After this discussion, the answer to the main research question will be given in this chapter.

References

Bohne, E., & Dietze, D. (2004). Pollution prevention and control in Europe revisited. *European Energy and Environmental Law Review, 13*(7).

Council Directive 96/61/EC of 24 September 1996 concerning integrated pollution prevention and control (1996) OJ L 257/26 (IPPCD).

Directive 2008/1/EC of the European Parliament and of the Council of 15 January 2008 concerning integrated pollution prevention and control (Codified version) (2008) OJ L 24/8.

Directive 2010/75/EU of the European Parliament and of the Council of 24 November 2010 on industrial emissions (integrated pollution prevention and control) (2010) OJ L 334/159 (IED).

Faure, M., & Lefevere, J. G. (1996). The draft directive on integrated pollution pollution prevention and control: An economic perspective. *European Energy and Environmental Law Review, 5*(4), 112–122.

Guruswamy, L. (1989). Integrating thoughtways: re-opening of the environmental mind. *Wisconsin Law Review*, 463.

Guruswamy, L. (1991). The case for integrated pollution control. *Law and Contemporary Problems, 54*, 41.

Guruswamy, L. (2000). Integration & (and) Biocomplexity. *Ecology LQ, 27*, 1191.

Hydra. https://www.britannica.com/topic/Hydra-Greek-mythology, Accessed 6 May 2022.

Koutalakis, C., Buzogany, A., & Börzel, T. A. (2010). When soft regulation is not enough: The integrated pollution prevention and control directive of the European Union. *Regulation & Governance, 4*(3), 329–344.

Li, Q., & Cai, W. (2006) The integration and expansion of an emission permit system in China (in Chinese: 论我国排污许可证制度的整合与拓展). *Environmental and Resources Law Review, 00*.

Li, Z., & Chen, X. (2019) On the institutional foundation and barriers for implementing an integrated emission permit system (in Chinese: 综合排污许可制度运行的体制基础及困境分析). *Journal of Political Science and Law, 01*.

Liu, N., & Wang, J. (2021). The regulation on the administration of pollutant discharge permits: Characteristics, challenges and responses (in Chinese: 《排污许可管理条例》的特点、挑战与应对). *Environmental Protection, 49*(9).

Michaels, R. (2019). The functional method of comparative law. In M. Reimann & R. Zimmermann (Eds.), *The Oxford Handbook of Comparative Law* (2nd ed., pp. 345–389). Oxford University Press. https://doi.org/10.1093/oxfordhb/9780198810230.001.0001.

Ministry of Environmental Protection (abolished on 17 March 2018), Administrative Measures on Emissions Permitting (for Trial Implementation) (in Chinese: 排污许可管理办法(试行)), 10 January 2018 (no longer in force).

Pallemaerts, M. (1996). The proposed IPPC Directive: Re-regulation or de-regulation? *European Energy and Environmental Law Review, 5*(6), 174–179.

Recent International Developments under the Montreal Protocol. https://www.epa.gov/ozone-layer-protection/recent-international-developments-under-montreal-protocol. Accessed 18 December 2019.

'Resouces' (in Chinese: 文件库). http://www.mee.gov.cn/wjk/?keyword=控制污染物排放许可制实施方案. Accessed 15 October 2020.

Roberts, M. W. (2017). Finishing the job: The Montreal protocol moves to phase down hydrofluorocarbons. *Review of European, Comparative and International Environmental Law, 26*(3), 220–230.

Shi, X. & Yang, B. (2021). Research on legislative coordination and normative co-governance structure of China's emission permit management system (in Chinese: 我国排污许可管理制度的立法协同与规范共治结构研究). *Journal of Dalian University of Technology (Social Sciences), 42*(05).

Smits, J. M. (2017). What Is legal doctrine?: On the aims and methods of legal-dogmatic research. In R. van Gestel, H.-W. Micklitz, & E. L. Rubin (Eds.), *Rethinking legal scholarship: A Transatlantic Dialogue* (pp. 207–228). Cambridge University Press.

State Council. Administrative Regulation on Emissions Permitting (in Chinese: 排污许可管理条例), 9 December 2020.

State Council. Implementation Plan for the Permit System for Controlling Emissions (in Chinese: 控制污染物排放许可制实施方案的通知 国办发〔2016〕81号), 10 November 2016.

The Montreal Protocol Evolves to Fight Climate Change. https://www.unido.org/sites/default/files/unido-publications/2023-01/The-Montreal-Protocol-Evolves-To-Fight-Climate-Change-en.pdf. Accessed 3 May 2024.

Van Hoorick, G. (2020). Environmental permits: Origins and nature and recent tendencies. In M. Faure (Ed.), *Elgar encyclopedia of environmental law* (pp. 226–236). Elgar.

Viñuales, J. E. (2019). Comparative environmental law: Structuring a field. In E. Lees & J. E. Viñuales (Eds.), *The Oxford handbook of comparative environmental law* (pp. 3–34). Oxford University.

Wiener, J. B. (2016). Precaution and climate change. *The Oxford Handbook of International Climate Change Law*, pp. 163–184.

Xie, W. (2018). Research on the implementation of China's pollutant discharge permit (in Chinese: 论我国排污许可证的执行). *Legal Forum, 33*(6).

Chapter 2
The Concept of an Integrated Environmental Permit

Abstract This chapter examines the theoretical insights have been developed regarding the integrated environmental permit in environmental law literature. This examination aims to identify the core elements of a regulatory framework for establishing an integrated environmental permit system, so as to provide a conceptual framework for analyzing regulatory attempts to create an integrated environmental permit system in the EU and China respectively, and, subsequently, for the comparative analysis between these two systems.

2.1 Introduction

This chapter examines the theoretical insights have been developed regarding the integrated environmental permit in environmental law literature.[1] This examination aims to identify the core elements of a regulatory framework for establishing an integrated environmental permit system, so as to provide a conceptual framework for analyzing regulatory attempts to create an integrated environmental permit system in the EU and China respectively, and, subsequently, for the comparative analysis between these two systems.

The examination in this chapter is divided into four steps. The first step provides an elaboration of what is understood in the academic literature thus far by the concept of 'integrated pollution prevention and control' (Sect. 2.2). When reviewing the literature regarding the concept of integrated pollution prevention and control, it became clear that most of the literature focuses on discussing 'how integrated pollution control might be achieved, not what it meant or why it mattered'.[2] Therefore, the elaboration of the concept of integrated pollution prevention and control in this

[1] Hence this chapter answers the first research question as presented in Sect. 1.2.3 of Chap. 1.

[2] Irwin observed this characteristic at the Brussels Symposium on Integrated Pollution Control. See Frances Irwin, 'Integrated Pollution Control in Europe and North America' in Nigel Haigh and Frances Irwin (eds), *Integrated pollution control in Europe and North America* (Conservation Foundation 1990), 11. By now, this observation is still the case: rather than seeking a precise definition of integrated pollution prevention and control, most studies tend to discuss how integrated pollution control might be achieved by deriving regulatory experiences from different jurisdictions.

X. Chen, *Towards an Integrated Environmental Permit in China*,
https://doi.org/10.1007/978-981-97-5188-4_2

chapter does not aim to provide a precise definition of integrated pollution prevention and control, but it focuses on the approaches to implementing integrated pollution prevention and control. In the environmental law literature, the term 'integration' appears in two senses: external and internal. Section 2.1 explains that, according to the literature, the concept of 'integrated pollution prevention and control' is distinguished from external integration and falls within internal integration. Section 2.2 provides for an elaboration on three legislative techniques to establishing internal integration.

Section 2.3 delves into how the concept of integrated pollution prevention and control might be achieved by means of a permit instrument. Bohne introduced three concepts to describe *the way* and *to what extent* a specific permit system can facilitate integrated pollution prevention and control: substantive integration, procedural integration, and organizational integration.[3] This section mainly borrows these three concepts to develop three perspectives to analyze *the way* and *to what extent* a specific permit system can facilitate integrated pollution prevention and control.

Section 2.4 discusses the challenge of applying the permit instrument and market-based instruments at the same time for pollution control aiming at an integrated approach. The literature review presented in this section shows that the interaction between a permit instrument and market-based instruments might affect the implementation of integrated pollution prevention and control.

Based on the above analysis, the final section sets out the conceptual framework for examining the integrated environmental permit in specific jurisdictions, such as, in this book, the EU and China. First, the section highlights the core elements of a regulatory framework for establishing an integrated environmental permit system, and it then develops focal analytical points for examining a legal framework for an integrated environmental permit. These focal analytical points create a conceptual framework to analyze regulatory attempts to establish an integrated environmental permit system in the EU and China and to support the comparative analysis between the two systems.

2.2 The Concept of Integrated Pollution Prevention and Control

This section investigates how the concept of 'integrated pollution prevention and control' is or can be understood, based on a literature review. The environmental law literature distinguishes the term 'integration' in two senses: external and internal. The following sub-sections will first clarify the difference between external and

[3] Eberhard Bohne, *The Quest for Environmental Regulatory Integration in the European Union: Integrated Pollution Prevention and Control, Environmental Impact Assessment and Major Accident Prevention* (Kluwer Law International 2006), Chap. 3. The reason for borrowing Bohne's conceptual framework is that this framework was established to analyze and compare regulatory integration in national permitting and inspection systems, which is relevant for the aim of this research. The level of inspection is beyond the scope of this research and thus is not discussed in detail.

internal integration and explain that the concept of integrated pollution prevention and control belongs to internal integration. Section 2.2 further describes different legislative techniques to establishing internal integration.

2.2.1 External and Internal Integration

This section aims to clarify the difference between external and internal integration and will explain that the focus of this book is on internal integration.

External integration refers to the integration of environmental concerns into other policy areas,[4] such as agriculture and transport, etc. The notion of external integration can be found in principle 4 of the Rio Declaration on Environment and Development: '[i]n order to achieve sustainable development, environmental protection shall constitute an integral part of the development process and cannot be considered in isolation from it'.[5] Hence, this principle, which emphasizes the concept of sustainable development, stresses that in (economic) development policies, the need to protect the environment should not be set aside and needs to be an 'integral' part. This notion is also enshrined in EU treaty provisions, establishing external integration as the major component of sustainable development, such as Article 11 TFEU and Article 37 of the Charter of Fundamental Rights of the European Union.[6]

The concept of internal integration exists next to external integration. Faure defined internal integration as:

> the ecological goal that, in the decision-making and balancing of interests with respect to the permitted amounts and quality of pollutants, the total effects of pollution emanating from the licensed activity on the various components of the environment are taken into account.[7]

In short, internal integration concerns the integrated decision-making with respect to environmental requirements *within* the field of environmental law. Hence, the concept of integrated pollution prevention and control, which at its core aims to avoid cross-media transfers of pollution, is an element of internal integration.

---

[4] Michael G. Faure, 'The Harmonization, Codification and Integration of Environmental Law: A Search for Definitions' (2000) 9 European Environmental Law Review 174, 178.

[5] Gyula Bándi, Principles of EU Environmental Law Including (the Objective of) Sustainable Development, in Marjan Peeters and Mariolina Eliantonio (eds), *Research Handbook on EU Environmental Law* (Edward Elgar 2020), 41.

[6] Article 11 TFEU (ex Article 6 TEC) prescribes that '[e]nvironmental protection requirements must be integrated into the definition and implementation of the Union's policies and activities, in particular with a view to promoting sustainable development'; Article 37 of the Charter of Fundamental Rights prescribes that '[a] high level of environmental protection and the improvement of the quality of the environment must be integrated into the policies of the Union and ensured in accordance with the principle of sustainable development'. For a comprehensive analysis on article 6 TEC, see Nele Dhondt, *Integration of Environmental Protection into other EC Policies: Legal Theory and Practice* (Europa Law Publishing 2003); and for a recent discussion on article 11 TFEU and article 37 of the Charter of Fundamental Rights, see Gyula Bándi (2020), 41.

[7] Michael G. Faure (2000), 181.

Furthermore, literature has pointed to the inter-relationship between the concepts of internal integration and external integration respectively. According to Irwin, if the environmental policy field is regulated in a fragmented way, it will be difficult to take the environmental concerns fully into account within other policy fields outside the environmental domain.[8] Hence, in this view, internal integration serves external integration. Bándi holds a similar opinion that 'internal integration might also be taken as a prerequisite of effective external integration, focusing on the environment as a system'.[9] In this vein, the level of internal integration can influence effective external integration between environmental sectors and other policy sectors.

2.2.2 Legislative Techniques for Internal Integration

Internal integration can be achieved using several legislative forms. First, internal integration can be strived for by means of harmonization. Faure distinguishes three different modes of how *harmonization* can contribute to integration:

(a) 'various separate procedures are approximated [...] and separate legal acts remain in existence';
(b) 'various substantive environmental laws are approximated'; or
(c) 'the number of licences is reduced'.[10]

Secondly, next to harmonization, internal integration can be strived for by *codification*, which refers to moving the content of sectoral environmental legislation into one environmental code.[11] The third option is *coordination*. This means that, in the situation where separate decision-making procedures are not harmonized or codified into one procedure, 'the legislature has provided for legal rules which force the various authorities to take into account the separate procedures or licences.'[12] The coordination aims to avoid that decisions made in separate procedures run counter to each other. The three legislative techniques—harmonization, codification, and coordination—can be used in a combined way. In cases where harmonization or codification take place, but it is not complete, coordination can serve as an important supplement to achieve internal integration.[13] Meanwhile, Faure also noted that the form of the legislation does not necessarily determine the achievement of internal integration. Instead, the substance of the provisions must be examined concerning the question whether they aim at internal integration.[14] In other words, whether internal

[8] Frances Irwin (1990), 8.

[9] Gyula Bándi (2020), 43.

[10] Michael G. Faure (2000), 181.

[11] Ibid. Codification is also considered as the ultimate form of harmonization, see ibid, 176.

[12] Ibid, 182.

[13] Ibid, 181.

[14] Ibid, 175. For example, Faure pointed out that '[a]n environmental legal system where all legislation is brought together in one code and is in that sense 'harmonised' may appear attractive at

integration will truly be achieved depends on how the provisions within one code or the provisions of coordination are designed.

2.2.3 *Interim Conclusion*

Internal integration is a different concept in comparison to external integration, which aims at integrating decision-making in relation to environmental requirements within the field of environmental law. However, it is observed that the more ambitious internal integration is, the better the environmental concern can be integrated into other policy concerns. Thus, internal integration serves external integration. Internal integration can take place using different legislative forms: harmonization, codification, and coordination. However, the form of the legislation does not necessarily determine the achievement of internal integration, but how the provisions within one code or the provisions of coordination will be designed. The remainder of this chapter will provide a conceptual framework on the basis of which the EU and China's emissions permit system can be investigated.

2.3 Three Perspectives for Analyzing a Permit System for Integrated Pollution Prevention and Control

This section delves into how, according to insights from the literature, the concept of an integrated approach towards pollution prevention and control might be implemented by means of a permit instrument. Bohne introduced three concepts to describe *the way* and *to what extent* a specific permit system can facilitate integrated pollution prevention and control: substantive integration, procedural integration, and organizational integration.[15] This section mainly borrows these three concepts to develop three analytical perspectives to analyze the permit system for integrated pollution prevention and control. The Sects. 2.3.1, 2.3.2, and 2.3.3 will explain the perspectives of substantive integration, procedural integration, and organizational integration. It is noted, however, that although the three perspectives are discussed respectively, they are closely connected according to Bohne: '[e]ffective procedural and organizational integration of the permit system is a prerequisite for substantive integration of permit decisions'.[16]

first sight, but it may be that in fact the decision-making takes place in a totally disintegrated and uncoordinated manner.'.

[15] Eberhard Bohne (2006), Chap. 3.

[16] Eberhard Bohne, 'The implementation of the IPPC Directive from a comparative perspective and lessons for its recast (Part I)' (2008) 5.1 JEEPL 1, 23.

2.3.1 *Substantive Integration*

Substantive integration focuses on the content of regulatory decisions, requiring the consideration of the interrelationships which exist among environmental media (air, water, and soil), in order to find the optimal environmental control techniques for an industrial installation or activity that can best protect the environment as a whole.[17] Substantive integration has two dimensions: the scope of integration and the environmental effectiveness of integration.[18] Below, the perspective of substantive integration will be further developed, first by discussing the scope of integration (Sect. 2.3.1.1) and then the environmental effectiveness of integration (Sect. 2.3.1.2). Moreover, the establishment of substantive integration faces the challenge of the incommensurability of environmental goods, which will be addressed in Sect. 2.3.1.3.

2.3.1.1 The Scope of Integration

The scope of integration, in other words, the extent of the internal integration, refers to what environmental elements and their interrelationships would be integrated in legislation and then permit decisions.[19]

The literature has distinguished different scopes of integration that can be established by legislators. Guruswamy argued that the scope of integration can be understood from the *narrow and strictly operational level,* at which an integrated approach would seek to find the optimal balance for disposing of the pollutants into different environment medias, to the *broad and strategic level,* at which an integrated approach would consider other environmental impacts, such as the use of energy and resources, or even all the environmental and ecological repercussions caused by most human activities.[20]

---

[17] Eberhard Bohne (2006), 37 and 40.

[18] Ibid, 38. The term 'the degree of integration' was used by Bohne in his book. In my phone interview with Professor Bohne on 13 November 2019, he explained that 'the degree of integration' in his work refers to the scope of environmental factors to be integrated. Hence, in this book, in order to avoid using various terms that refer to the same meaning, 'the scope of integration' is used in this book.

[19] Ibid. This is also discussed in the procedural integration by Bohne, which is explained later in this section. Bohne did not draw a line to distinguish substantive integration from procedural integration. They are just different dimensions to think about 'integrated pollution prevention and control'.

[20] Lakshman Guruswamy (1991), 49–50. Guruswamy illustrated different ranges by supposing that 'a plant has a coal-burning electric generator that discharges unacceptable levels of [SO_2]'. One of Desulphurization technologies that apply pulverized limestone can solve this problem, but it also results in large quantities of waste. According to Guruswamy, different ranges of integrated schemes can be applied in this situation:

> At the narrow and strictly operational level, an integrated approach would seek to find the optimal balance for disposing of the pollutants into the air, land or water. A more far-ranging level of an integrated approach could involve evaluation of the environmental effects of limestone quarrying or transportation. At the broad and strategic level, an integrated approach would weigh building coal-fired generators against other alternative sources of energy, or

Another analysis distinguishing the scope of integrated pollution prevention and control in a broad sense and a narrow sense is provided by Emmott and Haigh.[21] In the broad sense, they considered that 'one of the most detailed definitions of the broad concept of [integrated pollution prevention and control] is to be found in a Recommendation adopted by the OECD in 1991'.[22] This recommendation advises OECD member countries to:

> practice integrated pollution prevention and control, taking into account the effects of activities and substances on the environment as a whole and the whole commercial and environmental life cycles of substances when assessing the risks they pose and when developing and implementing controls to limit their release.[23]

In addition, this recommendation identifies certain aspects as essential for an effective integrated approach, which not only concerns pollution, but—taking a broad environmental scope—also takes energy efficiency, resource conservation and waste prevention into account.[24] With respect to examining what type is already established in practice, Emmott and Haigh found that the UK system adopted in Part I of the Environmental Protection Act 1990 and the system adopted at the EU level with the Integrated Pollution Prevention Control Directive[25] in 1996 represented a narrow scope of integrated pollution control compared to that put forward by the OECD.[26]

In addition to the research by Emmott and Haigh, Doppelhammer further observed that the concept of integrated pollution prevention and control, according to a broad scope definition, has been simply impossible to realize and has remained theoretical.[27] Hence, she argued that, for the purpose of implementing this concept, it is

---

would evaluate better energy conservation measures for not building generators. This broad strategic approach could be even extended because most social and economic activities have environmental and ecological repercussions.

[21] Neil Emmott and Nigel Haigh, 'Integrated Pollution Prevention and Control: UK and EC Approaches and Possible Next Steps' (1996) 8J. Envtl. L. 301, 301.

[22] Ibid. Also see Organisation for Economic Co-operation and Development (OECD), 'Recommendation of the Council on Integrated Pollution Prevention and Control' (1991) OECD/LEGAL/0256.

[23] OECD (1991), art I(1).

[24] Ibid, point 2 of Annex; Neil Emmott and Nigel Haigh (1996), 302.

[25] Council Directive 96/61/EC of 24 September 1996 concerning integrated pollution prevention and control [1996] OJ L 257/26.

[26] Neil Emmott and Nigel Haigh (1996), Sect. 2.3 argued that the UK system did not extend to the aims of resource conservation and energy efficiency and did not take any significant steps towards the incorporation of a life cycle approach; Sect. 2.4 claimed that although some steps had been taken by the IPPCD in the direction of the broad concept of integrated pollution prevention and control, it was not a complete implementation of the broad concept. One possible area for further steps could be the use of mass balance and life cycle approaches.

[27] Martina Doppelhammer, 'More Difficult than Finding the Way Round Chinatown? The IPPC Directive and its Implementation' (2000) 9 European Energy and Environmental Law Review 199, 200. At this time, there is no literature showing that this broad concept has been achieved in practice.

necessary to find the right scope of integration 'in relation to what can be achieved in a particular area at a particular time'.[28]

2.3.1.2 The Environmental Effectiveness of Integration

The environmental effectiveness of integration refers to a certain level of environmental quality as a whole to be achieved. An integrated approach must determine the level of environmental protection, otherwise various environmental factors and their interrelationship can be considered together 'at any level of environmental quality, even at a low level that may be detrimental to human health'.[29] In other words, thinking about integrated pollution prevention and control without setting the desired level of environmental protection would be shortsighted.

However, the core problem is that, according to the current legal literature, it is impossible to work with a single denominator to assess the level of environmental quality as a whole. Environmental goods are incommensurable, which means that 'there is no common denominator for the assessment of chemical, physical, and biological impacts on air, water, land, flora, fauna, human health and cultural assets'.[30] Due to the incommensurability of environmental goods, 'only media-specific environmental quality objectives can be quantified', which are often demonstrated as environmental quality standards.[31] Hence, since there is no single benchmark or criterion possible to measure the achievement of a certain level of protection of the environment as a whole, only a certain scope of substantive integration can be assessed in terms of the environmental effectiveness through media-specific environmental quality standards. In cases where there are no environmental quality standards, the decision for a specific project defines the level of environmental protection to be achieved.[32]

2.3.1.3 Incommensurability of Environmental Goods

As mentioned above, environmental goods are incommensurable. Therefore, an integrated approach to environmental protection 'must be based on the weighing and balancing of all relevant factors that result in the trade-offs between environmental goods'.[33] There are two options, from a substantive perspective, for deciding on the trade-offs between environmental goods:

[28] Ibid.

[29] Eberhard Bohne (2006), 38.

[30] Eberhard Bohne and Doris Dietze (2004), 199.

[31] Eberhard Bohne (2006), 41.

[32] Ibid.

[33] Eberhard Bohne and Doris Dietze (2004), 199.

- first, the *generic option* 'addresses several decision situations of the same kind, and weighs and balances prospective environmental and other effects in a generic and abstract way', whose 'results are generic trade-offs which apply to all defined cases'[34];
- second, the *case-specific option* 'is concerned only with the effects of a single case, and results in case-specific trade-offs'.[35]

The decisions taken in a generic way are usually by regional or national regulatory authorities, while the decisions taken in a case-specific way are usually by permitting authorities.[36] In short, the generic option is based on centralization (with the competence to set the general rules that have to be applied in permit decisions attributed to an authority at the central level), while the case-specific option is based on decentralization (with the competence to set the permit conditions attributed to decentralized authorities).

2.3.1.3.1 The Case-Specific Option

It is argued that the case-specific option helps to make optimal choices for achieving an integrated approach. Bohne explained that, because of the infinite specific factors (such as technical characteristics, local environmental conditions, etc.), case-specific decisions are better suited,[37] since generic decisions limit, by definition, the opportunity to make optimal choices.[38] A theoretical case provided by Bohne and Dietze can illustrate this point:

> suppose that an old power plant located on a small creek with many trout is heavily polluting the air because it cannot technically meet present [generic requirements][39] for air emissions reductions. Since a shut-down of the plant is precluded by legal reasons, the only way to improve the environmental situation is to replace the old plant with a new one equipped with modern emission reduction technology. It is assumed that compliance with binding [generic air emission standards] requires the application of technologies which will cause waste water discharges that kill the trout. In contrast, fixing air emission limit values which are slightly less stringent than [generic requirements] would avoid waste water discharges that kill the trout. Assuming that air emissions slightly exceeding [generic] emission limit values are still below present pollution levels, and compatible with air quality objectives, the trade-off in favour of the trout would ensure a higher level of protection for the environment as a whole than compliance with [generic] air emission standards.[40]

---

[34] Ibid.

[35] Ibid.

[36] Ibid, 200.

[37] Eberhard Bohne (2006), 41.

[38] Ibid.

[39] The original term used here is 'BAT-requirements' referring to generic requirements based on the generic determination of BAT. The concept of BAT is relevant in the EU emissions permit system, which is discussed in Chap. 3 and therefore is not discussed in this chapter.

[40] Eberhard Bohne and Doris Dietze (2004), 201.

In this theoretical case, the binding generic emission standards legally eliminate the choice of a technology that, although not meeting the generic binding requirements for air, can better protect the environment as a whole. Such an outcome is not compatible with the idea of an integrated approach.

In addition, Bohne tends to adhere to the economists' view that supports a case-specific approach, namely that generic decisions ignore 'the differences of marginal costs for environmental controls' and thus 'produce cost-ineffective solutions for environmental protection'.[41] Similarly, Faure and Lefevere also recognized that 'the costs to reach a similar environmental quality may well vary with location-specific circumstances',[42] and thus they argued for the differentiation of emission standards 'as long as the advantages of further differentiation outweigh the administrative and information costs that are incurred with a highly detailed standard-setting process.'[43]

In summary, the case-specific option serves optimal decision-making given the infinite peculiarities of individual situations and the possibility to try to find the most cost-effective solution in a specific situation for the protection of environment as a whole. However, the possibly huge administrative and information costs of this case-specific option are also relevant and may be a factor for a legislator to follow the generic approach.

2.3.1.3.2 The Generic Option

This discussion about the generic option can start with the criticism of the economic arguments that support the case-specific approach (also called the 'fine-tuning' approach). Latin criticized the economic arguments as an 'excessive preoccupation with theoretical efficiency' that pay little attention to the actual decision-making costs in a real 'second best' world.[44] Precisely, Latin argued that

> Decisionmaking costs are typically high for each environmental conflict because ecological systems are complex, interactions are subtle and may require many years to become evident, people or biospecies are exposed to many potentially harmful agents, relative costs and benefits are difficult to assess, and sharply conflicting values and priorities are the norm rather than the exception. Moreover, many thousands of environmental resource conflicts must be resolved each year; thus, the cumulative costs of environmental decisionmaking would be high even if the cost of each regulatory decision were not.[45]

Concerning the implementation, Latin observed that case-specific decisions in pursuit of efficiency:

---

[41] Eberhard Bohne (2006), 42.

[42] Michael G. Faure and Jürgen C. Lefevere (1996), 115–116.

[43] Ibid. Interestingly, the high administrative and information costs incurred by the case-specific decisions are the main argument against the case-specific option; see the next sub-section for a further discussion.

[44] Howard Latin, 'Ideal versus Real Regulatory Efficiency: Implementation of Uniform Standards and Fine-tuning Regulatory Reforms.' (1985) 37(5) Stanford Law Review 1267, 1270–1331.

[45] Ibid, note 16.

require more data, more sophisticated scientific and economic analyses, more agency expertise and resources, and more cooperation from regulated parties, which cannot be implemented effectively in many environmental protection contexts.[46]

According to this point of view, case-specific decisions that require the consideration of all relevant information to find the most cost-effective environmental controls would not be feasible. Following the opinion of Latin, Guruswamy further argued that decision-making 'should not be paralyzed by the complexities of scientific uncertainty'.[47] In addition, he also warned that 'the illusion that risk assessment is a purely scientific activity hides the political and policy judgments on which such risk assessment is based'.[48] In this vein, one can question how to ensure that a decision to reduce environmental requirements is really based on a purely scientifically integrated evaluation of all relevant specific factors but not an outcome of a political preference for economic development.

There may be arguments that the risk of reduced environmental requirements motivated by the economic preferences can be countered by imposing an obligation to reach environmental quality standards.[49] However, Lübbe-Wolff pointed out that setting environmental quality standards 'captures only part of the environmental quality situation that we ought to be interested in'.[50] With regard to the shortage of environmental quality objectives, generic binding control measures bring more environmental elements and their interrelationships under environmental regulation. In addition, Bohne acknowledges that it is often difficult to determine the correct environmental control requirements in a permit for achieving environmental quality standards, and thus he admits the necessity of generic environmental control measures.[51] However, he pointed out that it is questionable whether and to what extent generic requirements should be indicative or legally binding.[52]

In summary, the generic option is relevant given the drawbacks of the case-specific option. First, the cost-effectiveness of the case-specific option that requires all relevant information to be collected and analyzed is not always feasible in view of the real second best world (in other words, the application in practice of the case-specific option seems very complex, if not too complicated). In addition, due to the lack of information and knowledge, there is a risk that a decision to reduce environmental requirements for economic benefits may be easily disguised as an allegedly integrated case-specific environmental trade-off. Although some may argue that this risk can

---

[46] Ibid, 1304. This observation was derived from the experiences with the environmental regulatory programmes in the United States.

[47] Lakshman Guruswamy (1989), 507.

[48] Ibid, 506.

[49] For example, Michael G. Faure and Jürgen C. Lefevere (1996), 115 argued that the risk of a race to the bottom resulted from the prisoners' dilemma and can be fixed by imposing controls on the quality to be reached; Also Martina Doppelhammer (2000), 204 stated that the requirement of reaching environmental quality standards provides a 'safety net' to limit any 'race to the bottom'.

[50] Gertrude Lübbe-Wolff, 'Efficient environmental legislation-On different philosophies of pollution control in Europe' (2001) 13(1) Journal of Environmental Law 79, 86.

[51] Eberhard Bohne (2006), 42–43.

[52] Ibid.

be countered by the imposition of an obligation to reach environmental quality standards, these arguments are weakened by the fact of the shortage of environmental quality standards and the difficulty to determine individual environmental control measures in a permit to achieve environmental quality standards. With regard to the drawbacks of the case-specific option, generic requirements are necessary. However, it is still questioned whether and to what extent generic requirements should be indicative or legally binding, particularly considering that binding generic requirements can legally limit the choice of techniques that can better protect the environment as a whole.

2.3.2 *Procedural Integration*

While substantive integration focuses on the content of permit decisions, procedural integration focuses on the form of permit decisions. Procedural integration refers to the number of procedures where various regulatory subjects (e.g. air pollution control, control of waste water, waste management, soil protection, etc.) are evaluated and decided.[53] Bohne further pointed out that *full procedural integration* refers to incorporating various regulatory subjects exclusively into one procedure.[54] Whereas, in the case where various separate procedures exist for each decision subject, procedural integration can also be developed by means of establishing coordination mechanisms to achieve coherence among decisions that are made in various procedures.[55] The concept of procedural integration, which is similar to the legislative techniques in internal integration as distinguished by Faure concerning the form of permit decisions, does not necessarily indicate the achievement of internal integration.[56]

2.3.3 *Organizational Integration*

With regard to organizational integration, the focus is on the number of authorities and their competence in the decision-making process in a certain environmental activity. Bohne argued that a low number of authorities involved in the decision-making process and a clear competence structure indicate a high degree of organizational

---

[53] Ibid. Also see Eberhard Bohne, César Colino, and Andrea E. Pandolfini, 'The evolution of Integrated Permitting and Inspections of Industrial Installations in the European Union: An Empirical Comparative Analysis of Existing and Emerging Integrated Permitting Procedures, Structures and Decisions in EU Member States' (1998), 45.

[54] Eberhard Bohne (2006), 36–37.

[55] Ibid, 53–55. Also see Eberhard Bohne, César Colino, and Andrea E. Pandolfini (1998), 45.

[56] Michael G. Faure (2000), 182. Also see Sect. 2.2.2, which explains that the reduced number of licences, one of the modes of harmonization and coordination, are considered legislative techniques for internal integration.

integration.[57] In case several authorities are involved in the process of environmental decision-making for issuing permits, the question is how their competences relate to each other. The relationship among the authorities involved in the process of environmental decision-making can be classified according to: sole competence, lead competence, and shared competence.[58] 'Sole competence' means that 'one authority has the power to make all relevant decisions' concerning various environmental impacts from a particular installation, and 'to direct other […] authorities to provide information and services necessary for decision-making'.[59] Under the 'lead competence', an authority has to consult with other authorities without being legally bound by their opinions, and the first authority has the final say on substantive and procedural issues.[60] As to the 'shared competence', an authority has to consult with other authorities and is legally bound by their opinions.[61]

However, an analysis of the extent of organizational integration does not indicate the level of environmental protection that has to be achieved. It is even questionable whether a low number of authorities involved in the process of decision-making, which indicates a high degree of organizational integration, will guarantee better environmental protection. According to Peeters:

> With a separation of responsibilities among different authorities which are obliged to coordinate their decisions, the respective environmental concerns will have a better chance of being defended when compared to the situation where these environmental interests are integrated into one environmental decision.[62]

From this perspective, a low number of authorities involved in the decision-making process does not necessarily imply that all environmental elements are given sufficient weight. Hence, a low number of authorities does not guarantee that a high level of environmental protection will be achieved.

---

[57] Ibid, 37.

[58] Eberhard Bohne, César Colino, and Andrea E. Pandolfini (1998), 45.

[59] Ibid, 46.

[60] Ibid.

[61] Ibid.

[62] Marjan Peeters, 'Elaborating on integration of environmental legislation: the case of Indonesia' in Michael Faure and Nicole Niessen (eds), *Environmental Law in Development Lessons from the Indonesian Experience* (Edward Elgar 2006), 99.

2.4 The Challenge of Applying a Permit Instrument and Market-Based Instruments to Pollution Control from the Perspective of an Integrated Approach

In addition to the permit instrument, there are various instruments applied to industrial pollution control, including market-based instruments and information-based instruments.[63] The rationale for the coexistence of various instruments is that:

> Since most instruments have strengths and weaknesses in specific circumstances, combining instruments and regulatory actors into a mix allows them to take advantage of their strengths while compensating for their weaknesses.[64]

However, the coexistence of various instruments may also lead to a problem of fragmentation, whereby the response to the problem is divided among multiple instruments.[65] For example, literature found that, when there are both command and control regulation (such as the imposition of fixed performance levels on industry that might limit the opportunity for making optimal choices) and market-based instruments (such as tradable pollution rights that enable flexibility in the choice of control measures), their combined outcome will be at least sub-optimal.[66] In this vein, how the interactions between a permit system and other types of instruments can affect integrated pollution prevention and control deserves further analysis. In other words, when a legislator wishes to apply an instrument mix, particularly a combined use of a permit system and market-based instruments, to regulate industrial pollution, the issue of how to achieve an integrated outcome to protect the environment as a whole (and to avoid the transfer of pollution of one media to another) merits attention.

---

[63] Richard B. Stewart, 'Instrument Choice' in Daniel Bodansky, Jutta Brunnée, and Ellen Hey (eds), *The Oxford Handbook of International Environmental Law* (Oxford University Press 2008), 150–154.

[64] Judith van Erp, Michael Faure, Jing Liu, Markos Karavias, André Nolkaemper, and Niels Philipsen, 'Introduction: The Concept of Smart Mixes for Transboundary Environmental Harm' in Judith van Erp, Michael Faure, André Nolkaemper, and Niels Philipsen (eds), *Smart Mixes for Transboundary Environmental Harm* (Cambridge University Press 2019), 7–8.

[65] This is derived from Arnold's view of fragmentation that the response to the problem is divided, whether intentionally or unintentionally, among multiple actors, multiple instruments, or methods, and/or multiple aspects of the problem. See Craig Anthony Arnold, 'Fourth-generation environmental law: integrationist and multimodal.' (2010) 35 Wm. & Mary Envtl. L. & Pol'y Rev. 771, 776.

[66] Judith van Erp, Michael Faure, Jing Liu, Markos Karavias, André Nolkaemper, and Niels Philipsen (2019), 8.

2.5 Focal Points for the Analysis of a Legal Framework for an Integrated Environmental Permit

This concluding section highlights the core elements of a regulatory framework to establish an integrated environmental permit system based on the above analysis. It then develops focal analytical points for examining a legal framework for an Integrated Environmental Permit. These focal analytical points develop a conceptual framework for the examination of regulatory attempts to create an integrated environmental permit system in the EU and China, respectively, and then for the comparative analysis between the two systems.

Based on Sect. 2.2, the concept of integrated pollution prevention and control falls within the scope of internal integration, focusing on integrating decision-making about environmental requirements within the field of environmental law. From the legislative perspective, there are three approaches to establishing integrated pollution prevention and control, being harmonization, codification, and coordination of environmental legislation. However, the form of the legislation does not necessarily determine the attainment of internal integration, but the substance of the provisions has to be examined to determine whether they aim at internal integration. Section 2.3 of this chapter provides a conceptual framework on the basis of which the EU and China's emissions permit systems can be examined. As discussed in Sect. 2.3, the concept of integrated pollution prevention and control using an environmental permit instrument can be analyzed from three perspectives: substantive integration, procedural integration, and organizational integration. Regarding substantive integration, there are three focal points of analysis, namely the scope of integration, the environmental effectiveness of integration, and the approaches to addressing the incommensurability of environmental goods. In order to understand these focal points, the provisions describing the scope of protection of the permit system, the provisions prescribing the aim of the permit system, and the provisions prescribing the application for permits and the setting of permit conditions need to be analyzed. From the perspective of procedural integration, the analytical focus is on whether one procedure is required or, where several procedures exist, whether a coordination mechanism is established in the issuing of permits. The organizational perspective of integration requires an analysis of the number of authorities involved in issuing permits and their competence to issue a permit.

In addition to permit instruments, other instruments can be applied to industrial pollution control. The interaction between a permit instrument and other types of instruments may allow them to take advantage of their strengths while compensating for their weaknesses, but this may also lead to a problem of fragmentation. In particular, the outcome of the combined use of command-and-control regulation and market-based instruments tends to be at least sub-optimal. Therefore, how the interaction between a permit instrument and market-based instruments would affect integrated pollution prevention and control deserves further analysis.

References

Arnold, C. A. (2010). Fourth-generation environmental law: integrationist and multimodal. *William & Mary Environmental Law and Policy Review, 35*, 771.

Bohne, E., Colino, C., & Pandolfini, A. E. (1998). *The evolution of integrated permitting and inspections of industrial installations in the European Union: An empirical comparative analyses of existing and emerging integrated permitting procedures, structures and decisions in EU Member States*. First Interim Report to the European Commission. Deutsches Forschungsinstitut für öffentliche Verwaltung.

Bohne, E., & Dietze, D. (2004). Pollution prevention and control in Europe revisited. *European Energy and Environmental Law Review, 13*(7).

Bohne, E. (2006). *The quest for environmental regulatory integration in the European Union: integrated pollution prevention and control, environmental impact assessment and major accident prevention* (Vol. 10). Kluwer Law International BV.

Bohne, E. (2008). The implementation of the IPPC Directive from a comparative perspective and lessons for its recast (Part1). *Journal for European Environmental and Planning Law, 5*(1), 1–33.

Bándi, G. (2020). Principles of EU environmental law including (the objective of) sustainable development. In *Research Handbook on EU Environmental Law* (pp. 36–53). Edward Elgar Publishing.

Council Directive 96/61/EC of 24 September 1996 concerning integrated pollution prevention and control [1996] OJ L 257/26.

Dhondt, N. (2003). *Integration of environmental protection into other EC policies: Legal theory and practice* (Vol. 2). Europa Law Publishing.

Doppelhammer, M. (2000). More difficult than finding the way round Chinatown? The IPPC Directive and its implementation. *European Energy and Environmental Law Review, 9*(7).

Emmott, N., & Haigh, N. (1996). Integrated pollution prevention and control: UK and EC approaches and possible next steps. *Journal of Environmental Law, 8*, 301.

Faure, M., & Lefevere, J. G. (1996). The draft directive on integrated pollution pollution prevention and control: an economic perspective. *European Energy and Environmental Law Review, 5*(4).

Faure, M. (2000). The harmonization, codification and integration of environmental law: A search for definitions. *European Energy and Environmental Law Review, 9*(6).

Guruswamy, L. (1989). Integrating thoughtways: re-opening of the environmental mind. *Wisconsin Law Review*, 463.

Guruswamy, L. (1991). The case for integrated pollution control. *Law and Contemporary Problems, 54*, 41.

Irwin, F. (1990). Integrated pollution control in Europe and North America. In N. Haigh & F. Irwin (Eds.), *Integrated pollution control in Europe and North America* (pp. 3–31). Conservation Foundation.

Latin, H. (1984). Ideal versus real regulatory efficiency: Implementation of uniform standards and fine-tuning regulatory reforms. *Stanford Law Review, 37*, 1267.

Lübbe-Wolff, G. (2001). Efficient environmental legislation—On different philosophies of pollution control in Europe. *Journal of Environmental Law, 13*(1), 79–87.

Organisation for Economic Co-operation and Development (OECD) (1991) Recommendation of the Council on Integrated Pollution Prevention and Control. OECD/LEGAL/0256.

Peeters, M. (2006). Elaborating on integration of environmental legislation: the case of Indonesia. In M. Faure & N. Niessen (Eds.), *Environmental Law in Development. Lessons from the Indonesian Experience* (pp. 92–128). Edward Elgar. https://doi.org/10.4337/9781847202918.00009.

Stewart, R. B. (2008). Instrument Choice. In D. Bodansky, J. Brunnée, & E. Hey (Eds.), *The Oxford Handbook of International Environmental Law*. Oxford University.

van Erp, J., Faure, M., Liu, J., Karavias, M., Nollkaemper, A., & Philipsen, N. (2019). Introduction: The concept of smart mixes for transboundary environmental harm. In J. van Erp, M. Faure, A. Nollkaemper, & N. Philipsen (Eds.), *Smart mixes for transboundary environmental harm* (pp. 3–24). Cambridge University Press.

Chapter 3
The EU Regulatory Approach Regarding the Integrated Emissions Permit System

Abstract On the basis of the conceptual framework of an integrated environmental permit as identified in Chap. 2, this chapter examines how the EU emissions permit system that attempts to implement integrated pollution prevention and control has been developed in terms of its regulatory design and relevant case law. The examination is carried out from three perspectives: substantive integration, procedural integration, and organizational integration. In addition, how the interactions between the EU emissions permit system and the market-based instruments affect integrated pollution prevention and control is also analyzed.

3.1 Introduction

3.1.1 Aim of This Chapter

The idea of applying an integrated regulatory approach to control emissions by industry was introduced in 1996 by the Integrated Pollution Prevention and Control Directive (IPPCD),[1] and it was then transformed into the Industrial Emissions Directive (2010/75/EU) (IED) as of 24 November 2010.[2] Recital 3 of the IED states:

[1] Council Directive 96/61/EC of 24 September 1996 concerning integrated pollution prevention and control (1996) OJ L 257/26. This Directive was 'amended four times since it entered in force. The first amendment reinforced public participation in line with the Aarhus Convention. The second amendment clarified the relationship between the permit conditions established in accordance with the IPPC Directive and the EU greenhouse gas emission trading scheme. The last two amendments relate to changes regarding Comitology procedures and [European Pollutant Emission Register]'. This summary is taken from the website of European Commission, available at 'The IPPC Directive', https://ec.europa.eu/environment/archives/air/stationary/ippc/legis.htm, accessed on 23 June 2022. Directive 96/61/EC and its amendments were later codified in 2008: Directive 2008/1/EC of the European Parliament and of the Council of 15 January 2008 concerning integrated pollution prevention and control (Codified version) (2008) OJ L 24/8. In addition to the special note, the IPPCD in this chapter refers to Directive 96/61/EC.

[2] Directive 2010/75/EU of the European Parliament and of the Council of 24 November 2010 on industrial emissions (integrated pollution prevention and control) (2010) OJ L 334/159 (IED).

X. Chen, *Towards an Integrated Environmental Permit in China*,
https://doi.org/10.1007/978-981-97-5188-4_3

'[d]ifferent approaches to controlling emissions into air, water or soil separately may encourage the shifting of pollution from one environmental medium to another rather than protecting the environment as a whole'; '[i]t is, therefore, appropriate to provide for an integrated approach to prevention and control of emissions into air, water and soil, to waste management, to energy efficiency and to accident prevention.'[3] Under the IED, the permit serves as the central instrument to implement this integrated approach: 'Member States shall take the necessary measures to ensure that no installation [...] is operated without a permit',[4] and 'shall take the necessary measures to ensure that the permit conditions are complied with'.[5] Therefore, the adoption of the IPPCD and later the IED can be considered as an attempt to establish an integrated environmental permit. This chapter aims to provide an in-depth legal examination of the IED in order to understand *how the emissions permit system of the IED that attempts to implement an integrated environmental permit has been developed in terms of its regulatory design and relevant case law*.[6] It is noted that although the term 'emissions permit system' is used in this chapter, the following research analyzes the scope of the protection of the permit scheme by the IED, which will show that the integrated approach pursued by the IED does not concern emissions alone and moreover, that not all emissions are included.

3.1.2 Approach and Structure of This Chapter

In order to address the question of how the emissions permit system of the IED developed to implement integrated pollution and prevention control, the analysis of the IED in this chapter is conducted following the conceptual framework of an integrated environmental permit as identified in Chap. 2. As discussed in Chap. 2, a regulatory framework for establishing an integrated environmental permit system can be analyzed from three perspectives: substantive integration, procedural integration, and organizational integration. In addition, how the interactions between a permit instrument and market-based instruments affect integrated pollution prevention and control deserves analysis. Thus, the following sub-questions will be explored:

- Regarding the substantive integration,

---

[3] IED recital 3. Similar provisions were also laid down in recitals 7 and 8 IPPCD.

[4] See IED art 4. There is one exception for certain installations and activities using organic solvents, see IED recital 5:

> In order to ensure the prevention and control of pollution, each installation should operate only if it holds a permit or, in the case of certain installations and activities using organic solvents, only if it holds a permit or is registered.

[5] IED art 8.

[6] Hence this chapter answers the second research question as presented in Sect. 1.3 of Chap. 1.

Question 1: in view of the scope of integration, what is the scope of the environmental issues subject to the emissions permit system as developed by the IED?
Question 2: in view of the environmental effectiveness of integration, what is the level of environmental quality as a whole required by the emissions permit system as developed by the IED?
Question 3: in view of the incommensurability of environmental goods, what are the options adopted by the IED to make environmental trade-offs?

- Regarding procedural integration,

Question 4: does the IED require one permit procedure, or does it allow for several permit procedures?
Question 5: is there a coordination mechanism required by the IED?

- Regarding organizational integration, the IED does not provide rules on organizational arrangements, given the subsidiarity principle in EU law,[7] and thus the IED permit system will not be examined with regard to organizational integration.
- Regarding the interactions between the permit instrument and market-based instruments,

Question 6: According to the IED, how should emissions permitting interact with market-based instruments for pollution control in view of integration?

With the above analytical focus, the examination of the IED is structured as followed. Section 3.2 provides an introduction of the IED. The IED consists of general provisions and special provisions laying down rules for the emissions permit system for industrial installations and activities. These rules will be analyzed in the following sections from the perspective of substantive integration, procedural integration, and organizational integration.[8] It is noted that the Commission published a proposal to amend the IED on 5 April 2022.[9] The examination in this chapter is based on the

[7] The principle of subsidiarity is established in TEU art 5:

> Under the principle of subsidiarity, in areas which do not fall within its exclusive competence, the Union shall act only if and in so far as the objectives of the proposed action cannot be sufficiently achieved by the Member States, either at central level or at regional and local level, but can rather, by reason of the scale or effects of the proposed action, be better achieved at Union level.'

For further discussion on the principle of subsidiarity, see Helle Tegner Anker, 'Competences for EU Environmental Legislation: About Blurry Boundaries and Ample Opportunities' in Marjan Peeters and Mariolina Eliantonio (eds), *Research Handbook on EU Environmental Law* (Edward Elgar 2020), 20.

In addition, during the process of drafting the original IPPCD, the Commission also emphasized that there was no intention to intervene in the internal organization of the Member States. For a relevant discussion, see Sect. 5.1 of this chapter.

[8] See Sect. 2.3 of Chap. 2.

[9] Commission (EU), 'Proposal for a DIRECTIVE OF THE EUROPEAN PARLIAMENT AND OF THE COUNCIL amending Directive 2010/75/EU of the European Parliament and of the Council

current legislation. While there is an in-depth discussion of the current legislation, there will also be an exploration of the main changes in the proposed amendment in light of the purpose of this book.[10] Precisely, Sect. 3.3 examines the objective of the IED, so as to understand the scope of integration and the environmental effectiveness of integration (in the sense of the level of environmental quality as a whole to be achieved)[11] as pursued by the IED. However, the provision prescribing the objective of the IED does not provide for an exact explanation of the integrated approach to be pursued by the IED. Hence, it is necessary to delve into the detailed rules on the key stages of the permit procedure—application for the emissions permit (Sect. 3.4), issuing of the emissions permit (Sect. 3.5), and the setting of permit conditions (Sects. 3.6–3.8)—established by the IED. Section 3.9 analyzes how the rules on the interaction between the permit instrument as provided by the IED and the market-based instrument as provided by the Emissions Trading System Directive (Directive 2003/87/EC) (ETS Directive),[12] and the National Emission Reduction Commitments Directive (2016/2284/EU) (NEC Directive)[13] that also covers industrial emissions, would affect the implementation of integrated pollution prevention and control.

Based on the above analysis, Sect. 3.10 provides answers to the six sub-questions as listed above to clarify how the emissions permit system of the IED attempting to implement integrated environmental permits has been developed in terms of its regulatory design and relevant case law.

3.2 Introduction to the Industrial Emissions Directive

This section provides an introduction to the Industrial Emissions Directive (IED). With the IED, the EU legislator recast seven previously existing directives, including the IPPCD (Directive 2008/1/EC), the Large Combustion Plants Directive,[14] the

---

of 24 November 2010 on industrial emissions (integrated pollution prevention and control) and Council Directive 1999/31/EC of 26 April 1999 on the landfill of waste' COM(2022)156 final, 5 April 2022.

[10] For the discussion on the Commission's proposal for amending the IED, see Sects. 3.2.2, 3.3.1.3, 3.6, 3.7.4.3.1, 3.7.4.3.3, 3.7.4.4, 3.7.6, and 3.8 of this chapter.

[11] See Sect. 2.3.1.2 of Chap. 2.

[12] Directive 2003/87/EC of the European Parliament and of the Council of 13 October 2003 establishing a scheme for greenhouse gas emission allowance trading within the Community and amending Council Directive 96/61/EC (Text with EEA relevance) (2003) OJ L 275/32.

[13] Directive (EU) 2016/2284 of the European Parliament and of the Council of 14 December 2016 on the reduction of national emissions of certain atmospheric pollutants, amending Directive 2003/35/EC and repealing Directive 2001/81/EC (Text with EEA relevance) OJ L 344/1. The NEC Directive allows Member States to choose the instrument used to control emissions, which means that Member States may choose market-based instruments. This raises the problem of the interaction between different instruments. For a further discussion see Sect. 3.9 of this chapter.

[14] Directive 2001/80/EC of the European Parliament and of the Council of 23 October 2001 on the limitation of emissions of certain pollutants into the air from large combustion plants (2001) OJ L 309/1.

Waste incineration Directive,[15] the Solvent Emissions Directive,[16] and three Titanium Dioxide Industry Directives.[17] Chapters I and II of the IED represent the recast of the IPPCD (Directive 2008/1/EC) providing general provisions of the emissions permit system for controlling industrial pollution and chapters III to VI of the IED are the recast of the Large Combustion Plants Directive, the Waste Incineration Directive, the Solvent Emissions Directive, and the Titanium Dioxide Industry Directives, providing special provisions for controlling pollution from certain industrial installations and activities.

3.2.1 General Provisions for the Emissions Permit System

As indicated above, Chapters I and II of the IED provide general provisions for the emissions permit system, which originated in the IPPCD (Directive 2008/1/EC). The IPPCD (Directive 2008/1/EC), originally adopted in 1996, laid down a set of common rules for emissions permits to control industrial pollution. Under the IED, the permit also serves as the central instrument to implement an integrated approach.[18] It had been 'questioned why, given the subsidiarity principle, so much weight is put on the permit'.[19] To answer this question, the drafting background to the adoption of the IPPCD can be investigated. In the explanatory memorandum of the Commission proposal for adopting the IPPCD from 1993, the Commission described the improvement of industrial pollution prevention and control in all Member States to explain the need for action at the Community level.[20] According to the Commission at that time, a permit system for implementing an integrated approach had been developed in

---

[15] Directive 2000/76/EC of the European Parliament and of the Council of 4 December 2000 on the incineration of waste (2000) OJ L 332/91.

[16] Council Directive 1999/13/EC of 11 March 1999 on the limitation of emissions of volatile organic compounds due to the use of organic solvents in certain activities and installations (1999) OJ L 85/1.

[17] Council Directive 78/176/EEC of 20 February 1978 on waste from the titanium dioxide industry (1978) OJ L 54/19; Council Directive 82/883/EEC of 3 December 1982 on procedures for the surveillance and monitoring of environments concerned by waste from the titanium dioxide industry (1982) OJ L 378/1; Council Directive 92/112/EEC of 15 December 1992 on procedures for harmonising the programmes for the reduction and eventual elimination of pollution caused by waste from the titanium dioxide industry (1992) OJ L 409/11.

[18] IED art 4.

[19] Michael G. Faure and Jürgen G J Lefevere (1996), 118. They further argued that '[w]ould it not, given subsidiarity, have been preferable to prescribe an integrated approach towards the pollution problem, but leave freedom to the Member States to choose the legal instruments they consider most appropriate to effectuate this integrated approach'.

[20] Commission (EC), 'Proposal for a Council Directive on Integrated Pollution Prevention and Control' COM(93) 423 final, 14 September 1993, 6–9. I'm extremely grateful to Dr. Lorenzo Squintani who sent me this document and other documents relating to the enactment of the IPPCD. Most of them are not available on EU-Lex.

most Member States, including Belgium, France, Germany, Greece, Ireland, Luxembourg, the Netherlands, Portugal, and the United Kingdom.[21] However, the general evolution of the practices towards an integrated environmental permit system in the Member States had not been reflected in the Community legislation yet, and thus the Commission at that time considered that 'Member States having already introduced an integrated approach [would] be hindered by the existing media-oriented Community legislation'.[22] Thus, from the drafting background to the adoption of the original IPPCD, it can be inferred that the reason for choosing the permit system as a central instrument by the EU legislator was in order to adapt to the general practice towards an integrated environmental permit in Member States. The general provisions in chapters I to II of the IED (which originate from the IPPCD) prescribe the objective of achieving an integrated approach and lay down a set of rules regarding the stages of a permit procedure, including application for permits, the issuing of permits, the setting of permit conditions, and rules on the interaction between the IED permit instrument with the EU ETS, which are the focus of the analysis in this chapter.

3.2.2 Special Provisions for the Emissions Permit System

Chapters III to VI of the IED are the recast of the Large Combustion Plants Directive, the Waste incineration Directive, the Solvent Emissions Directive, and the Titanium Dioxide Industry Directives. These chapters provide special provisions for controlling pollution from combustion plants, waste incineration plants, and waste co-incineration plants and organic solvents, setting down minimum requirements for these sectors.[23] The recast of the IPPCD (Directive 2008/1/EC) incorporating these sectoral directives—by means of bringing several directives into one directive—aimed to solve the lack of coherence between the IPPCD (Directive 2008/1/EC) and other sectoral legislation on industrial emissions. At the end of 2005, the Commission

[21] Ibid. According to the Commission at that time, the systems in Italy and Spain did not reflect integration. The Commission at that time also found that Denmark had a system of integrated pollution control since 1974, but it did not explicitly mention whether a permit system for implementing an integrated approach had been developed in Denmark.

[22] Ibid, 10.

[23] The summary of chapters III–VI of the IED is taken from the website of European Commission, available at 'Industrial emissions',

https://eur-lex.europa.eu/EN/legal-content/summary/industrial-emissions.html, accessed on 11 April 2022.

In addition, the proposal of amending the IED published by the Commission inserts a new chapter on 'special provisions for rearing of poultry, pigs and cattle', see Commission (EU), COM(2022)156 final, 5 April 2022, chapter VI a.

launched a review process of the IPPCD (Directive 2008/1/EC) and related legislation on industrial emissions.[24] In the review, the Commission found that the lack of coherence between the IPPCD (Directive 2008/1/EC) and other sectoral legislation on industrial emissions led to 'difficulties in reconciling the different standards and approaches used, and confusion over differences in definitions'.[25] In particular, there was evidence that the emission limit values laid down in the sectoral legislation were in many cases applied as the 'default rule' without reference to the use of Best Available Techniques (BAT)[26] as set out in the IPPCD (Directive 2008/1/EC).[27] According to the Commission, this is because the general principles and special requirements regulating industrial emissions were prescribed separately in the IPPCD (Directive 2008/1/EC) and the sectoral directives, which 'make it easy and attractive for operators and authorities to simply focus on the latter'.[28] In order to address this problem, a single directive was proposed by the Commission in 2007 and the IED was adopted on 24 November 2010.[29] According to the theory as discussed in Chap. 2, codification, referring to moving the content of sectoral environmental legislation into one code, is one of the legislative techniques used to implement internal integration.[30] Since the contents of sectoral environmental legislation (the Large Combustion Plants Directive, the Waste incineration Directive, the Solvent Emissions Directive, and the Titanium Dioxide Industry Directives) and the IPPCD (Directive 2008/1/EC) were combined into the IED, this shows that the technique of codification was adopted by

---

[24] The Commission launched the review process of the IPPCD and related legislation on industrial emissions in its first IPPC report. In the first IPPC report, the Commission raised concerns about the slow implementation of this key piece of EU environmental policy and thus decided to launch an IPPC implementation action plan and review of the Directive. See Report from the Commission to the Council and the European Parliament—Report of the Commission on the implementation of Directive 96/61/EC concerning integrated pollution prevention and control COM(2005) 540 final, 3 November 2005, and its summary at 'Adoption on 3 November 2005 by the Commission of the first report on the implementation of the IPPC Directive', https://ec.europa.eu/environment/archives/air/stationary/ippc/ippc_report.htm, accessed on 30 May 2020.

The review process included 2003 Commission Communication, a number of studies undertaken by the Commission to inform the process, and a public consultation. For more information of the review process, see 'IPPC Review Process', https://ec.europa.eu/environment/archives/air/stationary/ippc/ippc_review_process.htm, accessed on 3 April 2020.

[25] Commission (EU), 'Commission Staff Working Document Accompanying document to the proposal for a Directive of the European Parliament and of the Council on industrial emissions (integrated pollution prevention and control) (recast) IMPACT ASSESSMENT' SEC(2007) 1679, 21 December 2007, 64.

[26] The concept of BAT has served as one of the general principles governing the basic obligations of the operator, see IPPCD art 3(a) and the IED art 11(b). The rules on the BAT under the IED will be discussed in detail in Sect. 3.7 of this chapter.

[27] Commission (EU), SEC(2007) 1679, 21 December 2007, 29.

[28] Ibid, 64.

[29] The proposal for adopting the IED published by the Commission in 2007 and its subsequent revisions before the final adoption of the IED will be discussed in the following sections, serving as one of the important sources for examining the EU legislative choice for integrated emission permits.

[30] See Sect. 2.2.2 of Chap. 2.

the EU legislator to implement integrated pollution prevention and control.[31] Within this codification, the minimum requirements as prescribed in chapters III to VI serve as 'a secondary ceiling' in specific cases, in particular when derogations from the rules on the BAT as laid down in chapter II are applied.[32]

3.2.3 Interim Conclusion

The IED recast seven previously existing directives, including the IPPCD (Directive 2008/1/EC) and other relevant sectoral legislation on industrial emissions. The reason for this legislative development was that, at its core, the sectoral directives were used in such a way[33] that an integrated assessment of how to control the emissions of an industry was not sufficiently achieved. The integration of sectoral directives into one directive, the IED, shows that the technique of codification was used by the EU legislator to achieve integrated pollution prevention and control. The IED consists of general provisions and special provisions of a permit system for industrial pollution prevention and control. The general provisions provide for the objective of an integrated approach pursued by the emissions permit system, the rules on the stages of emissions permit process, and rules on how the emissions permit system interacts with the EU ETS for industrial pollution control. The special provisions serve as 'a secondary ceiling', or, in other words, a safety net, in the specific case when the derogation clause laid down in chapter II is applied.

3.3 The Objective of the Integrated Approach Pursued by the Industrial Emissions Directive

As discussed in Sect. 3.1 of this chapter, the adoption of the Industrial Emissions Directive (IED) is an attempt to establish an integrated environmental permit. This section aims to examine what kind of integrated approach the IED aims to provide. The rationale for adopting an integrated approach is presented in the recital of the

[31] In addition to codification, coordination is also used for implementing internal integration in the IED, which will be discussed in Sect. 3.5 of this chapter.

[32] European Environmental Bureau (EEB), 'New Features under the Industrial Emissions Directive' 14 July 2011, 18–19. Also see Peter Vajda, 'Large combustion plants and their specific situation' in training package on Industrial Emissions Directive developed by the European Commission, explaining that minimum requirements set out in chapters III–VI serve as a safety net where a derogation clause in chapter II is applied, available at https://ec.europa.eu/environment/legal/law/12/videos_5.htm, accessed on 24 August 2021. Further discussion on derogation clause in chapter II and the minimum requirements is provided in Sects. 3.7.4.3.3 and 3.7.6 of this chapter.

[33] The emission limit values laid down in the sectoral legislation were in many cases applied as the 'default rule' without reference to the use of BAT as required by the IPPCD (Directive 2008/1/EC), see Sect. 3.2.2 of this chapter.

IED, already presented in Sect. 3.1 of this chapter but, given its importance, repeated here:

> *Different approaches to controlling emissions into air, water or soil separately may encourage the shifting of pollution from one environmental medium to another rather than protecting the environment as a whole. It is, therefore, appropriate to provide for an integrated approach to prevention and control of emissions into air, water and soil, to waste management, to energy efficiency and to accident prevention. Such an approach will also contribute to the achievement of a level playing field in the Union by aligning environmental performance requirements for industrial installations.*[34]

This recital shows that the IED not only aims at transforming the traditional sectoral approach into the integrated approach to 'achieve a high level of protection of the environment taken as a whole',[35] but also that a market concern of achieving a level playing field is at issue in its pursuit of an integrated approach.[36] Therefore, the examination in this section focuses on investigating the objective of protecting the environment as a whole at a high level (Sect. 3.1) and the concern of achieving a level playing field by aligning environmental performance requirements (Sect. 3.2). Section 3.3 provides for an interim conclusion.

3.3.1 The Objective of Protecting the Environment as a Whole at a High Level

The objective of the integrated approach, which is to protect the environment as a whole, at a high level, is prescribed in the provision of the subject matter of the IED:

> This Directive lays down rules on integrated prevention and control of pollution arising from industrial activities.
>
> It also lays down rules designed to prevent or, where that is not practicable, to reduce emissions into air, water and land and to prevent the generation of waste, in order to achieve a high level of protection of the environment taken as a whole.[37]

This provision very much resembles the provision addressing the purpose and scope of the IPPCD.[38] From the perspective of substantive integration, this provision

---

[34] IED recital 3.

[35] IED art 1.

[36] Frans Oosterhuis and Marjan Peeters, 'Limits to integration in pollution prevention and control' in Marjan Peeters and Rosa Uylenburg (eds), *EU Environmental Legislation: Legal Perspectives on Regulatory Strategies* (Edward Elgar 2014), 97.

[37] IED art 1.

[38] See IPPCD art 1:

> The purpose of this Directive is to achieve integrated prevention and control of pollution arising from the activities listed in Annex I. It lays down measures designed to prevent or, where that is not practicable, to reduce emissions in the air, water and land from the abovementioned activities, including measures concerning waste, in order to achieve a high

delineates two dimensions of an integrated approach pursued by the IPPCD and later the IED: the scope of integration and the environmental effectiveness of integration.[39] The following sub-sections examine the scope and the environmental effectiveness of an integrated approach pursued by the IED by investigating the literature, the drafting history, and relevant case law.[40]

3.3.1.1 The Scope of the Integrated Approach Pursued by the IED

The scope of integration refers to what environmental elements and their interrelationships would be integrated in permit decisions.[41] This sub-section aims to examine the scope of an integrated approach pursued by the IED by investigating the Directive itself, the drafting documents, case law, and relevant literature. As will be discussed below, different interpretations of the scope of an integrated approach pursued by the IED can be identified. Basically, these interpretation differences can be classified as a narrow interpretation of the scope of an integrated approach concerning pollution alone and a broad interpretation of the integrated approach concerning not just pollution. This will be explained below in Sects. 3.1.1.1 and 3.1.1.2 respectively.

3.3.1.1.1 The Narrow Interpretation

It has been argued in the literature that the scope of an integrated approach, as pursued by the IPPCD and later the IED, has to be interpreted in a narrow sense. In this interpretation, the scope concerns pollution control alone, which basically covers emissions into the air, water, and land. Doppelhammer considered that the scope of an integrated approach as pursued by the IPPCD 'may only be inferred from phrases such as "air, water, and land" and "the environment taken as a whole" in Article 1 [of the IPPCD]', but claimed that the definition of 'pollution' provided by the IPPCD 'contributes to delimiting the integrated concept'.[42] Bohne analyzed

---

> level of protection of the environment taken as a whole, without prejudice to Directive 85/337/EEC and other relevant Community provisions.

[39] Eberhard Bohne (2006), 37–38. This analysis investigated the provision on the purpose and scope of the IPPCD. The provision on the subject matter is almost the same as the provision on the purpose and scope of the IPPCD; this analysis is also applicable to the provision on the subject matter of the IED.

[40] Since the provision on the subject matter of the IED is almost the same as the provision on the purpose and scope of the IPPCD, the following analysis on the provision on the purpose and scope of the IPPCD is therefore also applicable to the provision on the subject matter of the IED.

[41] See Sect. 2.3.1.1 of Chap. 2.

[42] Martina Doppelhammer (2000), 201. The definition of pollution in the IPPCD and later the IED is the same, see IPPCD art 2(2) and IED art 3(2):

> the direct or indirect introduction, as a result of human activity, of substances, vibrations, heat or noise into air, water or land which may be harmful to human health or the quality of

the provision on the purpose and scope of the IPPCD and argued that the scope of the integrated approach pursued by the IPPCD was 'defined…by the emissions released into the air, water or land', which means that 'environmental effects not resulting from emissions (e.g. interventions into nature and landscape impairing the functioning of eco-system) are not subject to the integrated approach'.[43]

The narrow interpretation can also be derived from the drafting history of the provision on the purpose and scope of the IPPCD based on a textual analysis. The concept of an integrated approach was initially introduced by the Commission in 1993 with a seemingly broad definition of scope.[44] According to the Commission's explanatory memorandum on the proposal for the IPPCD from 1993:

> A key aim of integrated forms of control is to prevent or minimize the risk of harm to the environment taken as a whole.[45]

The aim 'to prevent or minimize the risk of harm to the environment taken as a whole'—which sounds very broad—seems to be inspired by the recommendation of integrated pollution prevention and control published by the Organisation for Economic Co-operation and Development (OECD) in January 1991.[46] This recommendation was mentioned by the Commission in its explanatory memorandum of the proposal for the IPPCD from 1993 to explain the need for action at the Community level to implement an integrated approach.[47] According to the recommendation of the OECD, the 'purpose of integrated pollution prevention and control is to prevent or minimise the risk of harm to the environment taken as a whole', which concerns not only pollution control but also energy efficiency and resource conservation.[48] However, it can be seen that neither the provision on purpose and scope under the IPPCD nor the provision on subject matter under the IED incorporates the phrase of 'to prevent or minimize the risk of harm', but only explicitly mention 'to prevent or, where that is not practicable, to reduce emissions into air, water and land and to prevent the generation of waste'.[49] In particular, during the drafting of the IPPCD, the aim to 'ensure the efficient use of raw materials, water and energy in industrial processes' was added by the European Parliament to the provision prescribing the

> the environment, result in damage to material property, or impair or interfere with amenities and other legitimate uses of the environment.

However, Doppelhammer did not explain how the definition of pollution in the IPPCD contributes to delimiting the integrated concept.

[43] Eberhard Bohne (2008), 9–10.

[44] Commission (EC), COM (93) 423 final, 14 September 1993.

[45] Ibid, 3.

[46] Organisation for Economic Co-operation and Development (OECD), 'Recommendation of the Council on Integrated Pollution Prevention and Control' (1991) OECD/LEGAL/0256.

[47] Commission (EC), COM (93) 423 final, 14 September 1993, 9.

[48] Neil Emmott and Nigel Haigh (1996), 302. Also see OECD (1991), art I(1) and point 2 of Annex, which was discussed in Sect. 2.3.1.1 in Chap. 2.

[49] IPPCD and IED art 1.

purpose and scope at its first reading for the adoption of the IPPCD.[50] Even though a more ambitious scope of an integrated approach, concerning not only emissions but also the use of raw materials, water and energy, had been put forward, it was not accepted[51] in the final provision regarding the purpose and scope of the IPPCD and the provision on subject matter under the IED. This indicates that the final legislative text, as adopted, does not intend to subject the use of raw materials, water, and energy to the integrated approach. At least, it does not do so explicitly.

3.3.1.1.2 The Broad Interpretation

The phrase 'environment as a whole' in the provision on the subject matter may imply a broader scope rather than that just covering pollution control. Tolsma claimed that biodiversity and nature could be involved by considering the definition of the term environment derived from the Habitat Directive.[52] However, Tolsma also pointed out that 'it seems quite clear that the permit accords no conditions that can be set to protect ecological values in the direct surroundings of the installation'.[53] Hence, to further clearly identify the scope of an integrated approach pursued by the IED, in addition to investigations on the provision on subject matter as laid down in article 1 IED, it is also necessary to investigate other rules related to the permit system of the IED.[54]

In light of this, case law indicates that the IPPCD had a broad objective, more specifically concerning the question what industrial activities have to be regulated

---

[50] European Parliament (EC), 'Legislative resolution embodying Parliament's opinion on the proposal for a Council Directive on integrated pollution prevention and control (Cooperation procedure: first reading)' COM (93)0423—C3-0363/93—00/0526(SYN) OJ C 18/82, 23 January 1995, amendment 7:

> The purpose of this Directive is to provide for measures minimize emissions from industrial installations belonging to the industrial sectors listed in Annex I and to ensure the efficient use of raw materials, water and energy in industrial processes within the Community, so as to achieve a high level of protection for the environment as a whole.

[51] It was rejected by the European Commission, see European Commission (EC), 'Amended proposal for a Council Directive concerning Integrated Pollution Prevention and Control' COM (95) 88 final—SYN 526, 15 May 1995, 1.

[52] Hanna D. Tolsma, *Integrated environmental permitting: Towards a coherent system of environmental law in the Netherlands* (Europa Law 2019), 20. Council Directive 92/43/EEC of 21 May 1992 on the conservation of natural habitats and of wild fauna and flora (1992) OJ L 206/7. The recital states: '[w]hereas the preservation, protection and improvement of the quality of the environment, including the conservation of natural habitats and of wild fauna and flora, are an essential objective of general interest pursued by the Community, as stated in Article 130r of the Treaty.'.

[53] Hanna D. Tolsma (2019), 20–21.

[54] A discussion on the other detailed rules of the IED permit system is provided in the following sections of this chapter.

under the IPPCD. In case C-473/07,[55] the court was asked: '[m]ust subheading 6.6(a) of Annex I to Directive 96/61[...], which applies to installations for the intensive rearing of poultry with more than 40,000 places, be interpreted as including within its scope quails, partridges and pigeons'?[56] To answer this question, the court examined the purpose of the IPPCD and held that the purpose of the IPPCD has been broadly defined.[57] Hence, the court considered that subheading 6.6(a) of Annex I could not be interpreted narrowly so as to exclude quail, partridge, and pigeon.[58] Misonne considered that this case shows that the requirement of a high level of protection of the environment taken as a whole is 'effective in preventing restrictive interpretations' that tend to narrow the scope of industrial activities to be regulated under the IPPCD, helping 'to insert quails, partridges, pigeons and gilts within the scope of the [IPPCD]'.[59]

This case shows that the IPPCD and later the IED have a broad objective, which is used as a starting point by the court to interpret a specific provision. According to this broad objective, the scope of the IED should not be interpreted narrowly to exclude industrial activities that are not explicitly prescribed in the Directive. However, since this case is more relevant with regard to the scope of industrial activities to be regulated under the IED, it is not clear whether this broad objective can also help to prevent a narrow interpretation of the scope of IED concerning pollution alone, and to provide for a broad scope of integration covering environmental issues that are not explicitly mentioned in the provision on subject matter under the IED, such as taking the use of energy into consideration.

In summary, the provision on subject matter in article 1 of the IED can be interpreted in a narrow sense or a broad sense. In the narrow sense, the focus of this provision on pollution control without explicitly mentioning other environmental elements such as energy efficiency or the reasonable use of resources, indicates a limited scope of the integrated approach. However, in the broad sense, this provision also prescribes the protection of the environment taken as a whole, which may imply a wider scope of environmental elements to be integrated rather than just covering pollution control. Thus far, the case law has not provided clarity on this matter.

---

[55] Case C-473/07 Association nationale pour la protection des eaux et rivières-TOS and Association OABA v Ministère de l'Ecologie, du Développement et de l'Aménagement durables [22 January 2009] ERC I-00319.

[56] Ibid [14].

[57] Ibid [26]–[27]. The court followed the opinion of Advocate General that the 'integrated approach is realised by appropriate coordination of the procedure and authorisation conditions for industrial installations whose potential for pollution is significant, making it possible to achieve the highest level of protection for the environment as a whole, which must in all cases include provisions minimising long-distance or transboundary pollution and ensure a high level of protection for the environment as a whole'.

[58] Ibid [27]. Also see Case C-585/10 Niels Møller v Haderslev Kommune [15 December 2011] ERC I-13407 [28]–[33], using the similar reasoning for interpreting subheading 6.6(a) of Annex I to Directive 96/61 as including gilts (female pigs after puberty and before farrowing) within its scope.

[59] Delphine Misonne, 'The Importance of Setting a Target: The EU Ambition of a High Level of Protection' (2015) 4(1) Transnational Environmental Law 11, 26–27.

3.3.1.2 The Environmental Effectiveness of an Integrated Approach Pursued by the IED

The environmental effectiveness of integration refers to a certain level of environmental quality as a whole to be achieved.[60] This sub-section examines the environmental effectiveness of the integrated approach pursued by the IED. In order to do so, the meaning of 'a high level of protection' as prescribed in the provision on subject matter in article 1 of the IED needs to be investigated.

'A high level of protection' is considered as one of the most important objectives of EU environmental law.[61] Article 191(2) of the TFEU provides that 'Union policy on the environment shall aim at a high level of protection taking into account the diversity of situations in the various regions of the Union.' This objective can also be found in article 114 of the TFEU, together with other important issues, including a high level of health, safety, and consumer protection.[62] Krämer put forward that a specific reference to a high level of protection in the EU treaty provisions prohibits the adoption of measures at the EU level that only provide for the lowest common denominator of environmental protection.[63]

From another perspective, a high level of protection indicates that the highest possible level of protection of the environment taken as a whole is not required. This can be derived from cases C-284/95 and C-341/95, where the court ruled that:

> whilst it is undisputed that Article 130t of the Treaty [now article 193 TFEU] requires Community policy in environmental matters to aim for a high level of protection, such a level of protection [...] does not necessarily have to be the highest that is technically possible. [...] Article 130t of the Treaty [now article 193 TFEU] authorises the Member States to maintain or introduce more stringent protective measures.[64]

From these two cases, a high level of environmental protection 'does not necessarily aim to ensure absolute, immediate, and global protection of the environment'.[65] Furthermore, the rationale for not requiring the highest level of protection is that

---

[60] See Sect. 2.3.1.2 of Chap. 2.

[61] Ludwig Krämer, *EU environmental law* (Sweet & Maxwell, 2015, 12–13); Geert Van Calster and Leonie Reins, *EU environmental law* (Edward Elgar, 2017, 12–13).

[62] TFEU art 114(3) prescribes that:

> The Commission, in its proposals envisaged in paragraph 1 concerning health, safety, environmental protection and consumer protection, will take as a base a high level of protection, taking account in particular of any new development based on scientific facts. Within their respective powers, the European Parliament and the Council will also seek to achieve this objective.

[63] Ludwig Krämer (2015), 12–13.

[64] Case C-284/95 Safety Hi-Tech Srl v S. & T. Srl. [14 July 1998] ECLI:EU:C:1998:352 [49]; Case C-341/95 Bettati v Safety Hi-Tech [14 July 1998] ECLI:EU:C:1998:353 [47].

[65] Elisa Moregera, 'Environmental law' in Catherine Barnard and Steve Peers (eds), European Union law (Oxford University Press 2020), 60.

Member States may introduce more stringent protective measures.[66] Member States are allowed to adopt more stringent measures at the national level by virtue of article 193 TFEU. However, Misonne showed concern that the rulings that do not require the highest level of protection can be 'easily misinterpreted as a permission, or even an obligation' of not imposing ambitious measures which potentially undermines the requirement of a high level of protection.[67]

In summary, 'a high level of protection of the environment taken as a whole' can be understood as the requirement of the environmental effectiveness of integration. It indicates that the lowest level of protection of the environment taken as a whole is not allowed, but the highest possible level of the environment taken as a whole is also not required. However, a concrete meaning of 'a high level of protection of the environment taken as a whole' cannot be identified in the IED. The theory shows that, due to the incommensurability of environmental goods, a high level of protection can only be quantified in a media-specific way, which is often demonstrated as environmental quality standards.[68] The IED laid down the rules on environmental quality standards,[69] which requires concrete levels of protection for certain environmental media. In this vein, the rule on environmental quality standards as laid down in the IED can provide for further insight into the effectiveness of integration, which will be discussed in Sect. 3.8.

3.3.1.3 The Objective of Zero Pollution

On 12 May 2021, the Commission published an action plan: 'Towards Zero Pollution for Air, Water and Soil', in which the IED is recognized as a main instrument to steer the EU towards zero pollution.[70] On 5 April 2022, the Commission published a proposal to amend the IED, which aims to progress towards zero pollution, 'thereby contributing to the objectives of reaching carbon neutrality, increased energy efficiency, a non-toxic environment and a circular economy'.[71] However, few changes are proposed in the subject matter of the IED.[72] Until now it is unclear whether

---

[66] Lorenzo Squintani, 'Beyond minimum harmonisation: gold-plating and green-plating of European environmental law' (Cambridge University Press 2019), 9.

[67] Delphine Misonne (2015), 20.

[68] See Sect. 2.3.1.2 of Chap. 2.

[69] IED art 3(6), art 18, and art 21(5)(c).

[70] Commission (EU), 'EU Action Plan: Towards Zero Pollution for Air, Water and Soil' COM(2021) 400 final, 12 May 2021, 10.

[71] Commission (EU), COM(2022)156 final, 5 April 2022, 4.

[72] Ibid, art 1, and see also ibid, 17—a short explanation:

> The amendment to Article 1 aims at explicitly clarifying that this Directive lays down rules designed to prevent or, where that is not practicable, to reduce emissions into air, water and land and to prevent the generation of waste, in order to achieve a high level of protection of the environment and of human health taken as a whole; consistent with Article 191 of the Treaty on the Functioning of the European Union (TFEU).

the revision including the policy ambition of zero pollution for a toxic-free environment will require—in a revised IED—a more ambitious level of protection in view of the environmental effectiveness of integration. While, as already indicated, the Commission has introduced the aim of zero pollution in its policy documents, it does not propose to insert this concept into the provisions of the IED. Also, the concerns regarding climate, energy, and circular economy policies cannot be read into the provision on the subject matter of the IED.

3.3.2 The Concern of Achieving a Level Playing Field

The concern of achieving a level playing field is added by the IED in its recital: an integrated approach will 'contribute to the achievement of a level playing field in the Union by aligning environmental performance requirements for industrial installations.'[73] Oosterhuis and Peeters considered that recital 3 of the IED shows that 'market integration by means of a level playing field has become part of the integrated permitting approach'.[74] Similarly, Braaksma and Tolsma claimed that 'reaching a level playing field within the EU by aligning environmental performance requirements for industrial installations is also an objective of the instrument.'[75]

According to the IED, a level playing field within the Union is to be achieved by aligning environmental performance requirements for industrial installations. This means that an integrated approach pursued by the IED will entail the alignment of environmental performance requirements at the EU level. The alignment of environmental performance requirements indicates that the IED intends to apply a generic option to deal with the incommensurability of environmental goods.[76] However, the necessity of aligning environmental performance requirements can be questioned in view of an integrated environmental permit. Theoretically, an integrated approach does not necessarily require a generic option, as it can also be implemented using case-specific decision-making which would lead to the differentiation of environmental performance requirements.[77] Furthermore, the literature also points out that

---

Although the proposed provision on the subject matter now explicitly refers to 'human health', this aim is already enshrined in the definition of pollution in the current IED. See IED art 3(2):

> 'pollution' means the direct or indirect introduction, as a result of human activity, of substances, vibrations, heat or noise into air, water or land which may be harmful to human health or the quality of the environment, result in damage to material property, or impair or interfere with amenities and other legitimate uses of the environment.

[73] IED recital 3.

[74] Frans Oosterhuis and Marjan Peeters (2014), 97.

[75] Lolke S. Braaksma and Hanna D. Tolsma, 'Integrated Pollution Prevention and Control: A Critical Legal Perspective on All-inclusive Integration' in: Marjan Peeters and Mariolina Eliantonio (eds), *Research Handbook on EU environmental law* (Edward Elgar 2020), 318.

[76] For an explanation of the generic option, see Sect. 3.3.1.3 of Sect. 3.2.

[77] See Sect. 2.3.1.3 of Chap. 2.

generic environmental performance requirements may limit the choice of technologies that can better protect the environment as a whole.[78] In particular, given the principle of subsidiarity, since the generic option is not perfect and another legislative choice can be to establish a case-specific option, it can be questioned why the alignment of environmental performance requirements at the EU levels is necessary.

3.3.3 Interim Conclusion

The IED aims at transforming the traditional sectoral approach to the integrated approach to achieve a high level of protection of the environment taken as a whole, but there is also a market concern of achieving a level playing field in the pursuit of an integrated approach.

The objective of protecting the environment as a whole at a high level, as prescribed in the provision on the subject matter of the IED delineates two dimensions of an integrated approach: the scope of an integrated approach and the environmental effectiveness of an integrated approach. In terms of the scope of an integrated approach pursued by the IED, the provision on subject matter can be interpreted in a narrow sense and a broad sense. In the narrow sense, since the provision on the subject matter of the IED focuses on pollution control without explicitly mentioning other environmental elements, such as energy efficiency or the reasonable use of resources, it may delimit the scope of an integrated approach within pollution control, basically covering emissions into the air, water, and land. In the broad sense, this provision also prescribes the protection of the environment taken as a whole, which may imply a broader scope of environmental elements to be integrated rather than just concerning pollution control alone.

In terms of the environmental effectiveness of an integrated approach pursued by the IED, ‘a high level of protection’ indicates that the lowest level of protection of the environment taken as a whole is not allowed, but the highest possible level of protection of the environment taken as a whole is not required (considering that Member States may adopt stricter measures). Nevertheless, the concrete meaning of protecting the environment taken as a whole in view of the scope and the environmental effectiveness of integration is not clear, and thus the examination of the detailed provisions adopted in the IED is needed.

The IED is also intended to implement an integrated approach by means of applying generic environmental performance requirements for industrial installations at the EU level and, thus, to contribute to ensuring a level playing field. This indicates that the IED intends to apply a generic option to deal with the incommensurability of environmental goods to implement an integrated approach. However, its necessity can be questioned. For further insights into the option as adopted by the IED to deal with the incommensurability of environmental goods, an analysis of the detailed rules for the permit system is needed.

[78] Ibid.

3.4 Rules on the Application for the Permit

As analyzed in Sect. 3.3, the provision prescribing the objective of the IED does not provide for an exact explanation of the integrated approach to be pursued by the IED. Hence, it is necessary to delve into the detailed rules on the key stages of the permitting procedure. This section examines the rules on the application procedure for a permit as laid down in the IED, which consists of three parts. First, Sect. 4.1 analyzes what environmental information has to be collected by the operators and then submitted to the competent authorities to set permit conditions. Section 4.2 explains that the rules on the application procedure for a permit can serve as a coordination tool from the perspective of procedural integration. The last section provides an interim conclusion.

3.4.1 The Obligatory Content of the Permit Application

Article 12(1) of the IED lists a set of information to be included in the application of the permit. This information includes, for example, the use or generation of raw materials and energy, the sources, nature, and quantities of emissions from the installation, a baseline report,[79] the techniques for controlling emissions, the measures for the management of waste, etc. With this provision, the IED provides for a broad scope of environmental elements to be collected by operators applying for the emissions permit, concerning not just emissions, but also other environmental elements, such as the use or generation of raw materials and energy. The requirements for the contents of an application for a permit help to 'enhance incentives for operator reflection on environmental performance', otherwise operators may tend to be ignorant.[80] According to the Commission in its explanatory memorandum of the IPPCD proposal from 1993, the incentives for operators to reflect on their environmental performance can derive from the requirement to make applications publicly available:

> as the application will be publicly available there will be every incentive on the operator to ensure that the application does not avoid the environmental issues (and that he is compared unfavourably with his competitors).[81]

---

[79] As defined by IED art 3(19), the 'baseline report' means 'information on the state of soil and groundwater contamination by relevant hazardous substances'.

[80] Maria Lee, *EU environmental law, governance and decision-making* (Bloomsbury 2014), 124.

[81] Commission (EC), COM(93) 423 final, 14 September 1993, 15. Later, in 1998, the Aarhus Convention was concluded which, in its article 6, also includes obligations to inform the public about permit-applications (article 6(2)(a) of this Convention). Hence, EU law already provided transparency provisions before the Aarhus Convention became applicable. IED art 24 and Annex IV prescribe the requirement of making the applications for permits publicly available.

In addition to this expectation that the publication of the permit application will encourage operators to reflect well on the environmental consequences of the installation,[82] the Commission also explained at that time that it is cheaper and simpler for operators to examine the options for the environmental protection thoroughly at the design stage of the plant.[83] In this vein, by prescribing the contents of the application for a permit, the IED aims to stimulate operators to consider their environmental performance in an integrated manner in the design of the plant, also in view of making cost-effective decisions.

In addition, according to the Commission in its explanatory memorandum of the IPPCD proposal from 1993, the obligatory contents of an application for a permit 'will allow the public authorities to further strengthen their knowledge about BAT'.[84] However, it can be questioned to what extent competent authorities can strengthen their knowledge about BAT in practice from the applications for emissions permit.[85] For example, in the IED, there is an obligation requiring applicants to submit a description of 'the main alternatives to the proposed technology, techniques and measures studied by the applicant in outline'.[86] Scholars consider that reference to the alternatives described in the applications 'seeks to steer regulators to include "green" production technologies',[87] but since the description of the alternative technologies is provided in summary, this 'weakens the requirement to engage in a serious consideration of the environmental consequences of different process technologies and to select the best one on environmental grounds'.[88]

3.4.2 The Coordination Tool for Achieving Procedural Integration

Neither the IPPCD nor the IED requires Member States to establish one single permit procedure; where there are several permit procedures (such as, for example, for water and for waste, respectively), it is required that the procedures should be fully coordinated.[89] According to the Commission, in its explanatory memorandum of the IPPCD proposal from 1993, the obligatory contents of the application for a permit was 'intended to help authorities with statutory responsibilities for a single

[82] However, there is no empirical evidence yet published in English that this incentive indeed 'works'.

[83] Commission (EC), COM(93) 423 final, 14 September 1993, 15.

[84] Ibid. 'BAT' stands for Best Available Techniques.

[85] No empirical evidence published in English can be found that competent authorities indeed strengthen their knowledge about BAT from the applications for emissions permits.

[86] IED art 12(1)(k).

[87] Elizabeth Fisher, Bettina Lange and Eloise Scotford, *Environmental law: text, cases & materials* (Oxford University Press 2019), 436.

[88] Ibid.

[89] IED art 5(2). For a further discussion on this provision, see Sect. 3.5 of this chapter.

environmental medium to take account of wider environmental issues'.[90] In this vein, the obligatory contents of the application for a permit was intended to serve as a coordination tool from the perspective of procedural integration, as it can facilitate different authorities in charge of sectoral procedures to take account of separate environmental decisions.

In addition, the provision concerning applications for permits in the IED mentions two specific directives, prescribing that when information produced in response to the two directives fulfills any of the requirements of this provisions, that information may be used in the application.[91] The first is a directive on the environmental impact assessment (EIA) (Directive 85/337/EEC on the assessment of the effects of certain public and private projects on the environment).[92] This EIA Directive was amended three times respectively in 1997,[93] in 2003,[94] and in 2009.[95] Directive 85/337/EEC and its three amendments were codified by Directive 2011/92/EU of 13 December 2011,[96] and the codification was amended in 2014 by Directive 2014/52/EU[97] (hereinafter 'EIA Directive'[98]). The EIA Directive aims to 'identify, describe and assess in an appropriate manner, in the light of each individual case, the direct and

[90] Commission (EC), COM(93) 423 final, 14 September 1993, 15.

[91] IED art 12(2).

[92] Directive 85/337/EEC of 27 June 1985 on the assessment of the effects of certain public and private projects on the environment (1985) OJ L 175/40 (EIA), which was amended three times in in 1997, 2003, and 2009. This initial Directive 85/337/EEC and its three amendments were codified by Directive 2011/92/EU of 13 December 2011. The codification was amended in 2014 by Directive 2014/52/EU.

[93] Directive 97/11/EC of 3 March 1997 amending Directive 85/337/EEC on the assessment of the effects of certain public and private projects on the environment (1997) OJ L 73/5.

[94] Directive 2003/35/EC of the European Parliament and of the Council of 26 May 2003 providing for public participation in respect of the drawing up of certain plans and programmes relating to the environment and amending with regard to public participation and access to justice Council Directives 85/337/EEC and 96/61/EC (2003) OJ L 156/17.

[95] Directive 2009/31/EC of the European Parliament and of the Council of 23 April 2009 on the geological storage of carbon dioxide and amending Council Directive 85/337/EEC, European Parliament and Council Directives 2000/60/EC, 2001/80/EC, 2004/35/EC, 2006/12/EC, 2008/1/EC and Regulation (EC) No 1013/2006 (2009) OJ L 140/114.

[96] Directive 2011/92/EU of the European Parliament and of the Council of 13 December 2011 on the assessment of the effects of certain public and private projects on the environment (2011) OJ L 26/1.

[97] Directive 2014/52/EU of the European Parliament and of the Council of 16 April 2014 amending Directive 2011/92/EU on the assessment of the effects of certain public and private projects on the environment (2014) OJ L 124/1.

[98] EIA Directive here only refers to the latest version of the EIA Directive, namely Directive 2011/92/EU amended by Directive 2014/52/EU. As to the previous Directives on the assessment of the effects of certain public and private projects on the environment, this book will indicate them specifically if they are discussed.

indirect significant [environmental] effects of a project'.[99] In the explanatory memorandum of the IPPCD proposal from 1993, the Commission explained that 'in order to avoid the unnecessary duplication of work, that any impact assessment undertaken by virtue of [EIA Directive], may be submitted to the competent authority as part of the IPC application'.[100] The IED provision concerning applications for permits also mentions Directive 96/82/EC on the control of major accident hazards involving dangerous substances,[101] which has been amended and repealed by Directive 2012/18/EU (hereinafter 'Seveso Directive').[102] The Seveso Directive aims at 'the prevention of major accidents which involve dangerous substances, and the limitation of their consequences for human health and the environment'.[103] Article 12(2) of the IED states that a safety report prepared in accordance with the Seveso Directive may be included in the application. The reason for such a suggestion is that, according to the Commission's explanatory memorandum of the IPPCD proposal from 1993, 'it is opportune to draw the attention of environmental regulators from the outset to safety management'.[104] From the perspective of procedural integration, the rule of allowing information produced in response to the other directives to be used in the application for a permit can facilitate the coordination between the IED and other directives.

3.4.3 *Interim Conclusion*

The IED lists a set of environmental information that must be included in the application for the permit. By prescribing the contents of the permit application, the IED aims to encourage operators to consider their environmental performance in an integrated manner in the design stage of the plant. Whether and to what extent these provisions indeed help to avoid ignorance by operators is not yet empirically tested.[105] This

[99] EIA Directive art 3(1). Further discussion on the interaction between the procedure for emissions permits as prescribed in the IED and the procedure for an environmental impact assessment as prescribed in the EIA Directive is provided in Sect. 3.5.2 of this chapter.

[100] Commission (EC), COM(93) 423 final, 14 September 1993, 16. 'IPC' stands for 'integrated pollution control'.

[101] Directive 96/82/EC of 9 December 1996 on the control of major-accident hazards involving dangerous substances (1996) OJ L 10/13.

[102] Directive 2012/18/EU of the European Parliament and of the Council of 4 July 2012 on the control of major accident hazards involving dangerous substances, amending and subsequently repealing Council Directive 96/82/EC (2012) OJ L 197/1. In the IPPCD, Directive 82/501/EEC of 24 June 1982 on the major accident hazards of certain industrial activities was mentioned in the provision on applications for permits at that time.

[103] Seveso Directive art 1.

[104] Commission (EC), COM(93) 423 final, 14 September 1993, 16.

[105] To my best knowledge, there is no peer reviewed published research on this matter. Moreover, with the increase of attention on the need to protect the environment and the need for Corporate Sustainable Responsibility, it may be that, over time, less ignorance (as suggested by Maria Lee) may evolve.

information is submitted to the authorities, which, according to the Commission, will allow the public authorities to strengthen their knowledge about BAT for setting permit conditions. The contents of the application for a permit do not just address emissions, but also other environmental elements, such as the use or generation of raw materials and energy. In view of the scope of integration, this means that a broad scope of environmental issues must be considered by the operators. In addition, the rules of allowing information produced in response to sectoral procedures to be used in the application for a permit also serve as a coordination tool from the perspective of procedural integration.

3.5 Rules on Issuing a Permit

This section examines the rules on the administrative decision to issue the emissions permit. In order to guarantee an effective integrated approach, the IED requires Member States to ensure that 'the conditions of, and the procedures for the granting of, the permit are fully coordinated where more than one competent authority or more than one operator is involved or more than one permit is granted'.[106] From the perspective of procedural integration,[107] this shows that the IED does not require one authority to be in charge of one permitting procedure, but prescribes a coordination mechanism to implement an integrated approach. Theoretically, the effective procedural integration of the permit system serves as a prerequisite for the substantive integration of permit decisions. Related to this, from the perspective of legislative techniques for internal integration in cases where codification takes place but is not complete, coordination can serve as an important supplement for achieving internal integration. Coordination occurs when the separate decision-making procedures are not harmonized but the legislature has provided legal rules which force the authorities to take the separate procedures into account.[108] Therefore, it can be asked to what extent coordination, as prescribed by the IED, can serve a prerequisite or a supplement for achieving an integrated approach.

The following sub-sections first examine the meaning of full coordination (Sect. 3.5.1) and then delve into the rules regarding the coordination within the EIA procedure (Sect. 3.5.2). The last section provides an interim conclusion.

[106] IED art 5(2).

[107] See Sect. 2.3.2 of Chap. 2.

[108] See Sect. 2.2.2 of Chap. 2.

3.5.1 The Meaning of Full Coordination

There are no detailed provisions provided by the IED to clarify what is intended by full coordination. In order to understand the meaning of full coordination, this sub-section investigates the drafting history and relevant literature.

In the initial proposal for a Council Directive on Integrated Pollution Prevention and Control from 1993, the proposed directive prescribed that:

> In order to facilitate an integrated approach, Member States shall appoint, where there is no single competent authority, a supreme competent authority to coordinate the licensing procedure. Member States may identify different supreme competent authorities for different categories of installations.[109]

According to the explanatory memorandum of the proposal, rather than requiring the establishment of a single environmental authority in each Member State, it was proposed that Member States identify a lead authority for all installations or for different categories of installation, and this would not affect the right of other competent authorities to set conditions in the permit.[110] Compared to the current article, the initial proposed article indicated a type of organizational arrangement, as it required Member States to appoint a supreme competent authority.[111] However, this requirement immediately entailed doubts or requests for clarification from the Council,[112] and it was then deleted by the Council.[113] During the first reading of the proposal by the Council, a further suggestion for full coordination was put forward by some delegations, namely introducing a mechanism to coordinate the various competent authorities, but this suggestion was subject to disagreement[114] and was not accepted in the end. Furthermore, compared to the current article, in the initial proposed article, the coordination of the content of the permit was not covered.[115] During the reading of the proposal by the Council, several delegations considered that the requirement

[109] Commission (EC), COM(93) 423 final, 14 September 1993, art 6.

[110] Ibid, 16.

[111] Although the European Commission emphasized that there was no intention to intervene in the internal organization of the Member States, it also claimed that, for the purposes of arriving at an 'integrated permit', it would be necessary to designate a 'coordinating' competent authority. See the Council (EC), 'OUTCOME OF PROCEEDINGS of Working Party on the Environment on 12 and 13 January 1994' (04.02) 4383/94, 28 January 1994, 5.

[112] Council (EC), 'OUTCOME OF PROCEEDINGS of Working Party on the Environment on 8 December 1993' (10.01) 11508/93, 21 December 1993, 3.

[113] The Council was requested to act on the proposal in June 1994, and the requirement of appointing a supreme authority was deleted in the drafting suggestions for article 6. See Council (EC), 'Working document ENV/94/22 on Proposal for a Council Directive on integrated pollution prevention and control–Meeting of the Working Party on the Environment on 15 June 1994' (14.06) SN 2860/94, Brussels, 10 June 1994.

[114] For example, the delegation from the Netherlands suggested introducing a mechanism to 'bring together the various competent authorities', while the German delegation felt that the arrangements should be left to the Member States. See Council (EC), (04.02) 4383/94, Brussels, 28 January 1994, 5.

[115] Commission (EC), COM(93) 423 final, 14 September 1993, art 6 prescribes that:

of procedural coordination did not sufficiently reflect the objective of achieving integration.[116] Based on this consideration, the United Kingdom delegation gave a more concrete suggestion to introduce a so-called arbitration system which, in the event of several competent authorities disagreeing on the conditions of the best environmental option to be chosen, would trigger a conciliation mechanism.[117] Its rationale was to avoid the separate determination of permit conditions, which could result in the full implementation of one condition jeopardizing the full implementation of the others. Take for an example the situation where there is one technique that reduces emissions into the air but increases emissions into water and another technique that reduces emissions into water but increases emissions into the air.[118] If the respective competent authorities in charge of air and water do not reach an agreement, and may apply different techniques separately for setting permit conditions at the same time, the result is that the full implementation of one set of conditions may prejudice the other conditions. To avoid this result, where there are two techniques regarding different environmental sectors that could not be enforced at the same time, only one should be chosen and specified in the permit.[119] However, this suggestion was also subject to disagreement and was not accepted in the end. Even though further concrete suggestions had been put forward, they were not discussed in more detail and the final provision remained vague. This may imply that the legislators did not intend to establish a concrete regulation on how to fully coordinate permit conditions

> In order to facilitate an integrated approach, Member States shall appoint, where there is no single competent authority, a supreme competent authority to coordinate the licensing procedure. Member States may identify different supreme competent authorities for different categories of installations.

[116] Particularly, the delegation from Denmark suggested that 'the substance of the permits, rather than procedures, should be co-ordinated'. See Council (EC), 'OUTCOME OF PROCEEDINGS of Working Party on the Environment on 15 June 1994' (11.07) 8019/94, Brussels, 28 June 1994, 7.

[117] Ibid.

[118] More specifically, see Commission (EC), 'Integrated Pollution Prevention and Control Reference Document on Economics and Cross-Media Effects', July 2006, 30, available at https://eippcb.jrc.ec.europa.eu/sites/default/files/2019-11/ecm_bref_0706.pdf, accessed on 3 November 2021:

> One technique might lead to emissions of methane to air corresponding to 0.01% of the total methane emissions to air in the (EU) sector and at the same time, a level of emissions of phenols to water corresponding to 1% of the total phenol emissions to water in the (EU) sector. Similarly, a second technique might lead to emissions of methane to air corresponding to 0.1% of the total methane emissions to air in the (EU) sector and emissions of phenols to water corresponding to 0.001% of the total phenol emissions to water in the (EU) sector. Compared to the first technique, the second thus leads to 10 times higher relative methane emissions to air but 1000 times lower relative phenol emissions to water.

[119] A similar definition is presented in the literature: coordination refers to 'a process in which efforts are made to utilize different elements in such a way that they do not run counter to one another, while the incongruities between those elements continue to exist'. See Otto, J. M., 'Implementation of Environmental Law: Harmonization, Environmental Management and Enforcement by the Courts, with References to Indonesia and the Netherlands' (1997) INDONESIAN J. ENVTL. L., 33, quoted by Michael G. Faure (2000), 176.

and procedures for the court to test it. This provides for the possibility of significant variation across Member States in the extent to which permitting officials in different environmental regulatory authorities really talk to each other when issuing separate parts of a permit.[120] According to the reports of the Commission on implementation, due to differences in the internal administrative organization of Member States, various degrees of coordination among Member States have been reported.[121] Related to this, it would be interesting to see how the coordination procedures for implementing the IED will be tested by the court. However, at this time, no case decided by the CJEU has presented a more precise definition of the full coordination of permit procedures.[122] Thus, it is not clear how the requirement of full coordination as prescribed by the IED truly requires procedural integration.

3.5.2 Coordination with the EIA Procedure

This section delves into the provisions prescribing coordination between the IED permit procedure and the EIA procedure as laid down by the IED and the EIA Directive.

According to article 5(3) of the IED, in the case of a new installation or a substantial change where the EIA Directive applies, any relevant information or conclusion of the EIA shall be examined and used for the purposes of granting the permit. This provision can be interpreted as a requirement of procedural integration, i.e. integrating the EIA procedure into the emissions permit procedure. However, the term 'relevant' in article 5(3) of the IED indicates that not all information or conclusion of the EIA shall be examined and used for the purposes of granting the emissions permit. Hence, this implies that full integration between the EIA procedure and the emissions permit procedure is not required by the IED. The IED does not provide a concrete explanation on what accounts for relevant EIA information. In this vein, Member States have discretion in deciding what EIA information is to be examined and used when issuing emissions permits. It can be further asked what the limits to such discretion are. Case law could provide a further interpretation on this matter.[123]

---

[120] Elizabeth Fisher, Bettina Lange and Eloise Scotford (2019), 435.

[121] Commission (EU), 'Report from the Commission on the implementation of Directive 2008/1/EC concerning integrated pollution prevention and control and Directive 1999/13/EC on the limitation of emissions of volatile organic compounds due to the use of organic solvents in certain activities and installations' COM(2010) 593 final, 25 October 2010, 4–5 providing two examples: 'Spain has nominated a main responsible authority which receives contributions from other authorities (e.g. municipalities, River Basin Authorities), whilst Austria has established an authority responsible for the overall permitting procedure and for appointing relevant experts for specific subject areas'. Also see Eberhard Bohne (2008), 18 providing more information about the national practice in terms of various degrees of coordination.

[122] It was found that nine cases decided by the CJEU indirectly referred to the article prescribing full coordination through art 5 of the IPPCD that prescribed requirements for the granting of permits for existing installations. These cases concern installations operating without a permit.

[123] Thus far, there is no case law from the CJEU providing further interpretations on this matter.

In addition, the EIA Directive provides for two options in terms of how to achieve the integration between the EIA procedure and the IED permit procedure:

(1) Coordinated procedure, under which Member States shall endeavor to coordinate the various individual assessments of the environmental impact of a particular project by designating an authority for this purpose; and
(2) Joint procedure, under which Member States shall endeavor to provide for a single assessment of the environmental impact of a particular project.[124]

A combination of the two procedures is also possible.[125] The option of a coordinated procedure, joint procedure, or a combination thereof, are also collectively known as a 'one-stop-shop'. These rules to adopt the 'one-stop-shop' approach is formulated as an option for Member States but not as an obligation. In practice, it is not evident that the 'one-stop-shop' has been widely established by the Member States.[126] In other words, it is not evident that procedural integration takes place in the implementation of the IED and the EIA Directive.

3.5.3 *Interim Conclusion*

According to the rules on granting of the emissions permit under the IED, Member States are not required to establish one procedure. Where more than one procedure exists, Member States shall establish a coordination mechanism for implementing an integrated approach. Very importantly, the IED prescribes that 'the conditions of, and the procedures for the granting of, the permit are fully coordinated … in order to guarantee an effective integrated approach by all authorities'.[127] However, the IED does not provide for further concrete provisions on how the full coordination mechanism should be established and thus leaves flexibility to Member States. Thus far, there is no case law from the CJEU providing further interpretations on this

---

124 EIA Directive art 2(3).

125 Ibid.

126 According to art 2(3) of the old EIA Directive (Directive 2011/92/EU), 'Member States may provide for a single procedure in order to fulfill the requirements of this Directive and the requirements of [IPPCD]'. The review of the old EIA Directive by the Commission found that most Member States have not established a single procedure and have not improved the coherence of their policy implementation. See Commission (EU), COMMISSION STAFF WORKING PAPER IMPACT ASSESSMENT Accompanying the document PROPOSAL FOR A DIRECTIVE OF THE EUROPEAN PARLIAMENT AND OF THE COUNCIL amending Directive 2011/92/EU on the assessment of the effects of certain public and private projects on the environment SWD(2012) 355 final, 26 October 2012, 16 and 87;

Also see Vajda's presentation on 'Implementation of the IED—most important legal issues', in the field of large combustion plants and landfills, it seems that not many Member States (among 20 Member States) take the 'one-stop-shop' approach. See Peter Vajda, 'Implementation of the IED—most important legal issues' in IED Workshop for national judges 11–12 November 2019, 26–27.

127 IED art 5(2).

matter. In practice, various degrees of coordination among Member States have been reported.

In addition, the IED prescribes that the relevant information produced in response to the EIA Directive has to be examined and used in the granting of emissions permits, which can be interpreted as the requirement of coordination between the EIA procedure and the IED permit procedure. However, the IED does not provide for concrete explanation on what accounts for relevant EIA information and thus leaves flexibility for the Member States. Thus far, there is no case law from the CJEU providing further interpretations on this matter. The EIA Directive suggests the so-called 'one-stop-shop' approach for achieving procedural integration: to establish a coordinated procedure or/and joint procedure. However, to adopt the 'one-stop-shop' approach is an option for Member States, but it is not an obligation. In practice, it is not evident that the 'one-stop-shop' has been widely established by Member States. In other words, it is not evident that the procedural integration between the EIA procedure and the IED permit procedure takes place in the implementation of the IED and the EIA Directive.

In summary, since the rules on the coordination as laid down by the IED are formulated in a vague manner, it is not clear how these rules truly require procedural integration, and thus it is also not clear whether these rules can serve a prerequisite or a supplement for achieving an integrated approach.

3.6 Rules on Setting Permit Conditions

This section and the following Sects. 3.7–3.8 examine the rules on setting permit conditions as laid down in the IED in order to gain further insight into the substantive integration pursued by the IED. Article 14 of the IED prescribes the content of permit conditions. First, it refers to the 'general principles governing the basic obligations of the operator' which are laid down in article 11 of the IED.[128] Member States and, more particularly, the competent authority in its decision on the permit, have to ensure that the permit includes all the measures necessary for compliance with these principles. The requirement of 'general principles governing the basic obligations of the operator' provides for a general description of the 'appropriate' or 'necessary' measures that have to be taken by the operator, including preventive measures taken against pollution[129]; measures taken regarding accidents and their consequences[130]; measures taken regarding the definitive cessation of activities[131]; measures taken regarding the generation and management of wastes[132]; and measures taken regarding

[128] IED art 14(1), art 11 and art 18.

[129] IED art 11(a).

[130] IED art 11(g).

[131] IED art 11(h).

[132] IED art 11(d) and art 11(e).

the efficient use of energy.[133] From this, it can be derived that the content of permit conditions does not concern pollution only, but it also requires the consideration of other environmental issues, such as the use of energy. The IED does not include the reasonable use of resources in the basic obligations of the operators.[134] In this vein, Oosterhuis and Peeters questioned 'to what extent the use of raw materials can be regulated with the permit'.[135] Related to this, the Commission proposes to include the efficient use of material resources and water into the basic obligations of the operator in the revision of the IED.[136] In addition, according to the general principles laid down in article 11 of the IED, operators have to apply the BAT.[137] In order to ensure the application of BAT by operators, the IED requires that permit conditions have to be set on the basis of BAT.[138] Hence, the concept of BAT serves one of the most important pillars for achieving an integrated approach.[139]

Operators are also obliged to ensure that no significant pollution is caused.[140] The IED does not further clarify what accounts for significant pollution, but does define pollution, which relates pollution to the damage to the quality of the environment.[141] In other words, to check the obligation of ensuring that no significant pollution is caused, a definition of a certain level of environmental protection is needed. Case law provides for further clarification on this issue. In Case C-375/21, the court followed the opinion of Advocate General that the EU legislature defines a high level of protection of the environment by setting environmental quality standards, and an exceedance of environmental quality standards cannot be regarded as insignificant pollution but is necessarily significant.[142]

---

[133] IED art 11(f).

[134] IED art 11.

[135] Frans Oosterhuis and Marjan Peeters (2014), 108. Oosterhuis and Peeters also noticed that the use of raw materials may play a role in the process of determining the BAT, as prescribed in IPPCD Annex IV point 9 and later the IED Annex III point 9, and questioned how it should exactly play a role in the permit conditions. For a further discussion on this matter, see Sect. 3.7.5.2 of this chapter.

[136] Commission (EU), COM (2022)156 final, 5 April 2022, art 1(8).

[137] IED art 11 (b).

[138] IED recital 12.

[139] Section 3.7 of this chapter provides an analysis on the detailed rules on the BAT for setting permit conditions in light of the question to what extent they facilitate an integrated approach.

[140] IED art 11(c).

[141] IED art 3(2) provides the definition of 'pollution':

> 'the direct or indirect introduction, as a result of human activity, of substances, vibrations, heat or noise into air, water or land *which may be* harmful to human health or *the quality of the environment*, result in damage to material property, or impair or interfere with amenities and other legitimate uses of the environment'. The *italic format* was added by the author for emphasis.

[142] Case C-375/21 Sdruzhenie "Za Zemyata—dostap do pravosadie" and Others [9 March 2023] ECLI:EU:C:2023:173, [50]. This case is also discussed in Sect. 3.7.4.3.3 and Sect. 3.8 of this chapter.

Furthermore, according to article 14(1) of the IED, Member States shall ensure that the permit includes all measures necessary for compliance with the requirements of article 18 of the IED, which basically regulates that if stricter conditions than those achievable by the use of the BAT are required by the environmental quality standards, additional measures shall be included in the permit.[143] In other words, the BAT is not the only basis for setting permit conditions, but environmental quality standards also play an important role in the setting of permit conditions for achieving integration.

In summary, the IED requires that the contents of permit conditions have to be set for compliance with the requirements of the general principles governing the basic obligations of the operator and for fulfilling the environmental quality standards. The requirement of the contents of permit conditions indicates two important substantive requirements: the BAT and environmental quality standards. How they possibly facilitate or require an integrated approach is discussed in detail in the following two sections.

3.7 Rules on the Best Available Techniques

3.7.1 Introduction

This section examines the rules on the Best Available Techniques for setting permit conditions. According to the IED, Member States, and, more particularly, the competent authority in its decision on the permit, have to ensure that operators apply the BAT.[144] This section starts with the rationale for introducing the concept of BAT into the IPPCD and later continuing with it in a slightly different way in the IED. It will be explained that the concept of BAT has been introduced with the aim of addressing the incommensurability of environmental goods by providing a common basis where the environmental impact on different environmental media can be weighed (Sect. 3.7.2). Therefore, the analysis of the (often detailed) rules on the determination of the BAT for the setting of permit conditions should focus on addressing the questions of what environmental impacts have to be weighed; and also how they have to be weighed, so as to provide for further insight into the scope of an integrated approach and the options to deal with the incommensurability of environmental goods as required by the IED.

The analysis of the detailed rules on the BAT is divided into five parts. It starts with analyzing the definition of BAT (Sect. 3.7.3), after which the concrete rules on

[143] IED art 18 prescribing that:

> Where an environmental quality standard requires stricter conditions than those achievable by the use of the best available techniques, additional measures shall be included in the permit, without prejudice to other measures which may be taken to comply with environmental quality standards.

[144] IED art 11 (b).

how to determine the BAT for setting permit conditions are analyzed. Sections 3.7.4 and 3.7.5 respectively investigate the rules on the use of so-called BREFs (BAT reference documents) and BAT conclusions for the determination of BAT in setting permit conditions and other rules on the determination of BAT in setting permit conditions. The IED also requires the setting of minimum requirements in the permit to be based on the integrated approach and the BAT, and thus rules on setting minimum requirements are also analyzed (Sect. 3.7.6). The final part (Sect. 3.7.7) provides an interim conclusion on how the rules on the BAT aim to serve the integrated approach.

3.7.2 The Rationale for the Concept of Best Available Techniques

This sub-section examines the rationale for the concept of BAT, on the basis of the drafting document of the Commission proposal for the IPPCD from 1993 that introduced the concept of BAT as well as the discussion of the concept in literature.

Before the introduction of the concept of BAT in the IPPCD, there was a similar concept—*Best Available Technology Not Entailing Excessive Costs* (BATNEEC)—in some EC directives, such as the Directive on the Combating of Air Pollution from Industrial Plants (84/360/EEC).[145] According to the explanatory memorandum of the Commission proposal for the IPPCD from 1993, there was no parallel application of BATNEEC to other environmental sectors, such as water and land, and thus it considered that 'the Community's legislation [was] unlikely to be as effective or as efficient as it might be, by encouraging the transfer of pollution from air to waste, rather than seeking to achieve the best environmental option.'[146] In order to address this issue, the Commission introduced the concept of BAT in its proposal for adopting the IPPCD from 1993 and explained that '[b]y requiring the use of BAT, [...] environmental problems can be estimated and compared on a common basis', and then 'the technology chosen or the method of operating an installation should be the best for the environment as a whole'.[147]

However, it is not clear what the Commission meant with environmental problems estimated and compared on a common basis, and this notion has not been used in the text of the IPPCD or the IED. As was explained in Chap. 2, due to the incommensurability of environmental goods, an integrated approach must be based on a weighing and balancing of all relevant factors that result in environmental trade-offs.[148] In light of this, the development of BAT-based permit conditions in the IPPCD and later the

[145] Council Directive 84/360/EEC of 28 June 1984 on the combating of air pollution from industrial plants (1984) OJ L 188/20, art 8 and art 13.

[146] Commission (EC), COM (93) 423 final, 14 September 1993, 4.

[147] Ibid, 3.

[148] See Sect. 2.3.1.3 of Chap. 2.

IED can be interpreted as providing for a common basis on which different incommensurable environmental impacts can be weighed and balanced by the competent authorities to seek optimal choices for the environment as a whole.[149]

Since the rationale for the BAT is to provide for a common basis where environmental impacts on different environmental media can be weighed and balanced in specific situations for which a permit is applied, two further questions arise: according to the IED, what environmental impacts on different environmental media have to be weighed in the permit decision in light of the common basis provided by the BAT; and how do they have to be weighed? The first question concerns the scope of an integrated approach required by the IED. According to the Commission in its explanatory memorandum of the proposal for the IPPCD from 1993, the concept of BAT was intended to work on several dimensions regarding emissions control,[150] energy efficiency,[151] and the rational use of resources.[152] This shows that the Commission at that time addressed the scope of applying BAT not only to pollution control, but also to other environmental issues, such as energy efficiency and the rational use of resources. Hence, the scope of applying the BAT can provide for further insight into the scope of an integrated approach as required by the IED.

The question of how environmental impacts have to be weighed concerns the options to deal with the incommensurability of environmental goods. Theoretically the generic option (with the competence to set the permit conditions attributed to an authority at the central level) and case-specific option (with the competence to set the permit conditions attributed to decentralized authorities) can be applied to weighing environmental impacts, and both options have strengths and weaknesses.[153] In this vein, the distribution of competence to determine the BAT for setting permit conditions can indicate the options to deal with the incommensurability of environmental goods as adopted by the IED.

In summary, the rationale for the concept of BAT is to deal with the incommensurability of environmental goods by providing a common basis where environmental impacts on different environmental media can be weighed and balanced, thus enabling the implementation of integrated pollution prevention and control. In this vein, the analysis of the (often detailed) rules on the determination of the BAT for setting permit conditions should focus on addressing the questions of what environmental impacts have to be weighed on different environmental media; and

---

[149] Eberhard Bohne (2008), 10–11.

[150] Commission (EC), COM(93) 423 final, 14 September 1993, 3 explained that the aim of BAT 'is to prevent emissions to air, water and land. Where it is not practicable to do so, the aim must then be to minimize emissions to the environment as a whole'.

[151] Ibid, 3–4 explained that 'In some cases it may be technically possible to reduce emissions from a particular installation further, but only at the environmental cost of requiring more energy to be used, with a resultant increase in emissions else where arising from power generation. This is a matter to consider in selecting what are the [BAT] for preventing or reducing emissions.'.

[152] Ibid, 4 explained that 'Techniques which use less, or less harmful, raw materials may be considered to be better for the environment as a whole (for example, those which use recycled materials efficiently), even though emissions from installations may be a little higher.'.

[153] See Sect. 2.3.1.3 of Chap. 2.

how they have to be weighed, so as to provide for further insight into the scope of an integrated approach and the options to deal with the incommensurability of environmental goods as required by the IED.

3.7.3 *The Definition of the BAT*

This section examines the definition of the BAT provided by the IED. The definition of the BAT consists of two parts: the general definition of the BAT; and the specific definitions of the terms 'techniques', 'available techniques', and 'best'. The following sub-sections examine the general definition and the specific definitions of the BAT on the basis of a literature review and the drafting history of the IED.

3.7.3.1 The General Definition of BAT

The IED provides for a general definition of BAT:

> the most effective and advanced stage in the development of activities and their methods of operation which indicates the practical suitability of particular techniques for providing the basis for emission limit values and other permit conditions designed to prevent and, where that is not practicable, to reduce emissions and the impact on the environment as a whole.[154]

From this general definition of the BAT, not much of a clear indication can be derived. At the least, it can be seen that, also with BAT, the integrated approach is pursued, since there is an explicit reference to 'the impact on the environment as a whole'.

3.7.3.2 The Specific Definition of BAT

In addition to the general description of the BAT, a separate definition of 'techniques', 'available techniques' and 'best' are also provided by the IED:

(1) 'techniques' includes both the technology used and the way in which the installation is designed, built, maintained, operated and decommissioned,
(2) 'available techniques' means those developed on a scale which allows implementation in the relevant industrial sector, under economically and technically viable conditions, taking into consideration the costs and advantages, whether or not the techniques are used or produced inside the Member State in question, as long as they are reasonably accessible to the operator,
(3) 'best' means most effective in achieving a high general level of protection of the environment as a whole.'[155]

---

[154] IED art 3(10).

[155] IED art 3(10).

These specific definitions are discussed in the following sub-sections.[156]

3.7.3.2.1 The Definition of 'Available Techniques'

The definition of 'available techniques' reflects the consideration of the cost-effectiveness of environmental protection. The wording 'taking into consideration the costs and advantages' requires 'a judgment on the extent to which the benefits to the environment of using BAT outweigh the costs'.[157]

The consideration of cost-effectiveness usually leads to the argument for the case-specific option of deciding on environmental trade-offs to implement integration.[158] Pallemaerts argued that 'the emphatic reference to economic viability almost calls for individualized cost–benefit analyses to justify permit conditions', which could bolster the discretionary power of Member States for determining case-specific BAT.[159] The background to the IPPCD—the Fifth Environmental Action Program (1993–2000) (EAP)[160]—also reinforces the view of the discretionary power intended to be left to Member States with regard to the local economic and social situation. The adoption of the fifth EAP took place nearly a year after the signature of the Maastricht Treaty. One of the main changes that the Maastricht Treaty brought was a central role for the subsidiarity principle. The subsidiarity principle, originally introduced only for environmental policy, was promoted as a general European law principle in the Maastricht Treaty.[161] This principle was significantly stressed as 'an important part' in the fifth EAP, and it called to 'take full account of the traditions and sensitivities of different regions and the cost-effectiveness of various actions'.[162] Particularly, the fifth EAP set different aims for less wealthy and developed regions, considering the need of economic and social development.[163] Hence, because of the different economic situation from country to country, by requiring the consideration of 'economic viability' in determining the availability of techniques, it may be difficult to reach the same interpretation of BAT within the EU. In other words,

---

[156] It is noted that the specific definitions of BAT provided by the IED are the same as those provided by the IPPCD, thus the analysis on the definitions provided by the IPPCD is also applicable to those provided by the IED.

[157] Steve Sorrell, 'The meaning of BATNEEC: interpreting excessive costs in UK industrial pollution regulation' (2002) 4(1) Journal of Environmental Policy & Planning 23, 34.

[158] See Sect. 2.3.1.3.1 of Chap. 2.

[159] Marc Pallemaerts (1996), 176.

[160] IPPCD recital 3.

[161] Mireille Bogaart, 'The emergence of the Framework Directive in EU environmental policy: An exploration of its function and characteristics' in Marjan Peeters and Rosa Uylenburg (eds), *EU Environmental Legislation: Legal Perspectives on Regulatory Strategies* (Edward Elgar 2014), 53.

[162] Commission (EC), 'Towards sustainability, A European Community programme of policy and action in relation to the environment and sustainable development' OJ C 138/5, 17 May 1993, executive summary para 32.

[163] Ibid, para 13.

the consideration of 'economically viable conditions' in the definition of 'available techniques' indicates the case-specific BAT.

However, there are also arguments for the generic interpretation of BAT. Faure and Lefevere investigated the drafting history of the IPPCD and found that the requirement of a cost–benefit analysis was initially laid down in the definition of 'best', but, in the final text of the IPPCD, the requirement of a cost–benefit analysis was moved from the definition of 'best' to the definition of 'available'.[164] They considered that this move showed that 'the Community [was] moving towards a European interpretation of BAT, rather than interpreting the principle on a differentiated case by case basis', since 'within a European market the availability of technology hardly differs from region to region'.[165] In addition, Fisher, Lange, and Scotford noticed that the wording 'in a relevant industrial sector' in the definition of 'available techniques' indicates the sector-wide BAT.[166] Similarly, Litten, who was the Head of the European IPPC Bureau,[167] also explained that 'the definition of "available" does not seem to require that the technique has to be economically and technically viable for every installation in order to be economically and technically viable for the sector'.[168] According to these opinions, the definition of 'available techniques' does not necessarily require the BAT to be varied with installation-specific circumstances, but it has a generic sector-wide feature.

In summary, it is not clear whether the definition of available techniques requires a case-specific BAT or generic BAT, although the discussion in the literature points mostly to the generic BAT. Case law could provide for more clarity in the interpretation of this issue.

---

[164] Michael G. Faure and Jürgen C. Lefevere (1996), 120.
Also see Commission (EC), COM(93) 423 final, 14 September 1993, art 2(10) defined 'best' as

> most effective in achieving a high level of protection for the environment as a whole, taking into account the potential benefits and costs which may result from action or lack of action;

and see IPPCD art 2(12)(b) prescribed that:

> "available" techniques shall mean those developed on a scale which allows implementation in the relevant industrial sector, under economically and technically viable conditions, taking into consideration the costs and advantages, whether or not the techniques are used or produced inside the Member State in question, as long as they are reasonably accessible to the operator.

[165] Michael G. Faure and Jürgen C. Lefevere (1996), 120.

[166] Elizabeth Fisher, Bettina Lange, and Eloise Scotford (2019), 446.

[167] The European IPPC Bureau was set up in 1997 to organize an information exchange between the European Commission, EU Member States, industry, and environmental non-governmental organizations on BAT used to control industrial pollution. IED art 13 prescribes information exchange, which is discussed in detail in Sect. 3.7.4.2.1.

[168] Donald Litten, 'Economic aspects of BAT' (2000) Paper presented at the 'International Workshop on Economic Aspects of BAT', Brussels, 10–11 February, quoted from Steve Sorrell, 'The meaning of BATNEEC: interpreting excessive costs in UK industrial pollution regulation' (2002) 4(1) Journal of Environmental Policy & Planning 23, 34.

3.7.3.2.2 The Definition of 'Best'

The term 'best' is defined as 'most effective in achieving a high general level of protection of the environment as a whole',[169] which reflects the aim of achieving 'a high level of protection of the environment taken as a whole'.[170] It is not clear what the difference is between 'a high **general** level of protection' as prescribed in the definition of 'best' techniques[171] and 'a high level of protection' as prescribed in the provision of subject matter.[172] The drafting history of the IPPCD may provide a clue. After the European Parliament deleted the requirement of an analysis of the cost and benefits from the definition of 'best' during its first reading for the adoption of the IPPCD from 1994,[173] the word 'general' was added into the definition of 'best' in the Council's common position from 1995.[174] The insertion of the word 'general' in the definition may indicate a decreased ambition in view of the level of protection. This view aligns with article 18 of the IED, which requires that if stricter conditions than those achievable by the use of the BAT are required by the environmental quality standards, additional measures shall be included in the permit. Environmental quality standards can also demonstrate a high level of environmental protection.[175] Hence, apparently, different levels of a high level of environmental protection can be discerned when analyzing the IED provisions. The requirement of the use of the BAT at least provides a minimum for a high level of protection, while the requirement depending on the environmental quality standards in the permit could provide for a higher level of environmental protection.

3.7.3.3 Interim Conclusion

The definition of the BAT provided by the IED is split into a general definition and specific definitions of the separate elements of BAT. The general definition of the BAT indicates that the integrated approach is pursued, since there is an explicit reference to 'the impact on the environment as a whole'. The specific definitions of BAT are relevant in view of the options for weighing to achieve an integrated approach and

---

[169] IED art 3(10).

[170] IED art 1.

[171] IED art 3(10)(c).

[172] IED art 1.

[173] Parliament (EC), 'Legislative resolution embodying Parliament's opinion on the proposal for a Council Directive on integrated pollution prevention and control (Cooperation procedure: first reading)' COM(93)0423-C3-0363/93-00/0526(SYN) OJ C 18/82, 23 January 1995, amendment 14 attempted to delete the wording of 'taking into account the potential benefits and costs which may result from action or lack of action' from the definition of 'best'.

[174] Council (EC), 'COMMON POSITION (EC) No 9/96 adopted by the Council on 27 November 1995 with a view to adopting Council Directive 96/.../EC concerning integrated pollution prevention and control', 25 March 1996, art 2(11).

[175] See Sect. 2.3.1.2 of Chap. 2. Also see the discussion on the rules on environmental quality standards, provided in Sect. 3.8 of this chapter.

the environmental effectiveness of integration. In view of the options for weighing for integration, the definition of 'available techniques' indicates that the BAT can be interpreted in a generic or case-specific way, although various arguments are given for the generic way. In view of the environmental effectiveness of integration, the definition of 'best techniques' indicates that the use of BAT may lead to a minimum indication of a high level of protection, but in view of environmental quality standards, a higher level than the BAT indicates could be necessary.

3.7.4 Rules on BREFs and BAT Conclusions

This section examines the rules regarding BREFs and BAT conclusions as laid down in the IED. According to the IED, BREFs, and BAT conclusions are documents containing detailed techniques and setting out environmental performance requirements associated with those techniques for industrial sectors.[176] BREFs are the result of information exchange organized by the Commission,[177] and BAT conclusions have to be adopted by the European Commission through comitology.[178] BAT conclusions shall be the reference for setting the permit conditions.[179] Hence, the use of BAT conclusions is the main approach to the determination of BAT for setting the IED permit conditions. BAT conclusions have to include parts of BREFs,[180] thus the BREFs are indirectly given legal weight in the setting of permit conditions.[181] Since the IED provides the legal obligation that BAT conclusions established at the EU level are the reference for setting permit conditions, and thus have legal relevance, it indicates that the IED adopts the generic approach to deal with the incommensurability of environmental goods in the setting of permit conditions.

[176] See IED art 3(12); see also.

BAT conclusions available at 'European IPPC Bureau', https://eippcb.jrc.ec.europa.eu/reference, accessed on 7 August 2020.

[177] IED art 13(1).

[178] IED arts 13(5) and 75. The term 'comitology' refers to the set of procedures through which the European Commission exercises the implementing powers conferred on it by the European Union (EU) legislator, with the assistance of committees of representatives from EU Member States. This description is taken from the website of the European Union, available at: 'Comitology', https://eur-lex.europa.eu/legal-content/EN/ALL/?uri=LEGISSUM:comitology, accessed on 23 June 2022.

[179] IED art 14(3).

[180] IED art 3(12) defines BAT conclusions as 'a document containing the parts of a BAT reference document laying down the conclusions on best available techniques, their description, information to assess their applicability, the emission levels associated with the best available techniques, associated monitoring, associated consumption levels and, where appropriate, relevant site remediation measures'.

[181] In addition, while the adoption of BAT conclusions through comitology are pending, the conclusions on BAT from BREFs adopted by the Commission prior to the date of the Directive's entry into force shall apply as BAT conclusions, except for the setting of emission limit values. See IED art 13(7).

The examination in this section consists of three parts. First, the rationale for BREFs and BAT conclusions are analyzed. Second, Sect. 3.7.4.2 provides for the examination of how these generic BAT documents have to be established. Third, how they have to be applied in the setting of permit conditions is investigated in Sects. 3.7.4.3 and 3.7.4.4. This examination aims to understand how the IED provisions on these generic BAT documents are designed to cope with the weighing of environmental impacts and to what extent an integrated approach can take place through the implementation of the rules on these generic BAT documents.

3.7.4.1 Rationale for BREFs and BAT Conclusions

This sub-section examines the rationale for BREFs and BAT conclusions as the main approach to the determination of BAT. The rationale for this option is stated in the recital of the IED:

> In order to determine [BAT] and to limit imbalances in the Union as regards the level of emissions from industrial activities, [BREFs] should be drawn up, reviewed and, where necessary, updated through an exchange of information with stakeholders and the [BAT conclusions should be] adopted through committee procedure.[182]

This shows that the approach by means of generic BAT documents established at the EU level not only aims to facilitate the determination of BAT, but it also aims to limit imbalances in the Union as regards the level of emissions from industrial activities. In the explanatory memorandum of the proposal for adopting the IED from 2007, the Commission considered that the rare use of generic BAT documents in the setting of permit conditions was the main reason for the insufficient implementation of BAT, and thus 'the environmental benefits originally intended have not been delivered'.[183] However, it can be questioned that as 'varied local conditions require varied local environmental regulation',[184] a mere variation from BREFs in the implementation of the IPPCD 'did not imply failure of the IPPCD in its own terms, but 'was even, arguably, an indicator of success'.[185] In other words, it can be questioned whether the generic option indicated in BAT documents can facilitate the implementation of an integrated approach in the definition of permit conditions. The following analysis of the rules on the establishment and application of the generic BAT documents can provide further insight into this issue.

---

[182] IED recital 13.

[183] Commission (EU), 'Proposal for a Directive of the European Parliament and of the Council on industrial emissions (integrated pollution prevention and control)' COM(2007) 844 final, 21 December 2007, 9.

[184] Maria Lee (2014), 120–121.

[185] Ibid.

3.7.4.2 Procedure for Adopting BREFs and BAT Conclusions

This sub-section examines the procedure for adopting BREFs and BAT conclusions. The provision that these generic BAT documents shall be the reference for setting the permit conditions indicates that the generic option for weighing environmental impacts is adopted by the IED. Theoretically, the generic option tends to be less adaptive than the case-specific option, because the former option is usually less likely to consider as much relevant information as the latter one.[186] Hence, in view of an integrated environmental permit, the focus of the examination on the procedure for adopting the generic BAT documents can be placed on investigating what environmental issues to consider in the generic weighing of environmental impacts.

3.7.4.2.1 Procedure for Adopting BREFs

The BREFs are the result of an exchange of information organized by the Commission between Member States, the industries concerned, non-governmental organizations promoting environmental protection, and the Commission.[187]

The information exchange is organized at two levels: at political and technical levels.[188] At the political level, the so-called Information Exchange Forum (IEF) is established to deal with the practical arrangements for the exchange of information.[189] At the technical level, the so-called Technical Working Group (TWG) is established to carry out the detailed work for the development of BREFs.[190] According to the IED, the Technical Working Group shall address 'the performance of installations and techniques in terms of emissions, […], consumption and nature of raw materials, water consumption, use of energy and generation of waste'.[191] This shows that a wide scope of environmental impacts are considered in the determination of BREFs.

This two-level organization for drafting BREFs is an effort to separate 'technical discussions' from political impacts, but the technical discussion was never simply 'technical' and is not free from choices with political consequences.[192] In this vein, the composition of the Information Exchange Forum and Technical Working Group becomes important.

---

[186] See Sect. 2.3.1.3.1 of Chap. 2.

[187] IED art 13(1).

[188] Martina Doppelhammer (2000), 246; Also see Harald Schoenberger, 'Integrated pollution prevention and control in large industrial installations on the basis of best available techniques-The Sevilla Process' (2009) 17 Journal of Cleaner Production 1526, 1527.

[189] IED art 13(3).

[190] IED art 13(2).

[191] IED art 13(2)(a).

[192] Maria Lee (2014), 120; Also see Bettina Lange, *Implementing EU Pollution Control: Law and Integration* (Cambridge University Press 2008), Chap. 5.

The Information Exchange Forum

According to the IED, in order to ensure an effective and active exchange of information resulting in high-quality BREFs, '[t]he Commission shall establish and regularly convene a forum composed of representatives of Member States, the industries concerned and non-governmental organizations promoting environmental protection'.[193] However, the IED does not provide for concrete rules on the selection of Information Exchange Forum members. Hence, the selection of Information Exchange Forum members falls within the competence of the Commission. In 2011, the Information Exchange Forum was established by Commission Decision (2011/C 146/03).[194] According to this decision, the members of the Information Exchange Forum shall have an acceptable degree of European representation and be appointed by the Director General of DG environment (DG Environment is a European Commission department specifically for environmental matters).[195] However, it is not clear what accounts for 'an acceptable degree of European representation'.

Kimmel did an interview with a Commission official who provided a further explanation that the members of the Information Exchange Forum shall 'possess technical skills and knowledge'.[196] Kimmel considered that this criterion seems to privilege industrial groups 'that possess resources needed to professionally organize themselves and acquire technical skills',[197] while NGOs usually 'have a lack of funds in order to have experts participating in the working groups'.[198] Hence, this can lead to the unequal position taken by different parties in the Information Exchange Forum. In practice, environmental organizations do take up a relatively small position in the composition of the Information Exchange Forum (only 5 environmental organizations out of 88 organizations, compared to 83 trade and business associations).[199]

The Technical Working Group

The Technical Working Group consists of Member States, the industries concerned, NGOs promoting environmental protection, and the Commission.[200] However, the IED does not provide a concrete rule for how these different types of members

[193] IED recital 14 and art 13(3).

[194] Commission (EU), 'Decision of 16 May 2011 establishing a forum for the exchange of information pursuant to Article 13 of the Directive 2010/75/EU on industrial emissions' OJ C 146/3, 17 May 2011.

[195] Ibid, art 4.

[196] Jens Kimmel, 'Assessing the Democratic Quality of New Modes of EU Governance: the Industrial Emissions Directive as a Test Case' (2018) 17(2) European Political Science 240, 247. This information is gathered in the author's interview with a Commission official.

[197] Ibid, 247–248.

[198] Ibid.

[199] See 'Register of Commission Expert Groups and Other Similar Entities', https://ec.europa.eu/transparency/expert-groups-register/screen/expert-groups/consult?do=groupDetail.groupDetail&groupID=2611&NewSearch=1&NewSearch=1, accessed on 5 May 2024.

[200] IED art 13(1).

of the Technical Working Group should be selected. The IED confers an implementing power on the Commission to adopt guidance on the collection of data, drawing up BREFs, and on quality assurance by means of implementing acts.[201] In 2012, the Commission adopted a guidance document on the collection of data, on drawing up BREFs, and on quality assurance (hereinafter 'BAT guidance'),[202] which provides more detailed instructions on information exchange. In particular, it provides a detailed specification on the establishment of a Technical Working Group.[203] According to the BAT guidance, Technical Working Group members are nominated by the representatives in the Information Exchange Forum.[204] Kimmel found that, in practice, the right to nominate Technical Working Group members 'often constitutes a right to designate since this nomination is an exclusive [Information Exchange Forum] member's right without any conditions'.[205] In this vein, it can be inferred that, under this nomination procedure, the number of members defending environmental interests in the Technical Working Group would be small,[206] and thus their roles in shaping the BREFs may be relatively weak. Related to this, a targeted online survey was launched to gather the views of Member State authorities, industry and other type of organizations (e.g. NGO, research body) on the BREF process.[207] For the question of whether the BREF process has sufficiently considered the environmental benefits of techniques, the survey results show that industry were more positive than NGOs.[208]

In summary, according to the IED, the BREFs are the result of an exchange of information. The information exchange addresses various environmental issues concerning not just emissions only, but also other environmental issues such as the use of energy and resources, which indicates a relatively wide scope of generic weighing to achieve an integrated approach. The information exchange shall be organized by the Commission between Member States, the industries concerned, ENGOs, and the Commission. However, the IED does not provide concrete rules on how to organize the information exchange, and the selection of participants in the

---

[201] IED art 13(3).

[202] Commission (EU), Implementing Decision (EU)2012/119 of 10 February 2012 laying down rules concerning guidance on the collection of data, on drawing up BAT reference documents, and on quality assurance referred to in Directive 2010/75/EU of the European Parliament and of the Council on industrial emissions (2012), OJ L 63/1.

[203] Ibid, Chaps. 2 and 4.

[204] Ibid, 23.

[205] Jens Kimmel (2018), 248. The author interviewed a Commission official who said that 'The [member organizations) of the Forum nominate people and they become members, that's it.'.

[206] Ibid, 249 providing two examples regarding this inference: During the drawing up of BREF for Large Combustion Plants, 'the [European Environmental Bureau (an ENGO)] had a delegation size of two while the number of people representing a sector of industry was approximately 60, whereas in the Refineries BREF, the [European Environmental Bureau] was defending public environmental interests against 40 industry delegates'.

[207] Ricardo, 'Support to the evaluation of the Industrial Emissions Directive (Directive 2010/75/EU) Final report', March 2020, 2.

[208] Ibid, 105.

BREF drafting process falls within the competence of the Commission. In practice, the selection rule established by the Commission tends to result in environmental organizations taking up a relatively small position compared to the industrial groups in the composition of the organization for information exchange, and thus the role of environmental organizations in shaping the BREFs seems to be relatively weak. This shows that the procedure for adopting BREFs may imply that the views of environmental organizations play only a limited role in the generic weighing of environmental impacts.

3.7.4.2.2 Procedure for Adopting BAT Conclusions

BAT conclusions shall be adopted through the comitology.[209] Compared to the procedure for adopting BREFs, the procedure for adopting BAT conclusions is relatively closed, since the comitology only includes representatives from all Member States and the Commission. The rationale for adopting this relatively closed procedure can be derived from the drafting history of the IED.

The concept of BAT conclusions to be adopted through comitology was introduced by the Council during its first reading to adopt the IED in 2010.[210] According to the Council at that time, the introduction of comitology would ensure the involvement of all Member States in the adoption of BAT conclusions.[211] During the European Parliament at its second reading for adopting the IED from 2010, the Parliament proposed that the Commission shall adopt the BAT conclusion by means of delegated acts instead of implementing acts.[212] The main difference between implementing acts, as proposed by the Council, and delegated acts, as proposed by the Parliament, is that, for the former, the parliamentary supervision can almost be excluded in relation to the exercise of implementing powers by the Member States.[213] The proposal for adopting BAT conclusions by delegated acts was not accepted in the end, but

[209] IED art 13(5).

[210] Council (EU), 'Position (EU) No 1/2010 of the Council at first reading with a view to the adoption of a Directive of the European Parliament and of the Council on industrial emissions (integrated pollution prevention and control) Adopted by the Council on 15 February 2010 (Text with EEA relevance)' OJ C 107E/1, 27 April 2010.

[211] Ibid, 107.

[212] Parliament (EU), '***II RECOMMENDATION FOR SECOND READING on the Council position at first reading for adopting a directive of the European Parliament and of the Council on industrial emissions (integrated pollution prevention and control) (recast) (11962/2009 – C7-0034/2010 – 2007/0286(COD))' A7-0145/2010, 6 May 2010, amendment 21. The European Commission also expressed a similar opinion that BAT conclusions are of general application and seek to supplement the basic act with certain new non-essential elements, and thus their adoption should fall under the procedure of delegated acts instead of implementing acts, in Council (EU), OJ C 107E/1, 27 April 2010, 109.

[213] Kieran Bradley, 'Delegation of Powers in the European Union: Political Problems, Legal Solutions?' in Carl Fredrik Bergström and Dominique Ritleng (eds), *Rulemaking by the European Commission: The New System for Delegation of Powers* (Oxford University Press 2016), Chap. 4.

the IED provides for BAT conclusions adopted through comitology.[214] From the drafting history, it can be seen that the introduction of comitology is relevant in light of helping to ensure that the adoption of the binding BAT conclusions is largely controlled by the Member States.

This can be further illustrated by Case C-172/19 P, in which Euracoal (an industrial organization) sought to appeal against an order that dismissed its action for annulment of the implementing decision of the Commission to adopt the BAT Conclusion for large combustion plants.[215] Euracoal alleged that its capability to sue is derived from an infringement of its procedural standing, which it had in the context of the relevant exchange of information regarding the development of the BAT conclusions.[216] However, the court ruled that, although Euracoal had a right to be heard and had been heard during the information exchange, such a right did not create an obligation for the comitology to implement Euracoal's proposals.[217] This case shows that the introduction of the procedure for adopting BAT conclusions through comitology brings the generic determination of BAT into a relatively closed political fora.

Nevertheless, it is not appropriate to say the adoption of BAT conclusions is completely controlled by the Member States and the Commission. According to the definition of BAT conclusions provided by the IED, BAT conclusions have to contain parts of BREFs laying down BAT conclusions.[218] This means that the industries and ENGOs can indirectly exert their influence on the content of BAT conclusions through their engagement in the adoption of BREFs. However, the indirect influence of the industries and ENGOs on the content of BAT conclusions is relatively weak. The wording 'containing parts of BREFs' in the definition of BAT conclusions indicates that some parts of BREFs may be excluded from BAT conclusions adopted through the comitology procedure. For example, split views of BAT and environmental performance levels can be recorded in BREFs, but they do 'not form parts

---

[214] IED art 13(5) and art 75.

[215] Case C-172/19 P Association européenne du charbon et du lignite (Euracoal) v European Commission [31 January 2020] ECLI:EU:C:2020:66. This case is only available in Germany and French. I analyzed this case using google to translate it into English. There is no discussion of this case in English literature. This case is an appeal case from Case T-739/17 Euracoal and Others v Commission ECLI:EU:T:2018:959, which is partly discussed in Sect. 3.7.4.3.3.

[216] Case C-172/19 P: Appeal brought on 22 February 2019 by Association européenne du charbon et du lignite (Euracoal) against the order of the General Court (Third Chamber) delivered on 13 December 2018 in Case T-739/17 Association européenne du charbon et du lignite (Euracoal) and Others v European Commission OJ C 164/25, 13 May 2019, 26.

[217] Case C-172/19 P Association européenne du charbon et du lignite (Euracoal) v European Commission [31 January 2020] ECLI:EU:C:2020:66 [37].

[218] IED art 3(12). The full text reads:

> 'BAT conclusions' means a document containing the parts of a [BREF] laying down the conclusions on [BAT], their description, information to assess their applicability, the emission levels associated with the [BAT], associated monitoring, associated consumption levels and, where appropriate, relevant site remediation measures.

of the BAT conclusions, and therefore will not carry legal weight'.[219] The IED does not provide for further specifications as to what parts of BREFs must be included in BAT conclusions and thus it falls within the competence of the comitology.

In view of an integrated approach, the relatively closed procedure provided for through comitology for adopting BAT conclusions may not necessarily be a bad thing, particularly considering the fact of the unequal position of members defending industrial and environmental interests in the process of information exchange.[220] Fisher, Lange, and Scotford considered that this relatively closed comitology 'reduces the influence of industry at the crucial decision-making stage of adopting BAT conclusions or BAT guidance'.[221] In this vein, the BAT conclusions may tend to be less preferable for industry.

In summary, next to information exchange, the IED introduces a relatively closed procedure—the comitology—for adopting legal binding BAT conclusions. According to the literature, this relatively closed procedure tends to help to reduce undesirable influences on information exchange and in particular reduces the influences from industry.

3.7.4.2.3 Interim Conclusion

According to the IED, BREFs need to be developed on the basis of information exchange among Member States, industries, Environmental NGOs, and the Commission. The scope of this information exchange includes various environmental issues, and not just emissions only, but also other environmental issues such as the use of energy and resources, which indicates a relatively wide scope of generic weighing for an integrated approach.

In practice, information exchange is not as inclusive as it appears in its regulatory design. This can be indicated by unequal positions in the information exchange that are taken up overwhelmingly by industrial organizations and just a few environmental organizations. Next to information exchange, the IED introduces a relatively closed procedure—the comitology—for adopting legally binding BAT conclusions. This relatively closed procedure tends to help to reduce undesirable influences on information exchange, and in particular reduces influences the industry.

3.7.4.3 Rules on Applying BAT Conclusions for Setting Emission Limit Values

According to the IED, in the setting of emission limit values in the permit, the authorities have to ensure that the emissions levels as described in the BAT conclusions are

---

[219] Jens Kimmel (2018), 252.

[220] See Sect. 3.7.4.2.1 of this chapter.

[221] Elizabeth Fisher, Bettina Lange, and Eloise Scotford (2019), 443.

not exceeded.[222] Therefore, emission limit values have to be set directly on the basis of the emissions levels as described in the BAT conclusions. This sub-section examines the rules on emissions levels as described in the BAT conclusions for setting emission limit values.

This examination consists of four parts. First, it starts with the definition of emission levels associated with the BAT and as specified in BAT conclusions. The second part delves into how the emission levels associated with the BAT have to be applied in setting emission limit values. The third part provides an analysis of the possibility of a derogation from these BAT-associated emission levels provided by the IED, followed by an interim conclusion.

3.7.4.3.1 The Definition of Emission Levels Associated with the BAT

The IED defines 'emission levels associated with the BAT' as:

> the range of emission levels obtained under normal operating conditions using a [BAT] or a combination of [BATs], as described in BAT conclusions, expressed as an average over a given period of time, under specified reference conditions.[223]

According to this definition, emission levels associated with the BAT as laid down in BAT conclusions have to be expressed as a range of emission levels. The rationale for this is explained by the Commission in its BAT guidance:

> A range may reflect the differences within a given type of installation (e.g. differences in the grade/purity and quality of the final product, differences in design, construction, size and capacity of the installation) that result in variations in the environmental performances achieved when applying BAT.[224]

It also states that '[i]t is preferable to use a true range rather than an expression of the type " < X", because this gives less information.'[225] Hence, providing clear information is also a key point in laying down emission levels expressed as ranges, rather than as single values. By prescribing that emission levels have to be formulated as ranges, the IED allows the variations in emission levels to be achieved, rather than pursuing uniform levels across the Union.

In particular, the ranges of emission levels associated with BAT as specified in BAT conclusions appear very wide. This implies that, even if competent authorities are obliged to set emission limit values that ensure that the emission levels specified in the BAT conclusions are not exceeded, due to the wide ranges of these mandatory emission levels, quite a significant level of flexibility is still available for making decisions in accordance with case-specific situations. This flexibility is indicated by the case law. In Case T-739/17, the action for the annulment of Commission Implementing Decision (EU) 2017/1442 of 31 July 2017 establishing best available

---

[222] IED art 15(3).

[223] IED art 3(13).

[224] Commission (EU), Implementing Decision (EU)2012/119 (2012), OJ L 63/1, 20.

[225] Ibid.

techniques (BAT) conclusions for large combustion plants was dismissed as inadmissible due to the lack of a direct concern.[226] However, this case is relevant given the court's considerations about the discretion of national authorities in applying BAT conclusions in setting permit conditions. The range of emission levels associated with BAT, as specified in the BAT conclusion for large combustion plants provides for the discretion of national authorities, which is the reason that the criterion of direct concern was not fulfilled.[227] For example, according to the BAT conclusion for combustion plants, the yearly average BAT-associated emission levels for SO_2 emissions into the air from an existing plant with a total rated thermal input of over 300 MW_{th} and for a PC boiler are 10–130 mg/Nm^3.[228] There is no further specification provided by this BAT conclusion on how to set a corresponding emission limit value for SO_2 emissions into the air between 10 and 130 mg/Nm^3. The court reasoned that the emission limit values mentioned in the BAT conclusions are provided within a range with an upper and a lower limit and, therefore, Member States have discretion within this range of values.[229]

It can be further examined whether the flexibility provided by the wide range of mandatory emission levels can help to find the best option for protecting the environment as a whole. Theoretically, due to the variation of local-specific situations, the case-specific option for an integrated approach will lead to a variation of emission limit values across Member States. In practice, the emission limit values in the permits are largely set towards the least stringent end of the ranges of emission levels

---

[226] Case T-739/17 Euracoal and Others v Commission [13 December 2018] ECLI:EU:T:2018:959. This case is only available in German and French. I analyzed this case using google to translate from German into English. There is no discussion of this case in English literature. This case is also discussed in Sects. 3.7.4.3.2 and 3.7.4.3.3 of this chapter. The case was decided on appeal on 31 January 2020: Case C-172/19 P Association européenne du charbon et du lignite (Euracoal) v European Commission [31 January 2020] ECLI:EU:C:2020:66, which is discussed in Sect. 3.7.4.2.2 of this chapter.

[227] TFEU art 263(4) prescribes that:

> [a]ny natural or legal person may, under the conditions laid down in the first and second paragraphs, institute proceedings against an act addressed to that person or which is of direct and individual concern to them, and against a regulatory act which is of direct concern to them and does not entail implementing measures.

[228] Commission (EU), 'Implementing Decision (EU) 2017/1442 of 31 July 2017 establishing best available techniques (BAT) conclusions, under Directive 2010/75/EU of the European Parliament and of the Council, for large combustion plants' C/2017/5225, OJ L 212/1, 32.

[229] Case T-739/17 Euracoal and Others v Commission [13 December 2018] ECLI:EU:T:2018:959 [97]:

> Zweitens bewegen sich die in den BVT-Schlussfolgerungen genannten Emissionsgrenzwerte innerhalb einer Bandbreite mit einer Ober- und einer Untergrenze, was die Kläger im Übrigen selbst anerkennen. Die Mitgliedstaaten verfügen folglich über ein Ermessen im Rahmen dieser Wertbandbreite.

associated with BAT as described in BAT conclusions.[230] Hence, it is not evident that the flexibility entailed by the wide range of mandatory emission levels has led to case-specific decision-making. In its proposal to revise the IED, the Commission considered that the emission limit values in the permits that are largely set closer to the least stringent end of the ranges of emission levels associated with BAT as described in BAT conclusions result in 'under-delivery of emissions reduction',[231] and thus the Commission proposed that the competent authorities should set the emission limit values at the lowest end of the relevant BAT associated emission levels.[232] In this vein, it appears that the revision is intended to require a more ambitious level of protection.

In summary, emission levels associated with the BAT that have to be set in the permit take the form of ranges of levels. The ranges of emission levels associated with BAT as specified in BAT conclusions appear to be very wide. In view of an integrated approach, this means that quite a large degree of flexibility is left to Member States, which is supposed to facilitate case-specific decision-making to find the best solution to protect the environment as a whole. However, given the fact that emission limit values are largely set towards the least stringent end of the ranges of emission levels associated with BAT, as described in BAT conclusions, it is not evident that this flexibility has caused the setting of emission limit values to be adapted to the variation of local-specific situations.

3.7.4.3.2 The Use of Emission Levels Associated with the BAT

The IED requires that, in the setting of emission limit values, permitting authorities have to ensure that emissions levels as described in the BAT conclusions are not exceeded.[233] In order to ensure the attainment of emission levels as described in BAT conclusions, two methods of setting emission limit values are further prescribed:

[230] Commission (EU), Commission Staff Working Document Evaluation of the Industrial Emissions Directive SWD (2020) 181 final, 23 September 2020, 70.

[231] Commission (EU), COM (2022)156 final, 5 April 2022, 18–19.

[232] Ibid, art 1(12):

> The competent authority shall set the strictest possible emission limit values that are consistent with the lowest emissions achievable by applying BAT in the installation, and that ensure that, under normal operating conditions, emissions do not exceed the emission levels associated with the best available techniques (BAT-AELs) as laid down in the decisions on BAT conclusions referred to in Article 13(5). The emission limit values shall be based on an assessment by the operator analysing the feasibility of meeting the strictest end of the BAT-AEL range and demonstrating the best performance the installation can achieve by applying BAT as described in BAT conclusions.

[233] IED art 15(3).

(1) '[E]mission limit values shall be expressed for the same or shorter periods of time and under the same reference conditions as those emission levels associated with the [BAT]'[234]; or
(2) Setting emission limit values that differ from emission levels associated with the BAT in terms of values, periods of time, and reference conditions.[235]

The rationale for setting different emission limit values is stated in the recital of the IED: '[i]t is important to provide sufficient flexibility to competent authorities to set emission limit values'.[236] Particularly, Bohne considered that this provides for the possibility of setting emission limit values that exceed emissions levels specified in the BAT conclusions.[237] This view can be supported by the difference between emission limit values and emission levels associated with the BAT distinguished by the European Parliament in its first reading to adopt the IED in 2009: emission limit values in the permit correspond to a maximum over a specific short period or under specific circumstances, while emission levels associated with the BAT represent an average value.[238] Hence, according to the European Parliament at that time, emission limit values in the permit may 'exceed emission levels associated with the [BAT]' in a specific short period or under specific circumstances and, 'make it possible to achieve the emission levels associated with the [BAT]' on average.[239] Therefore, the requirement of attaining emission levels as described in the BAT conclusions will not necessarily lead to applying uniform emission limit values within the Union. In this vein, a certain degree of flexibility is left to Member States in the setting of emission limit values. This degree of flexibility is also indicated by the case law. In Case T-739/17, the court ruled that Member States, on the basis of art 15(3)(b), have a margin of discretion, which allows them to set emission limit values that differ from emission levels associated with the BAT in terms of values, periods of time, and reference conditions.[240] In view of an integrated approach, the possibility of setting different emission limit values at the national level can leave room for case-specific decisions.

In cases where the flexible approach of setting different emission limit values is applied, the IED prescribes that Member States shall ensure that the permit includes emission monitoring requirements specifying that 'results of emission monitoring

---

[234] IED art 15(3)(a).

[235] IED art 15(3)(b).

[236] IED recital 15.

[237] A phone interview with Professor Bohne on 13 November 2019.

[238] Parliament (EU), REPORT on the proposal for a directive of the European Parliament and of the Council on industrial emissions (integrated pollution prevention and control) (recast) (COM (2007)0844 – C6-0002/2008 – 2007/0286(COD) A6-0046/2009 6 February 2009, justification of amendment 4.

[239] Ibid. For example, the initial emission can be very high but short lived. This example is borrowed from the Draft guidance on Article 15 of Industrial Emission Directive (2010/75/EU) established by the Irish environmental protection agency in 2016, see https://www.epa.ie/publications/licensing--permitting/industrial/ied/draft_guidance_art15_IED.pdf, 6, accessed on 15 January 2022.

[240] Case T-739/17 Euracoal and Others v Commission [13 December 2018] ECLI:EU:T:2018:959 [99]–[100]. This case is also discussed in Sects. 3.7.4.3.1 and 3.7.4.3.3 of this chapter.

are available for the same periods of time and reference conditions as for the emission levels associated with the BAT'.[241] A summary of these results which allows for a comparison with the emissions levels associated with the BAT has to be supplied regularly, and at least annually for assessment, by the operators to the competent authority, in order to ensure the attainment of emission levels associated with the BAT.[242] In other words, competent authorities should ensure that the permitted emission levels, based on the yearly average should not exceed the emission levels associated with the BAT. In addition, the results of emissions monitoring have to be made available to the public.[243]

In summary, the IED establishes a mandatory status for the emissions levels as described in the BAT conclusions, but a degree of flexibility still exists as Member States are allowed to set different emission limit values, which can leave room for case-specific decisions in view of an integrated approach. Where the flexible approach is applied, additional emission monitoring requirements have to be included in the permit, to ensure compliance with emissions levels as described in the BAT conclusions at least annually.

3.7.4.3.3 Derogation from the Emission Levels Associated with BAT

The IED provides the possibility for derogation from the emission levels specified in the BAT conclusions, in order to take certain specific circumstances into account.[244] This shows that the case-specific option to deal with the incommensurability of environmental goods is also adopted by the IED. According to the IED, the derogation is allowed where the achievement of these emission levels 'would lead to disproportionately higher costs compared to the environmental benefits'.[245] Such a derogation has to be based on an assessment, taking into account the geographical location or the local environmental conditions of the installation concerned, or the technical characteristics of the installation concerned.[246] However, the IED does not provide clear rules on what accounts for disproportionate higher costs nor on what kinds of technical characteristics, geographical location, and local environmental conditions account for valid conditions for granting a derogation. In fact, the European Parliament, at its second reading to adopt the IED in 2010 attempted to provide more concrete rules in terms of the conditions for applying a derogation.[247] In terms of the assessment of costs and environmental benefits, the European Parliament proposed that only costs that were ***not*** taken into consideration in the exchange of information

---

[241] IED art 14(1)(c)(ii).

[242] IED art 14(d)(ii) and art 15(3).

[243] IED art 24(3)(b).

[244] IED recital 16 and art 15(4).

[245] IED art 15(4).

[246] IED (n 2) art 15(4)(a)(b).

[247] Parliament (EU) (11962/2009 – C7-0034/2010 – 2007/0286(COD) A7-0145/2010, 6 May 2010, amendment 30).

resulting in the BREFs are allowed to be considered in deciding whether to grant a derogation.[248] In addition, the European Parliament at that time also proposed that a derogation may apply only where the geographical location, the local environmental conditions, and the technical characteristics of the installation concerned ***prevent*** the implementation of BAT described in the BREFs.[249] Even though these more concrete rules that could further restrict the application of a derogation were proposed, they were not accepted in the final text. This may imply that the legislators did not intend to establish a concrete regulation on the assessment of costs and environmental benefits for the court to test the granting of a derogation.

In addition, the IED also prescribes substantive limits for the application of a derogation and procedural requirements. Substantive limits include the fulfillment of minimum emission limit values set out in the Annexes to the Directive, the need to prevent significant pollution, and the achievement of a high level of protection of the environment as a whole.[250] Case law provides further clarification on the limits of no significant pollution occurring and achieving a high level of protection of the environment as a whole. In Case C-375/2, the court interpreted that the rules on environmental quality standards put into concrete terms the achievement of a high level of protection of the environment as a whole, and an exceedance of environmental quality standards can be regarded as significant pollution.[251] Accordingly, the court ruled that the granting of a derogation requires a comprehensive assessment taking account of all sources of pollutants and their cumulative effect, in order to ensure it does not cause any exceedance of environmental quality standards.[252] The court also specified that where the air quality standards are exceeded, such a derogation may be granted only where the requirements in the air quality plans are complied with.[253] However, the environmental quality standards set by the EU legislature only captures part of the environmental quality situation. In the cases where no concrete environmental quality standard exists, the limits of no significant pollution occurring and achieving a high level of protection of the environment as a whole are quite open-ended, and thus they will be difficult to enforce.[254] Therefore, quite a significant level of flexibility is left to Member States in the determination of conditions for granting a derogation, which may entail a risk of reducing the level of environmental protection.

Where the application of a derogation is proposed, Member States are also subject to some procedural requirements. They shall ensure that early and effective public

---

[248] Ibid.

[249] Ibid.

[250] IED art 15(4), inter alia prescribing:

> The competent authority shall in any case ensure that no significant pollution is caused and that a high level of protection of the environment as a whole is achieved.

[251] Case C-375/21 Sdruzhenie "Za Zemyata - dostap do pravosadie" and Others [9 March 2023] ECLI:EU:C:2023:173, [50]–[51].

[252] Ibid, [54].

[253] Ibid, [63].

[254] Maria Lee (2014), 121.

participation is provided for in relation to the decisions on whether to grant a derogation.[255] Where the derogation is granted, the competent authority shall document in an annex to the permit conditions the reasons for the derogation including the result of the assessment and the justification for the conditions imposed[256] and make it publicly available.[257] This requirement responds to the Commission's concern that there may have been no good reasons for the derogation.[258] Furthermore, Member States shall report to the Commission on the granting of a derogation.[259] Based on the information provided by the Member States, the Commission may adopt a guidance to further clarify how the derogation should be granted.[260] At this time, the Commission has not yet exercised such power,[261] although it has been recommended that it should do so.[262] However, even though the Commission would exercise this power to establish a guidance in the future, it can be questioned whether this guidance would be followed. The European Environmental Bureau considered that it would be 'an empty mandate', since it is adopted as a guidance.[263] Related to this, the Commission proposed that the Commission shall adopt an implementing act to establish a standardized methodology to further clarify how the derogation should be granted.[264]

Since quite some flexibility exists for Member States in the determination of whether to grant a derogation, it can be asked whether the possibility of applying a derogation would facilitate competent authorities to make case-specific assessments, so as to find the best option for protecting the environment as a whole. In practice, it is found that cross-media effects have been considered for granting such a derogation in some Member States. For example, Slovakia reported that the fact that a '[r]eduction of emissions of one pollutant causes increase in emissions of other pollutant, or it impacts transfer of emissions to another component of the environment' is considered when granting a derogation; and Slovakia and the United Kingdom reported that the fact that a 'reduction of emissions of one pollutant causes higher consumption of resources (energy, water, fuel) or generation of waste' was considered for granting

255 IED art 24(1)(c).

256 IED art 15(4).

257 IED art 24(2)(f).

258 Maria Lee (2014), 122.

259 IED art 72(1).

260 IED art 15(4) prescribing: '[o]n the basis of information provided by Member States in accordance with Article 72(1), in particular concerning the application of this paragraph, the Commission may, where necessary, assess and further clarify, through guidance, the criteria to be taken into account for the application of this paragraph'.

261 On 5 May 2024, there was no guidance yet on this issue.

262 Amec Foster Wheeler Environment and Infrastructure UK Limited and Milieu Limited, Assessment and summary of the Member States implementation reports for the IED, IPPCD, SED and WID: Industrial Emissions Directive Final Report, 5 March 2016, stating that: 'Member States also reported that clarifications, guidance or examples of cost–benefit analysis provided by the European Commission would be useful'. This report is based on the information contained in the reports submitted by Member States for the first reporting period under the IED.

263 European Environmental Bureau (EEB) (2011), 7.

264 Commission (EU) COM(2022)156 final, art 1(12).

a derogation.[265] These examples indicate that the case-specific weighing among environmental impacts is achieved by means of applying a derogation.

In summary, the possibility for a derogation from the emission levels specified in BAT conclusions is provided by the IED, which allows certain specific circumstances to be taken into account. This derogation provision is formulated vaguely, which leaves quite a lot of flexibility for Member States in determining whether to grant a derogation.[266] In view of an integrated approach, the flexibility for Member States to apply a derogation makes case-specific decisions possible, but it may also entail a risk of reducing the level of environmental protection due to the shortage of environmental quality standards.

3.7.4.3.4 Interim Conclusion

The IED establishes a strong mandatory status for the emissions levels as described in the BAT conclusions. At the same time, quite some flexibility is also provided because of the wide range of emission levels as described in the BAT conclusions, the rule of setting different emission limit values, and the derogation clause, which makes the case-specific weighing of environmental impacts at the national level possible within certain conditions. However, only limited evidence is reported in practice indicating that such flexibility contributes to a case-specific weighing of environmental impacts with regard to integrated pollution prevention and control.

3.7.4.4 Rules on Applying BAT Conclusions for Setting Other Permit Conditions

The IED requires that BAT conclusions shall be the reference for setting permit conditions.[267] However, except for the concrete rules on how to apply emission levels associated with the BAT in BAT conclusions provided by article 15, the IED does not provide a clear rule on how to apply the other requirements of BAT conclusions, such as energy efficiency levels associated with the BAT,[268] in setting permit conditions for regulating environmental issues other than emissions. As a result, there is limited evidence of their use in national practice.[269] In some Member States, the requirements of BAT conclusions other than emission levels are interpreted as

---

[265] See Amec Foster Wheeler Environment and Infrastructure UK Limited, Final report of Application of IED Article 15(4) derogations, March 2018, 40–43.

[266] To what extent courts will scrutinize such decisions is not clear; an examination of national case law falls outside the scope of this research. The CJEU preliminary ruling will hopefully provide some insight into the judicial assessment of derogation decisions.

[267] IED art 14(3).

[268] For example, energy efficiency levels associated with the BAT are specified in Commission Implementing Decision (EU) 2017/1442 (2017) OJ L 212/1, 28–29.

[269] Commission (EU), Commission Staff Working Document Evaluation of the Industrial Emissions Directive SWD(2020) 181 final, 23 September 2020, 50. There is no CJEU case on this matter.

being non-binding and thus they are not included in the permit.[270] This shows that, compared to the BAT-associated emission levels, other environmental conditions as specified in BAT conclusions are given a relatively weak legal weight in national practice. From the perspective of an integrated approach, it can be questioned to what extent environmental issues that are not covered by BAT-associated emission levels would be weighed on a common basis with those that are covered by BAT-associated emission levels. The evaluation of the IED by the Commission pointed out that, while it is relatively obvious that the IED has resulted in effective outcomes concerning emissions control, 'there is very little information available on what impact the IED may have had in addressing non-emissions aspects such as: energy, water and material use, as well as waste generation'.[271]

However, it is debatable whether the national practice of interpreting some parts of BAT conclusions as non-binding correctly implements article 14(3) of the IED, which requires BAT conclusions to be the reference for setting permit conditions. Sanden pointed out that BAT conclusions are made by a decision of the EU Commission, and, according to article 288(4) of the TFEU,[272] they shall be binding in their entirety.[273] According to this view, the national practice to interpret some contents of BAT conclusions as non-binding cannot be considered as being a correct implementation of the IED.

With regard to the use of energy, the issue becomes more complicated. While detailed energy efficiency levels are specified in some BAT conclusions that shall be the reference for setting permit conditions,[274] the IED allows Member States to refrain from imposing requirements relating to energy efficiency.[275] Oosterhuis and Peeters observed that, although the IED has no obligation to conduct an integrated permit assessment that would lead to energy efficiency requirements under the IED,[276] given the explicit emphasis in the IED on energy efficiency being part of an integrated approach,[277] they hold the view that energy considerations should play a role when determining the specific emission limit value for an installation.[278] Following this view, one can argue that if a Member State has decided to make use of the possibility to refrain from adopting energy efficiency measures in the IED

270 Ibid, 50.

271 Ibid, 70 and 72.

272 TFEU art 288(4) reads: 'A decision shall be binding in its entirety. A decision which specifies those to whom it is addressed shall be binding only on them.'.

273 Joachim Sanden, 'Coherence in European Environmental Law with particular regard to the Industrial Emissions Directive' (2012) 21 European Energy and Environmental Law Review 220, 234.

274 For example, energy efficiency levels associated with the BAT are specified Commission Implementing Decision (EU) 2017/1442 (2017) OJ L 212/1, 28–29.

275 IED art 9(2) prescribes that '[f]or activities listed in Annex I to Directive 2003/87/EC, Member States may choose not to impose requirements relating to energy efficiency in respect of combustion units or other units emitting carbon dioxide on the site'.

276 Frans Oosterhuis and Marjan Peeters (2014), 101.

277 IED recital 3.

278 Frans Oosterhuis and Marjan Peeters (2014), 101.

permit, competent authorities still shall refer to energy efficiency levels as specified BAT conclusions when determining the specific emission limit value for an installation, although explicit conditions regarding energy efficiency are not required to be included in the permit.[279] Related to this, the proposal of revising the IED by the Commission suggests deleting the provision that allows Member States not to impose requirements relating to energy efficiency.[280]

The proposal of revising the IED by the Commission attempts to provide further concrete rules on applying BAT conclusions to set other permit conditions by suggesting that:

> the competent authority shall set environmental performance limit values that ensure that, under normal operating conditions, such performance limits values do not exceed the environmental performance levels associated with BATs as laid down in the BAT conclusions.[281]

As stated above, the Commission suggests to delete the IED provision that allows Member States not to impose requirements relating to energy efficiency,[282] aiming at 'making any requirements relating to energy efficiency mandatory'.[283] In this vein, if these proposed amendments will be adopted, the rules on applying BAT conclusions to set other permit conditions and the legal status of relevant environmental conditions regarding energy, water, and material use as specified in BAT conclusions will be clearer and stricter, so as to make a more effective contribution to resource and energy efficiency and a circular economy in the Union.[284]

In summary, the IED does not provide for concrete rules on how to apply BAT conclusions for setting permit conditions other than emission limit values. As a result, other environmental requirements as specified in the BAT conclusions are given a relatively weak legal position in national practice. From the perspective of an integrated approach, this means that environmental issues that are not covered by BAT-associated emission levels are not weighed on a common basis with those that are covered by BAT-associated emission levels, which indicates a limit to an integrated approach. Meanwhile, the Commission has proposed to strengthen the obligation of Member States to include environmental conditions regarding energy, water, and material use in the permit.

[279] Nevertheless, it is questionable whether it is possible for the court to test whether energy efficiency levels as specified BAT conclusions have really played a role in setting specific emission limit values for an installation. No preliminary reference has been made to the CJEU yet.

[280] Commission (EU), COM(2022)156 final, art 1(7).

[281] Ibid, art 1(12).

[282] Ibid, art 1(7).

[283] Ibid, the explanatory memorandum, 17.

[284] Ibid, recital 16.

3.7.4.5 Interim Conclusion

The IED provides for a strong legal status for the EU generic BAT documents (BREFs and BAT conclusions) in the determination of BAT, which indicates, from the perspective of an integrated approach, that the generic option for the weighing of environmental impacts is adopted by the IED. The procedure of adopting these generic BAT documents shows that various environmental issues, including emissions, energy use, resource use, and the generation of waste, are weighed in a generic way. However, the process of adopting these generic BAT documents appears to be less inclusive, where the environmental organizations play a relatively weak role compared to industrial organizations. This may negatively affect the generic weighing of environmental impacts for the implementation of an integrated approach.

Despite a strong legal status for the EU generic BAT documents, Member States have different degrees of flexibility in the use of these documents, which allows Member States to make case-specific decisions. However, in practice, the flexibility does not seem to have led to a case-specific weighing to discover techniques that can better protect the environment as a whole. In particular, this flexibility tends to make environmental issues that are not covered by BAT-associated emission levels hold less weight in the setting of permit conditions compared to those that are covered by BAT-associated emission levels, which can hinder an integrated approach.

3.7.5 Other Rules on the Determination of BAT for Setting Permit Conditions

The IED provides for rules on setting permit conditions on the basis of a BAT not described in the BAT conclusions in the two following cases. First, it allows authorities to 'set stricter permit conditions than those achievable by the use of [BAT] as described in the BAT conclusions'.[285] Secondly, 'where an activity or a type of production process […] is not covered by any of the BAT conclusions or where those conclusions do not address all the potential environmental effects of the activity or process', permit conditions shall be set on the BAT by giving special consideration to the criteria listed in Annex III.[286]

[285] IED art 14(4).

[286] IED art 14(6).

3.7.5.1 Setting Stricter Permit Conditions Than Those Achievable Based on BAT Conclusions

Article 14(4) allows permit conditions to be set stricter than those achievable based on BAT conclusions.[287] This provision helps to ensure compliance with local environmental quality standards and to account for local circumstances.[288] In view of an integrated approach, this can be understood as the IED providing the possibility for Member States to make a case-specific determination to follow more ambitious local environmental policies. However, to set stricter permit conditions than those achievable based on BAT conclusions is formulated as an option for Member States, but it is not an obligation. In light of this, Member States may not have strong enough incentives to apply stricter local BAT. Moreover, Koutalakis, Buzogany, and Börzel found that the consideration of local conditions to determine BAT requires 'significant cognitive, material and political capacities of both state regulators and industry'.[289] In other words, authorities are faced with great difficulties to develop case-specific BAT and, as a result, they tend to make use of BAT conclusions as 'a tempting refuge' from applying BAT locally.[290] In practice, few cases of applying stricter permit conditions based on article 14(4) of the IED can be found. According to the data provided on the Industrial Emissions Portal, just 115 records out of 344,414 permits indicated stricter conditions pursuant to article 14(4) of the IED.[291]

3.7.5.2 Setting Permit Conditions on the BAT Determined on the Basis of Annex III

According to article 14(6) of the IED, in the case 'where an activity or a type of production process [...] is not covered by any of the BAT conclusions or where those conclusions do not address all the potential environmental effects of the activity or process', the IED requires that permit conditions shall be set on the BAT determined by giving special consideration to the criteria listed in Annex III. The criteria listed in Annex III include:

---

[287] Generally, Member States are allowed to adopt measures aimed at environmental protection that are more stringent than measures already adopted at the EU level in light of TFEU art 193. For a further discussion on TFEU art 193, see Leonie Reins, Where Eagles Dare: How Much Further May EU Member States Go under Article 193 TFEU, in Marjan Peeters and Mariolina Eliantonio (eds), *Research Handbook on EU Environmental Law* (Edward Elgar 2020).

[288] Ricardo (2020), 125.

[289] Charalampos Koutalakis, Aron Buzogany and Tanja A. Börzel (2010), 332 and 338.

[290] Maria Lee (2014), 120. Also see a national example in Sweden. Pettersson and Söderholm found that 'the Swedish courts have chosen to lean heavily on the BREF documents in determining BAT, and there are thus few (if any) attempts to go beyond these requirements'. Maria Pettersson and Patrik Söderholm, 'Industrial pollution control and efficient licensing processes: the case of Swedish regulatory design' (2014) 6(8) Sustainability 5401, 5410–5415.

[291] Data is available at: 'European Industrial Emissions Portal', https://industry.eea.europa.eu/, last updated in January 2024, accessed on 5 May 2024.

1. the use of low-waste technology;
2. the use of less hazardous substances;
3. the furthering of recovery and recycling of substances generated and used in the process and of waste, where appropriate;
4. comparable processes, facilities or methods of operation which have been tried with success on an industrial scale;
5. technological advances and changes in scientific knowledge and understanding;
6. the nature, effects and volume of the emissions concerned;
7. the commissioning dates for new or existing installations;
8. the length of time needed to introduce the best available technique;
9. the consumption and nature of raw materials (including water) used in the process and energy efficiency;
10. the need to prevent or reduce to a minimum the overall impact of the emissions on the environment and the risks to it;
11. the need to prevent accidents and to minimise the consequences for the environment;
12. information published by public international organisations.'[292]

It is noted that not all of the environmental issues listed in Annex III of the IED are included in the basic obligations of the operators as prescribed in article 11 of the IED. For example, the 'consumption and nature of raw materials (including water)' used in the process is not mentioned in the list of basic obligations of the operator,[293] but it plays a role in the process of determining the BAT as prescribed in the IED Annex III point 9. Thus, it can be questioned how the use of raw materials should exactly play a role in the permit conditions.[294] In addition, the criteria listed in Annex III of the IED are general in nature, and thus they leave flexibility for the Member States. Giljam considered that these general criteria 'allow[s] for a (relatively) flexible BAT concept, which enables a state-of-the-art interpretation of the required high protection of the environment as a whole'.[295] Based on this opinion, this flexibility may be advantageous for the case-specific option to achieve an integrated approach. However, it appears that this is not the case in practice. It is found that the BAT conclusions provide 'far fewer conclusions on water usage than there are on emissions to water'.[296] This means that, in the area of water use, Member States have more room to develop local BAT pursuant to article 14(6) and the criteria listed in Annex III, compared to that in the area of controlling emissions into water, which is supposed to facilitate a state-of-art interpretation of BAT. However, there is very

[292] IED 3(11), art 14(5)(a), and art 14(6), and Annex III.

[293] IED art 11.

[294] Frans Oosterhuis and Marjan Peeters (2014), 108.

[295] Renske A. Giljam, 'Better BAT to Bolster Ecosystem Resilience: Operationalizing Ecological Governance through the Concept of Best Available Techniques' (2017) 26(1) Review of European, Comparative & International Environmental Law 5, 7.

[296] Ricardo (2020), 173.

little information available on what impact the IED may have had in addressing water use.[297]

Two limits to the flexibility of applying BAT not described in the BAT conclusions for setting permit conditions are required: the emission levels associated with the BAT as laid down in the BAT conclusions shall be attained; and where the BAT conclusions do not contain emission levels associated with the BAT, a level of environmental protection equivalent to the BAT described in the BAT conclusions shall be ensured.[298] In view of an integrated approach, it is questionable whether the environmental issues covered by the BAT conclusions would be given more weight in setting permit conditions than those that are not covered by the BAT conclusions.

3.7.5.3 Interim Conclusion

The IED provides the possibility for setting stricter permit conditions than those achievable based on BAT conclusions, which allows for more ambitious case-specific decisions. However, setting stricter permit conditions than those achievable based on BAT conclusions is formulated as an option for Member States, but it is not an obligation. In light of this, Member States may not have strong enough incentives to apply stricter local BAT. It has also been found that permitting authorities may not have enough capacity to develop case-specific BAT in practice.

In cases where there is no generic requirement provided the BAT conclusion, the IED requires that permit conditions shall be set on the BAT determined by a set of general criteria. The general criteria allow for a flexible BAT concept, which enables case-specific decisions. However, in practice, there is very little information available on what impact the IED may have had in addressing environmental issues that are not covered by the BAT conclusions. From the perspective of an integrated approach, it is questionable whether the environmental issues covered by the BAT conclusions would be given more weight in setting permit conditions than those that are not covered by the BAT conclusions.

3.7.6 Rules on Setting Minimum Emission Limit Values Based on the BAT

A set of minimum emission limit values are established in the Annexes to the IED.[299] These minimum emission limit values serve as ‘a European safety network whose

[297] Commission (EU), SWD(2020) 181 final, 23 September 2020, 72.

[298] IED art 14(5).

[299] IED Annexes V–VIII. In addition to minimum emission limit values, the IED also provides for a set of minimum requirements for rules on monitoring and compliance. These requirements are less relevant with regard to weighing environmental impacts. Thus will not be discussed in this section.

rules may not be breached by any installation'.[300] According to the IED, the Commission should present legislative proposals for establishing or updating Union-wide minimum requirements for emission limit values based on an assessment of the implementation of the BAT by certain activities or of the impact of those activities on the environment as a whole.[301] This shows that the proposals for Union-wide minimum emission limit values have to be based on an integrated approach and the BAT. The minimum emission limit values are established at the EU level, which indicates the use of the generic option to deal with the incommensurability of environmental goods in setting permit conditions.

According to the IED, minimum emission limit values have to be adopted or amended through the ordinary legislative procedure. The fact that this legislative procedure has to be followed does not encourage the update of minimum emission limit values to adapt to the development of BAT. This can be seen from the experience with the previous sectoral directives that were repealed by the IED. In the Impact Assessment report related to the IED proposal, it was found that the application of the minimum emission limit values of the sectoral directives lagged behind the level of BAT.[302] One reason for this, according to the Impact Assessment report, is that the minimum requirements '[could] only be revised or set through the EU co-decision process', which 'is necessarily a lengthy process, [...] and does not encourage adjustments to technological progress towards BAT on a regular basis'.[303] It is interesting to note that, in the process of adopting the IED, faster and easier procedures than the legislative procedure were proposed. At the first reading by the European Parliament to adopt the IED in 2009, the Parliament proposed that minimum emission limit values should be set by the Commission through a comitology subject to parliamentary scrutiny.[304] However, this proposal was rejected by the Council at its first reading to adopt the IED in 2010 with the reason that 'the ordinary legislative procedure is the appropriate procedure for the amendment of emission limit values',[305] while the setting of legally-binding emission limit values using comitology subject to parliamentary scrutiny 'could lead to excessive reliance on the values so set, rather than the application of BAT, as well as to an increased administrative burden'.[306] During the second reading of the European Parliament to adopt the IED in 2010, the European Parliament attempted to require the emission limit values as already established under

[300] Parliament (EU), 'REPORT on the proposal for a directive of the European Parliament and of the Council on industrial emissions (integrated pollution prevention and control) (recast)' (COM(2007)0844 – C6-0002/2008 – 2007/0286(COD) A6-0046/2009, 6 February 2009, 48).

[301] IED recital 41 and art 73(1).

[302] Commission (EU), SEC(2007) 1679, 21 December 2007, 29–30.

[303] Ibid.

[304] Parliament (EU), 'Position of the European Parliament adopted at first reading on 10 March 2009 with a view to the adoption of Directive 2009/.../EC of the European Parliament and of the Council on industrial emissions (integrated pollution prevention and control) (recast)' P6_TC1-COD(2007)0286 OJ C 87E/192, 1 April 2010, art 68 and art 69.

[305] Council (EU), OJ C 107E/1, 27 April 2010, 106.

[306] Ibid.

the proposed IED to be supplemented or amended by means of delegated acts.[307] This proposal was also not adopted. In short, the drafting history shows that the legislator—particularly, the Council—was not willing to adopt a relatively adaptive procedure to update the minimum emissions limit values.

The scope of minimum emission limit values as set out in the IED is based on the sectoral directives that it codified. By now, the IED has established minimum emission limit values for combustion plants, waste co-incineration plants, installations and activities using organic solvents, and installations producing titanium dioxide,[308] while other sectors have not been subject to these minimum emission limit values under the IED, which indicates a narrow scope from the perspective of an integrated approach. The proposal of revising the IED by the Commission does not set forth a broad scope of minimum emission limit values.[309]

In summary, a set of minimum emission limit values is established based on an assessment of the implementation of the BAT for certain activities or of the impact of those activities on the environment as a whole in the Annexes to the IED, serving as 'a European safety network'. These minimum emission limit values are established through the EU legislative procedure, which indicates the use of the generic option to deal with the incommensurability of environmental goods in setting permit conditions. The scope of these minimum emission limit values is relatively narrow, covering combustion plants, waste co-incineration plants, installations and activities using organic solvents, and installations producing titanium dioxide. They can be amended using a possibly lengthy legislative procedure. Although it was acknowledged that a lengthy legislative procedure would make minimum emission limit values lag behind the development of BAT, and more adaptive procedures were proposed in the drafting process, the legislative procedure for amending minimum emission limit values was finally adopted.

3.7.7 Interim Conclusion

The rationale for the concept of BAT is to deal with the incommensurability of environmental goods by providing a common basis related to which the environmental impact on different environmental media can be weighed. The IED requires a relatively wide scope of environmental impacts to be weighed, addressing not just emissions but also other environmental issues, such as the use of energy and resources. In terms of the options to deal with the incommensurability of environmental goods, a combined use of the generic approach and the case-specific approach is adopted by the IED.

---

[307] Parliament (EU), (11962/2009 – C7-0034/2010 – 2007/0286(COD) A7-0145/2010, 6 May 2010, amendment 64).

[308] See IED Annexes V–VIII.

[309] Commission (EU), COM(2022)156 final, 5 April 2022.

The adoption of the generic approach is mainly indicated by the mandatory status of the generic BAT documents, as well as the Union-wide minimum requirements for emission limit values as prescribed in the Annexes to the IED. First, the EU generic BAT documents include the BREFs and the BAT conclusions. The BREFs need to be developed based on information exchange among Member States, industries, Environmental NGOs, and the Commission, while the BREFs serve as the basis for establishing BAT conclusions through the comitology. The BAT conclusions shall be the reference for setting the permit conditions and, particularly, in the setting of emission limit values in the permit, the authorities have to ensure that emissions levels as described in the BAT conclusions are not exceeded. Meanwhile, there are various degrees of flexibility for Member States in the application of generic BAT conclusions in the setting of permit conditions. The flexibility makes some of these generic requirements to some extent indicative and thus leaves room for case-specific decision-making, which can facilitate an integrated approach. Precisely, some flexibility is given to Member States in the application of BAT conclusions for setting emission limit values in the permits because of the relatively wide range of the generic BAT associated emission levels; the provisions allowing emission limit values different from the generic BAT associated emission levels; the provision allowing emission limit values stricter than the generic BAT associated emission levels; and the provisions allowing a derogation from the generic BAT associated emission levels. In addition, a large degree of flexibility is available given that there is no clear rule on how to apply BAT conclusions in setting permit conditions to regulate environmental issues other than emissions. In cases where no generic requirement exists, more flexibility is available, which also indicates the case-specific approach adopted by the IED. However, in practice, it is not evident that the application of flexibility can guarantee case-specific decision-making resulting in optimal decisions for the protection of the environment as a whole. Instead of the variation of emission limit values across Member States, the emission limit values in the permits are largely set towards the least stringent end of the ranges of emission levels associated with BAT as described in BAT conclusions, which is considered an under-delivery of emissions reductions. In addition, few cases of applying stricter permit conditions based on the IED provision which allows emission limit values that are stricter than the generic BAT associated emission levels can be found in practice. In the non-emissions aspect, where Member States enjoy more flexibility, there is very little information available on what impact the IED may have had in addressing non-emissions issues such as energy, water, and material use, as well as waste generation.

Although it is not evident that the application of flexibility can guarantee case-specific decisions serving integration, an absolute binding generic option may not be favourable, since few cases have shown that the flexibility provided by the rules on the derogation from the emission levels associated with BAT is applied for case-specific decision-making considering cross-media effects. In other words, abandoning the flexible approach would obviously result in the disadvantage that an integrated approach in case-specific situations would not be reached. Meanwhile, a set of minimum emission limit values are established based on an assessment of the implementation of the BAT in certain activities or the impact of those activities on the environment as a whole in the Annexes to the IED, serving as 'a European safety network'. These Union-wide minimum requirements for emission limit values, established through the EU legislative procedure, indicate an absolute binding generic approach in the setting of permit conditions. In other words, no flexibility is available in the implementation of Union-wide minimum emission limit values. In this vein, updating these generic requirements could face great difficulties. One concern is that they must be amended through a possibly lengthy legislative procedure. Although it was acknowledged that a lengthy legislative procedure would make minimum emission limit values lag behind the development of BAT, and while a more adaptive procedure was proposed in the drafting process, the EU legislator chose to keep the ordinary legislative procedure for amending minimum emission limit values.

3.8 Rules on Environmental Quality Standards

Environmental quality standards are relevant in view of the permit conditions that must be set based on the BAT. If stricter conditions than those achievable using the BAT are required by the environmental quality standards, additional measures shall be included in the permit.[310] This requirement was introduced in the IPPCD and is continued with the IED. According to the Commission in its explanatory memorandum to the proposal of the IPPCD from 1993, the reason for introducing environmental quality standards is that 'quality standards provid[ed] a wider overview, assessing the effectiveness of BAT in protecting the environment'.[311] As discussed in Sect. 3.7.1, the rationale for the concept of BAT is to deal with the incommensurability of environmental goods by providing a common basis where environmental impacts on different environmental media can be weighed. Theoretically, an integrated approach must determine the effectiveness of environmental protection, otherwise, various environmental impacts can be weighed together at any level of environmental quality, and even at a low level of environmental quality.[312] Due to the incommensurability of environmental goods, a certain level of environmental protection can only be quantified in a media-specific way, which often takes the form of environmental quality standards.[313] Thus, the requirement to include stricter conditions in the permit if it is needed for the achievement of environmental quality

---

[310] IED art 18:

> Where an environmental quality standard requires stricter conditions than those achievable by the use of the best available techniques, additional measures shall be included in the permit, without prejudice to other measures which may be taken to comply with environmental quality standards.

[311] Commission (EC), COM (93) 423 final, 14 September 1993, 5.

[312] Section 2.3.1.2 of Chap. 2.

[313] Ibid.

standards indicates that the IED requires a concrete level of environmental protection to be achieved with the integrated permit.

The IED defines environmental quality standard as 'the set of requirements which must be fulfilled at a given time by a given environment or particular part thereof, as set out in Union law'.[314] Furthermore, case law interprets that the environmental quality standards are 'linked to the qualitative characteristics of the elements protected'.[315] The rules on environmental quality standards as prescribed by the IED make a link between the IED and other EU environmental legislation and, hence, can be seen as a form of coordination among several pieces of EU environmental legislation. For example, there is a link between the IED and the Water Framework Directive (2000/60/EC) (WFD) with regard to environmental quality standards.[316]

In practice, few cases of applying stricter permit conditions based on article 18 of the IED have been reported. According to the data provided on the Industrial Emissions Portal, just 39 records out of 344,414 permits indicated stricter conditions due to the objective of the environmental quality standards.[317] The lack of reported cases may be explained by two alternative hypotheses: either the BAT requirements are sufficient to achieve environmental quality standards; or article 18 of the IED requiring stricter permit conditions is not fully implemented in practice. The former

---

[314] IED art 3(6).

[315] Joined cases C-165/09 to C-167/09 Stichting Natuur en Milieu and Others v College van Gedeputeerde Staten van Groningen (C-165/09) and College van Gedeputeerde Staten van Zuid-Holland (C-166/09 and C-167/09) [26 May 2011] ECR I-4599 [61]–[62]. See also the Opinion of AG Kokott [55]–[63].

[316] Commission (EU), 'Fitness Check of the Water Framework Directive and the Floods Directive' (2019) SWD(2019) 439 final, 10 December 2019, 90. See also Directive 2000/60/EC of the European Parliament and of the Council of 23 October 2000 establishing a framework for Community action in the field of water policy (2000) OJ L 327/1 (WFD) art 10:

> The combined approach for point and diffuse sources
>
> 1. Member States shall ensure that all discharges referred to in paragraph 2 into surface waters are controlled according to the combined approach set out in this Article.
>
> 2. Member States shall ensure the establishment and/or implementation of:
>
> (a) the emission controls based on best available techniques, or
>
> (b) the relevant emission limit values, or
>
> (c) in the case of diffuse impacts the controls including, as appropriate, best environmental practices set out in:
>
> -Council Directive 96/61/EC of 24 September 1996 concerning integrated pollution prevention and control,
>
> [...]
>
> 3. Where a quality objective or quality standard, [...] requires stricter conditions than those which would result from the application of paragraph 2, more stringent emission controls shall be set accordingly.'

[317] Data is available at: https://industry.eea.europa.eu/, last update in January 2024, accessed on 5 May 2024.

hypothesis appears implausible, as there is evidence showing that the BAT requirements are not always sufficient to achieve environmental quality standards. In the area of water quality, the fitness check of the WFD shows that:

> [s]everal Member State representatives have expressed concern that it is difficult to set conditions that are stricter than the best available technique-associated emission levels (BAT-AELs) set under the IED, which are not always sufficient.[318]

The difficulty may be explained by the vagueness of article 18 of the IED. It is apparently not clear what accounts for the cases where an environmental quality standard requires stricter conditions than those achievable by the use of the BAT. It is known that industrial installations are not the only sources of pollution, as other sources of pollution such as transport are also relevant. In this vein, Groothuijse and Uylenburg considered that 'the Member State is not always obliged to set stricter permit conditions for installations, as it may also take other measures to ensure compliance with the [environmental quality standards], such as the reduction of diffuse sources of pollution'.[319] In addition, to deduce the correct permit conditions from environmental quality standards properly is also subject to great uncertainty, 'due to the complex interrelationships of physical, chemical and biological factors which influences the transport, dispersion and accumulation of pollutants in the environment'.[320] In other words, it is not clear what additional measures shall be included in the permit to achieve the environmental quality standards. The proposed revision of article 18 of the IED by the Commission does not provide further clarification on this issue, either.[321]

In summary, from the above analysis, the IED requires concrete levels of protection for specific environmental media to be achieved by suggesting that stricter measures must be included in the permit if this is required in order to achieve the environmental quality standards adopted in other EU legislation. This indicates that

---

318 Commission (EU), (2019) SWD (2019) 439 final, 10 December 2019, 90.

319 Frank Groothuijse and Rosa Uylenburg, 'Everything according to plan? Achieving environmental quality standards by a programmatic approach' in Marjan Peeters and Rosa Uylenburg (eds), *EU Environmental Legislation: Legal Perspectives on Regulatory Strategies* (Edward Elgar 2014), 119.

320 Eberhard Bohne (2006), 43.

321 Commission (EU), COM (2022)156 final, 5 April 2022, art 18:

> Where an environmental quality standard requires stricter conditions than those achievable by the use of the best available techniques, additional measures shall be included in the permit with a view to reducing the specific contribution of the installation to the pollution occurring in the relevant area.
>
> Where stricter conditions have been included in the permit in accordance with the first paragraph, regular monitoring of the concentration of relevant pollutants in the receiving environment resulting from operations of the installations concerned shall be required from the operator, and the results of such monitoring shall be transmitted to the competent authority. Where monitoring and measurement methods for the concerned pollutants are set out in other relevant Union legislation, such methods shall be used for the purpose of the monitoring referred to in this paragraph.

the IED requires concrete levels of environmental protection to be achieved with the integrated permit. In practice, it is not evident that this requirement to include stricter permit conditions in accordance with the need to achieve environmental quality standards is fully implemented in practice. One reason for this insufficient implementation in practice may be the vagueness of article 18 of the IED: it is not clear what happens in cases where an environmental quality standard requires stricter conditions; nor is clear what additional measures shall be included in the permit for the achievement of environmental quality standards. Hence, due to the vagueness, it can be questioned whether the IED truly requires the environmental effectiveness of integration in the sense of concrete levels of environmental quality standards to be achieved for specific media.

3.9 Interaction with Market-Based Instruments

There is an overlap between the integrated emissions permit instrument as pursued by IED and market-based instruments as prescribed by the Emissions Trading System Directive (Directive 2003/87/EC)[322] and the National Emission Ceilings Directive (2016/2284/EU) (NEC Directive).[323,324] This section examines the interaction between the industrial emissions permit as prescribed by the IED and the market-based instrument for controlling industrial pollution from the perspective of an integrated approach. The following sub-sections delve into how the industrial emissions permit system has to interact with instruments as prescribed in the ETS Directive and the NEC Directive, followed by an interim conclusion in the last section.

3.9.1 The Interface with the Emissions Trading System Directive

In 2003, the Emissions Trading System Directive (2003/87/EC) (ETS Directive) was adopted, establishing the EU system for greenhouse gas emission allowance trading, 'in order to promote reductions of greenhouse gas emissions in a cost-effective and economically efficient manner'.[325] The ETS Directive requires that 'the conditions of, and procedure for, the issue of a greenhouse gas emissions permit are coordinated with those for the permit provided for in [the IPPCD and later the IED]',[326] but it does not provide a further concrete explanation on the coordination. In addition, the ETS Directive amended the IPPCD, requiring that the emissions permit shall not

[322] Directive 2003/87/EC.

[323] Directive (EU) 2016/2284.

[324] Elizabeth Fisher, Bettina Lange, and Eloise Scotford (2019), 455.

[325] ETS Directive, art 1.

[326] ETS Directive art 8.

include an emission limit value for direct emissions of Green House Gases (hereinafter 'GHGs') from installations that are covered by the ETS Directive, 'unless it is necessary to ensure that no significant local pollution is caused'.[327] This requirement is also laid down in article 9(1) of the IED.[328] The rationale for this requirement is to avoid the duplication of regulation.[329] In addition, literature has pointed out that this requirement helps to avoid that 'the freedom of operators to decide whether to reduce emissions or to buy allowances [would get] frustrated by "command and control" emission limits imposed by the IPPC/IED permit'.[330] Hence, the provision aims to help cost-effectiveness, being a core aim of the ETS Directive.[331] However, this prohibition to establish an emission limit value in the IED permit also implies a restriction to an integrated approach. In other words, it is not possible to include the emission limit values of GHGs in the integrated assessment for the industrial emissions permit decision unless this is necessary to avoid significant local pollution.[332] It has been found that, due to the prohibition of setting GHGs emission limit values in the IED permits, the generic BAT documents, which are the outcomes of generic trade-offs, seldom specify BAT associated emission levels for GHGs and pay little attention to 'the synergies that may be achievable for addressing other pollutant emissions through decarbonisation techniques'.[333] This can be considered as evidence that the prohibition of setting GHGs emission limit values to some extent hinders the control of GHGs from being integrated with the control of other pollutant emissions.

Nevertheless, according to recital 10 of the IED,

> In accordance with Article 193 of the Treaty on the Functioning of the European Union (TFEU), this Directive does not prevent Member States from maintaining or introducing more stringent protective measures, for example [GHGs] requirements, provided that such measures are compatible with the Treaties and the Commission has been notified.'

Oosterhuis and Peeters considered that this may, theoretically, provide the possibility for Member States to impose GHGs emission requirements in the IED permit, although these 'GHGs emission requirements most likely may not take the form

---

[327] Ibid, art 26.

[328] IED art 9(1) prescribes:

> Where emissions of a greenhouse gas from an installation are specified in Annex I to Directive 2003/87/EC in relation to an activity carried out in that installation, the permit shall not include an emission limit value for direct emissions of that gas, unless necessary to ensure that no significant local pollution is caused.

[329] IED recital 9.

[330] Frans Oosterhuis and Marjan Peeters (2014), 100.

[331] See ETS Directive art 1.

[332] However, the possibility of including emission limit values of GHGs to avoid significant local pollution is, for instance, not relevant when regulating CO_2, an important greenhouse gas, since emissions of CO_2 do not produce local environmental effects.

[333] Commission (EU), SWD (2020) 181 final, 23 September 2020, 71–72.

of emission limit values in an IE permit (unless the view can be held that a directive cannot restrict Article 193 TFEU).'[334] Related to this, Squintani, Holwerda, and Graaf found that the main problem for Member States to rely on Article 193 TFEU to impose GHGs emission limit values in the IED permit is that GHGs emission limit values 'are likely to jeopardize the ETS's non-environmental objectives of cost-effectiveness and economic efficiency', thus these measures 'would probably to an infringement of EU law'.[335] In this vein, they further claimed that:

> 'Whether the CJEU will indeed consider that [GHGs emission limit values] do not respect the ETS Directive's objectives of cost-effectiveness and economic efficiency probably depends on the importance the CJEU will attach to these non-environmental objectives'.[336]

Whereas, putting the legal uncertainties related to article 193 TFEU aside, Macrory considered that 'Member States still possessed the freedom to impose nation[al] emission standards under non-IPPC laws'.[337] Following this idea, Fisher, Lange, and Scotford pointed out that article 26 of the ETS Directive 'only prohibits Member States from imposing [emission limit values under the IED], but not under other national legislation or rules'.[338] Therefore, they questioned 'whether the IED really does prevent Member States from setting emission limit values for GHGs in permits',[339] but on this important matter no judicial assessments have been provided yet.

In short, the ETS Directive requires a coordination between the greenhouse gas emissions permit and the permit provided for in the IED, but it does not provide a further concrete explanation on the coordination. Meanwhile, the imposition of emission limit values for GHGs in the emissions permit would risk legal challenges, and thus it is questionable whether or to what extent the greenhouse gases covered by the ETS market-based instrument can be integrated with the emissions permit instrument as prescribed by the IED.

---

[334] Frans Oosterhuis and Marjan Peeters (2014), 102.

[335] Lorenzo Squintani, Marijn Holwerda and Kars de Graaf, 'Regulating greenhouse gas emissions from EU ETS installations: what room is left for the member states?', in Marjan Peeters, Mark Stallworthy and Javier De Cendra de Larragán (eds), *Climate law in EU member states: towards national legislation for climate protection* (Edward Elgar 2012), 86.

[336] Ibid, 87.

[337] This opinion by Richard Macrory is available in the first report of emissions performance standards published by House of Commons of the United Kingdom 24 November 2010, paras 5–9, https://publications.parliament.uk/pa/cm201011/cmselect/cmenergy/523/523uw.pdf, accessed on 29 March 2022.

[338] Elizabeth Fisher, Bettina Lange, and Eloise Scotford (2019), 456.

[339] Ibid.

3.9.2 *The Interface with the National Emission Reduction Commitments Directive*

In 2016, a new National Emission Reduction Commitments Directive (2016/2284/EU) (NEC Directive) was adopted,[340] replacing the earlier one (2001/81/EU).[341] A programmatic approach was adopted by the NEC Directive, which allows Member States to decide how they will meet their emission reduction commitments for five important air pollutants.[342] In other words, Member States are allowed to choose instruments to meet their emission reduction commitments. Fisher, Lange, and Scotford were concerned that:

> [I]f Member States choose to achieve NEC Directive caps through national trading regimes in NOx and SOx, permitting authorities may lose [...] the power to impose technology standard based emission limits in environmental permits for installations covered by the IED that emit NOx and SOx.[343]

In this vein, a question of how to integrate a BAT-based instrument with an emission trading instrument would arise if Member states indeed would be allowed to use national emissions trading systems. During the process of drafting the IED, the Council's Position at the first reading in 2010 attempted to mention the use of market-based instruments in the recital, which can be illustrated by the following text:

> In order to prevent, reduce and, as far as possible, eliminate pollution arising from industrial activities in the most cost-effective way while ensuring a high level of protection of the environment as a whole, in particular through the implementation of best available techniques, the possibilities for market-based instruments such as trading in nitrogen oxides and sulphur dioxide emissions could be explored.[344]

However, this proposed recital was deleted by the European Parliament at its second reading to adopt the IED in 2010, as it considered that.

> Introducing marked based instruments would further complicate the legislation. Furthermore, nitrogen oxides and sulphur dioxide emissions have local and/or regional impacts and can therefore not be subject to trading at an EU scale.[345]

In the end, the market-based instrument for controlling nitrogen oxides and sulphur dioxide emissions is not mentioned in the IED. Therefore, it is not clear how the

---

340 Directive (EU) 2016/2284.

341 Directive 2001/81/EC of the European Parliament and of the Council of 23 October 2001 on national emission ceilings for certain atmospheric pollutants (2001) OJ L 309/22.

342 NEC Directive art 1 and art 6. The five important air pollutants are: sulphur dioxide (SO^2), nitrogen oxides (NOx), non-methane volatile organic compounds (NMVOC), ammonia (NH^3), and fine particulate matter (PM2,5).

343 Elizabeth Fisher, Bettina Lange, and Eloise Scotford (2019), 457.

344 Council (EU), OJ C 107E/1, 27 April 2010, recital 37.

345 Parliament (EU), (11962/2009 – C7-0034/2010 – 2007/0286(COD) A7-0145/2010, 6 May 2010, amendment 6).

BAT-based instrument as prescribed by the IED will have to interact with an eventual national emission trading instrument that may be adopted by Member States under the NEC Directive. Case law could play a role to clarify this issue. In the Joined Case C-165/09 to C-167/09, the CJEU ruled that Member States are not obliged to include the national emission ceilings as laid down the NEC Directive among the conditions for granting the IPPCD permit.[346] This case reinforces the great flexibility that Member States enjoy to choose their measures to meet national emission ceilings, but it does not deal with how various instruments taken by Member States have to interact with the integrated emissions permit as pursued by IED.

3.9.3 Interim Conclusion

The IED to some extent overlaps with the ETS Directive and NEC Directive. While the IED provides for the permit instrument to control emissions, the ETS Directive provides for an emission trading system for a set of GHGs. The ETS Directive requires the coordination between the greenhouse gas emissions permit and the permit provided for in the IED, but it does not provide for a further concrete explanation on the coordination. Meanwhile, the imposition of emission limit values for GHGs in the emissions permit would face legal challenges, and thus it is questionable whether or to what extent the greenhouse gases covered by the ETS market-based instrument can be integrated with the emissions permit instrument as prescribed by the IED.

The NEC Directive leaves it up to Member States to choose instruments to control the emissions of five pollutants, but it does not clearly prescribe how the integrated emissions permit instrument as pursued by the IED would have to interact with the other instruments taken by Member States, in particular the market-based instrument, in the emissions control. It is not clear how the ambiguous regulation on their interaction may affect the implementation of integrated pollution prevention and control.

3.10 Conclusion on the EU Emissions Permit System Towards an Integrated Environmental Permit

This chapter aims to address the question of how the emissions permit system of the IED attempting to implement an integrated environmental permit has been developed in terms of its regulatory design and relevant case law. In order to address this question, this chapter provided an in-depth legal examination of the IED on the basis

[346] Joined Cases C-165/09 to C-167/09 Stichting Natuur en Milieu and Others v College van Gedeputeerde Staten van Groningen (C-165/09) and College van Gedeputeerde Staten van Zuid-Holland (C-166/09 and C-167/09) [26 May 2011] ECR I-4599 [76].

of the conceptual framework of an integrated environmental permit as identified in Chap. 2. Below, a conclusion will be provided.

3.10.1 Substantive Integration Under the EU Emissions Permit System

This section provides answers to the three questions regarding substantive integration: the scope of integration, the environmental effectiveness of integration, and the options for environmental trade-offs.

3.10.1.1 The Scope of Integration Under the EU Emissions Permit System

In view of the scope of integration, what is the scope of the environmental issues that are subject to the emissions permit system as developed by the IED? Sect. 3.3 shows that the IED is aimed at 'integrated prevention and control of pollution arising from industrial activities', 'in order to achieve a high level of protection of the environment taken as a whole.'[347] This aim, from the perspective of the scope of integration, can be interpreted in a narrow sense and a broad sense.[348]

In the narrow sense, the objective of the IED focuses on pollution control, basically covering emissions into the air, water, and land. In the broad sense, the objective of the IED addresses the protection of the environment taken as a whole, which may imply a broader scope of environmental issues to be integrated rather than that just pollution control alone.

Meanwhile, the examination of the rules on the application for a permit as laid down by the IED shows that the IED requires a relatively wide scope of environmental issues to be included in the application for the permit, covering not just emissions, but also other environmental elements, such as the use or generation of raw materials and energy.[349] By prescribing a wide scope for the contents of the permit application, the IED aims to encourage operators to consider their environmental performance in an integrated manner in the design of the plant, but whether and to what extent these rules indeed help to avoid ignorance by operators is not yet empirically tested.[350] In addition, the IED requires that the contents of permit conditions have to comply with the requirements of general principles governing the basic obligations of the operator, which concern a relatively wide scope of environmental issues: not just emissions but also other environmental issues, such as the use of energy.[351] However,

[347] IED art 1.

[348] See Sect. 3.3 of this chapter.

[349] See Sect. 3.4 of this chapter.

[350] Ibid.

[351] See Sect. 3.6 of this chapter.

the IED does not include the reasonable use of resources in the basic obligations of the operators, and thus it can be questioned to what extent the use of raw materials can be integrated into the emissions permit.[352] The IED prescribes that the permit conditions have to be set on the basis of the BAT. The definition of the BAT indicates that the integrated approach is pursued, since there is an explicit reference to 'the impact on the environment as a whole'.[353] The other detailed rules on the BAT show that the scope of an integrated approach as required by the IED does not concern emissions only, but also other environmental impacts, including consumption of raw materials, water consumption, use of energy, and generation of waste, in the environment as a whole.[354] However, in practice, in relation to the non-emissions aspect, there is very little information available on what impact the IED may have had in addressing non-emissions issues such as: energy, water, and material use, as well as waste generation.[355]

Since there are legal challenges to imposing emission limit values for the GHGs that are covered by the ETS market-based instrument in the emissions permit, it is questionable whether and to what extent these GHGs can be integrated with the emissions permit instrument as prescribed by the IED.[356]

Hence, the answer to question 1 is: the scope of environmental issues subject to the IED permit system concerns not just emissions but also other environmental issues, such as the use of energy and resources. Meanwhile, the imposition of emission limit values for the GHGs that are covered by the ETS market-based instrument in the IED emissions permit would face legal challenges, which may hinder these GHGs limits from being integrated with the emissions permit instrument and thus constitute a limit to the scope of integration.

3.10.1.2 The Environmental Effectiveness of Integration Under the EU Emissions Permit System

In view of the environmental effectiveness of integration, what is the level of environmental quality as a whole required by the emissions permit system as developed by the IED? The objective of the IED is to 'achieve a high level of protection of the environment taken as a whole'.[357] This objective indicates that the lowest level of protection of the environment taken as a whole is not allowed, but a highest possible level of the environment taken as a whole is also not required (since Member States are allowed to adopt stricter measures).[358] Meanwhile, Sect. 3.8 shows that the IED

[352] Ibid.

[353] See Sect. 3.7.3 of this chapter.

[354] See Sect. 3.7 of this chapter.

[355] See Sects. 3.7.5.1 and 3.7.5.2 of this chapter. This will further discussed later in this section in view of the options for environmental trade-offs.

[356] See Sect. 3.9.1 of this chapter.

[357] IED art 1.

[358] See Sect. 3.3.1.2 of this chapter.

requires concrete levels of protection for specific environmental media to be achieved with the integrated emissions permit by suggesting that stricter measures have to be included in the permit if this is required in order to achieve environmental quality standards adopted in other EU legislation. In practice, it is not evident that this requirement to include stricter permit conditions in accordance with the need of achieving environmental quality standards is fully implemented, given the fact that although the emission levels associated with the best available technique[359] are not always sufficient for achieving environmental quality standards, few cases of applying stricter permit conditions based on article 18 of the IED have been reported.[360] One reason for the insufficient implementation in practice may be the vagueness of article 18 of the IED: it is not clear what happens in cases where an environmental quality standard requires stricter conditions; nor is clear what additional measures shall be included in the permit to achieve environmental quality standards.[361]

Hence, the answer to question 2 is: the IED aims to 'achieve a high level of protection of the environment taken as a whole', which indicates that the lowest level of protection of the environment taken as a whole is not allowed, while the highest possible level of the environment taken as a whole is not required. Meanwhile, the achievement of concrete levels of environmental quality for specific media (demonstrated as the environmental quality standards in Union law) are required by the IED. However, the rules on how to achieve these environmental quality standards are formulated in a relatively vague manner. Hence, it can be questioned to what extent the environmental effectiveness of integration can be guaranteed by the IED, particularly given the fact that although the emission levels associated best available technique are not always sufficient to achieve environmental quality standards, few cases of applying stricter permit conditions based on article 18 of the IED have been reported.

3.10.1.3 The Options for Environmental Trade-Offs Under the EU Emissions Permit System

In view of the incommensurability of environmental goods, what are the options adopted by the IED to make environmental trade-offs? Sect. 3.7 shows that the rationale for the concept of BAT prescribed by the IED is to deal with the incommensurability of environmental goods by providing a common basis where environmental impacts on different environmental media can be weighed. The rules on the BAT for setting permit conditions indicate that a combined use of the generic option, which addresses several decision situations of the same kind, and weighs and balances prospective environmental and other effects in a generic and abstract way and results

[359] The BAT associated emission levels set under the IED will also discussed later in this section in view of the options for environmental trade-offs.

[360] Ibid.

[361] See Sect. 3.8 of this chapter.

in generic trade-offs which apply to all defined cases,[362] and the case-specific option, which is concerned only with the effects of a single case and results in case-specific trade-offs,[363] is adopted by the IED. The adoption of the generic option is mainly indicated by the mandatory status of the EU generic BAT documents as well as the Union-wide minimum requirements for emission limit values as prescribed in the Annexes to the IED.[364] The EU generic BAT documents include the BREFs and the BAT conclusions.[365] The BREFs need to be developed on the basis of an information exchange between Member States, industries, Environmental NGOs, and the Commission,[366] and the BREFs serve as the basis for establishing BAT conclusions through the comitology.[367] The BAT conclusions shall be the reference for setting the permit conditions, and, particularly, in setting emission limit values in the permit, the authorities have to ensure that emissions levels as described in the BAT conclusions are not exceeded.[368] Meanwhile, Member States have various degrees of flexibility in the application of generic BAT conclusions to set permit conditions, which makes some of these generic requirements indicative, to some extent, and thus leaves room for case-specific decision-making. Precisely, a small degree of flexibility is given to Member States in the application of BAT conclusions in setting emission limit values in the permits by the relatively wide range of the generic BAT associated emission levels[369]; the provisions allowing emission limit values different from the generic BAT associated emission levels[370]; the provision allowing emission limit values stricter than the generic BAT associated emission levels[371]; and the provisions allowing a derogation from the generic BAT associated emission levels.[372] In addition, a significant degree of flexibility is available, given that there is no clear rule on how to apply BAT conclusions in setting permit conditions to regulate environmental issues other than emissions.[373] In cases where no generic requirement exists, more flexibility is available,[374] which also indicates that a case-specific approach is facilitated by the IED. However, in practice, it is not evident that flexibility can guarantee case-specific decision-making that serves optimal decisions for the protection of the environment as a whole. Instead of the variation of emission limit values across Member States, the emission limit values in the permits are largely set towards the least stringent end of the ranges of emission

[362] See Sect. 2.3.1.3 of Chap. 2.

[363] Ibid.

[364] See Sect. 3.7 of this chapter.

[365] See Sect. 3.7.4 of this chapter.

[366] See Sect. 3.7.4.2.1 of this chapter.

[367] See Sect. 3.7.4.2.2 of this chapter.

[368] See Sect. 3.7.4 of this chapter.

[369] See Sect. 3.7.4.3.1 of this chapter.

[370] See Sect. 3.7.4.3.2 of this chapter.

[371] See Sect. 3.7.5.1 of this chapter.

[372] See Sect. 3.7.4.3.3 of this chapter.

[373] See Sect. 3.7.4.4 of this chapter.

[374] See Sect. 3.7.5.2 of this chapter.

levels associated with BAT as described in BAT conclusions, which is considered to be an under-delivery of emissions reductions.[375] In addition, few cases of applying stricter permit conditions based on the IED provision allowing emission limit values stricter than the generic BAT associated emission levels can be found in practice.[376] It was found that authorities may not have enough capacity to develop case-specific BAT in practice and, as a result, they tend to make use of generic BAT conclusions as 'a tempting refuge' from applying BAT locally.[377] In the area of emissions control, where Member States enjoy less flexibility due to the relatively clear binding generic requirements, it is relatively obvious that the implementation of the IED has resulted in positive outcomes of emissions reduction,[378] while in the non-emissions area, where Member States enjoy more flexibility, there is very little information available on what impact the IED may have had in addressing non-emissions aspects such as: energy, water, and material use, as well as waste generation.[379]

Though it is not evident that the application of flexibility can guarantee the case-specific decisions serving integration, an absolute binding generic option may not be favourable, since a few cases have shown that the flexibility allowed by the rules on the derogation from the emission levels associated with BAT is applied for the case-specific decision-making considering cross-media effects.[380] In other words, abandoning the flexible approach would obviously have a disadvantage that an integrated approach in case-specific situations cannot be reached. Meanwhile, a set of minimum emission limit values are established on the basis of an assessment of the implementation of the BAT to certain activities or of the impact of those activities on the environment as a whole in the Annexes to the IED, serving as 'a European safety network'.[381] These Union-wide minimum requirements for emission limit values, established through the EU legislative procedure, indicate an absolute binding generic approach in setting permit conditions. In other words, no flexibility is available in the implementation of Union-wide minimum emission limit values. Updating these generic requirements could face great difficulties. They have to be amended using a possibly lengthy legislative procedure.[382] Although it was acknowledged that a lengthy legislative procedure would make minimum emission limit values lag behind the development of BAT, and more adaptive procedure were proposed in the drafting process, the legislative procedure for amending minimum emission limit values was finally adopted.[383]

Hence, the answer to question 3 is: in view of the incommensurability of environmental goods, a combined use of the generic option and the case-specific option is

---

[375] See Sect. 3.7.4.3.1 of this chapter.

[376] See Sect. 3.7.5.1 of this chapter.

[377] Ibid. The wording of 'a tempting refuge' is borrowed from Maria Lee (2014), 120.

[378] See Sect. 3.7.4.4 of this chapter.

[379] Ibid. Also see Sect. 3.7.5.2 of this chapter.

[380] See Sect. 3.7.4.3.3 of this chapter.

[381] See Sect. 3.7.6 of this chapter.

[382] Ibid.

[383] Ibid.

adopted by the IED to make environmental trade-offs. The adoption of the generic approach is indicated by the mandatory status of the EU generic BAT documents as well as the Union-wide minimum requirements for emission limit values as prescribed in the Annexes to the IED. The adoption of the case-specific approach is indicated by various degrees of flexibility provided to Member States in setting permit conditions on the basis of the BAT. In practice, it is not evident that flexibility guarantees the case-specific decision-making that serves optimal decisions for the protection of the environment as a whole. Meanwhile, abandoning the flexible approach is not favourable, as it would obviously have a disadvantage that an integrated approach in case-specific situations cannot be reached, particularly given the fact that a few cases in practice have shown that the flexibility is applied for case-specific decision-making considering cross-media effects.

3.10.2 Procedural Integration Under the EU Emissions Permit System

There are two questions regarding procedural integration: does the IED require one permit procedure, or does it allow for several permit-procedures; and is there a coordination mechanism required by the IED? Sect. 3.5 shows that, according to the rules on granting an emissions permit under the IED, Member States are not required to establish one procedure, and, where more than one procedure exists, Member States shall establish a coordination mechanism for implementing an integrated approach. However, the IED does not provide further concrete provisions on how the coordination mechanism should be established and thus leaves flexibility for the Member States. Thus far, there is no case law from the CJEU providing further interpretations on this matter. In practice, various degrees of coordination among Member States have been reported.[384]

In addition, the IED allows information produced in response to sectoral procedures to be used in the application for a permit to also serve as a coordination tool from the perspective of procedural integration.[385] Moreover, the IED prescribes that the relevant information produced in response to the EIA Directive has to be examined and used in granting an emissions permit, which can be interpreted as the requirement of coordination between the EIA procedure and the IED permit procedure.[386] However, the IED does not provide a concrete explanation on what accounts for relevant EIA information, and thus leaves flexibility for the Member States.[387] The EIA Directive suggests the so-called 'one-stop-shop' approach to achieve procedural integration: to establish a coordinated procedure and/or joint procedure. However, to adopt the 'one-stop-shop' approach is an option for Member States, but it not as

384 See Sect. 3.5.2 of this chapter.

385 See Sect. 3.4.2 of this chapter.

386 See Sect. 3.5.2 of this chapter.

387 Ibid.

an obligation. In practice, it is not evident that the 'one-stop-shop' has been widely established by Member States.[388] Therefore, it is not evident that the procedural integration between the EIA procedure and the IED permit procedure takes place in practice in the implementation of the IED and the EIA Directive.

Hence, the answers to questions 4 and 5 are: in view of procedural integration, the IED does not require one procedure to be established, but it requires the Member State to establish a coordination mechanism for implementing an integrated approach where more than one procedure exists. Meanwhile, the IED establishes the coordination with other Directives, particularly including the EIA Directive. However, given that the rules on the coordination as laid down by the IED are formulated in a vague manner, it can be questioned how these rules truly require procedural integration through coordination. In practice, various degrees of coordination of the conditions and the procedures for granting the permit have been reported among Member States. It is also not evident that the procedural integration between the EIA procedure and the IED permit procedure takes place in practice in the implementation of the IED and the EIA Directive.

3.10.3 The Interaction Between the Emissions Permit System and the Market-Based Instruments for Pollution Control in the EU

In view of the interaction between the IED emissions permits and the market-based instruments for pollution control, Sect. 3.9 shows that the IED to some extent overlaps with the ETS Directive and NEC Directive. While the IED provides for a permit instrument to control emissions, the ETS Directive provides for an emission trading system for a set of GHGs. The ETS Directive requires coordination between the greenhouse gas emissions permit and the permit provided for in the IED, but it does not provide for a further concrete explanation on the coordination. Meanwhile, the imposition of emission limit values for GHGs in the emissions permit would risk legal challenges, and thus it is questionable whether or to what extent the greenhouse gases covered by the ETS market-based instrument can be integrated with the emissions permit instrument as prescribed by the IED.

The NEC Directive leaves it up to Member States to choose instruments to control emissions for five pollutants, but it does not clearly prescribe how the integrated emissions permit instrument as pursued by the IED would have to interact with the other instruments adopted by Member States, in particular the market-based instrument, in the emissions control. It is not clear how the ambiguous regulation on their interaction may affect the implementation of integrated pollution prevention and control.

Hence, the answer to question 6 is: it is not entirely clear how the emissions permits have to interact with the market-based instruments for pollution control in

[388] Ibid.

view of integration, but it is at least clear that there are legal challenges to integrate the greenhouse gases covered by the ETS market-based instrument into the emissions permit instrument as prescribed by the IED.

In conclusion, the IED can to some extent be considered as providing possibilities for controlling emissions in an integrated way through the permit instrument. The emissions permit system as developed by the IED regulates a broad scope of environmental issues (including not just emissions but also other environmental issues, such as the use of energy and resources). Moreover, the IED adopts a combined use of a generic approach and a case-specific approach to environmental trade-offs. In order to pursue certain levels of environmental effectiveness of integration, the IED requires concrete levels of environmental quality for specific media (demonstrated as the environmental quality standards in Union law) to be achieved with the emissions permit system. Meanwhile, the IED requires a coordination mechanism to be established to implement procedural integration. In practice, some positive outcomes in terms of controlling various emissions in a generic way can be clearly identified in the implementation of the IED. Nevertheless, it is not evident that the rules on the coordination mechanism, the rules on the level of environmental protection, the rules on the case-specific decision-making and the rules on the interaction with the market-based instruments has had a positive impact on the implementation of integration in practice, and thus more effort is needed to improve these rules.

References

Adoption on 3 November 2005 by the Commission of the first report on the implementation of the IPPC Directive. https://ec.europa.eu/environment/archives/air/stationary/ippc/ippc_report.htm. Accessed 30 May 2020.

Amec Foster Wheeler Environment & Infrastructure UK Limited and Milieu Limited. (2016). Assessment and summary of the Member States implementation reports for the IED, IPPCD, SED and WID: Industrial Emissions Directive Final Report, 5 March 2016.

Amec Foster Wheeler Environment & Infrastructure UK Limited. (2018). Final report of Application of IED Article 15(4) derogations, March 2018.

Anker, H. T. (2020). Competences for EU environmental legislation: about blurry boundaries and ample opportunities. In *Research Handbook on EU Environmental Law* (pp. 7–21). Edward Elgar Publishing.

Braaksma, L. S., & Tolsma, H. D. (2020). Integrated pollution prevention and control: A critical legal perspective on all-inclusive integration. In: *Research Handbook on EU Environmental Law* (pp. 313–327). Edward Elgar Publishing.

Bradley, K. (2016). Delegation of powers in the European Union: political problems, legal solutions. In *Rulemaking by the European Commission: the new system for delegation of powers* (pp. 55–84). Oxford University Press.

Bogaart, M. (2014). The emergence of the framework directive in EU environmental policy: An exploration of its function and characteristics. In *EU environmental legislation* (pp. 48–69). Edward Elgar Publishing.

Bohne, E. (2006). The quest for environmental regulatory integration in the European Union: integrated pollution prevention and control, environmental impact assessment and major accident prevention (Vol. 10). Kluwer Law International BV.

Bohne, E. (2008). The implementation of the IPPC Directive from a comparative perspective and lessons for its recast (Part 1). *Journal for European Environmental and Planning Law, 5*(1), 1–33.
Case C-172/19 P Association européenne du charbon et du lignite (Euracoal) v European Commission [31 January 2020] ECLI:EU:C:2020:66.
Case C-172/19 P: Appeal brought on 22 February 2019 by Association européenne du charbon et du lignite (Euracoal) against the order of the General Court (Third Chamber) delivered on 13 December 2018 in Case T-739/17 Association européenne du charbon et du lignite (Euracoal) and Others v European Commission OJ C 164/25, 13 May 2019.
Case C-284/95 Safety Hi-Tech Srl v S. & T. Srl. [14 July 1998] ECLI:EU:C:1998:352.
Case C-341/95 Bettati v Safety Hi-Tech [14 July 1998] ECLI:EU:C:1998:353.
Case C-375/21 Sdruzhenie "Za Zemyata - dostap do pravosadie" and Others [9 March 2023] ECLI:EU:C:2023:173.
Case C-473/07 Association nationale pour la protection des eaux et rivières-TOS and Association OABA v Ministère de l'Ecologie, du Développement et de l'Aménagement durables [22 January 2009] ERC I-00319.
Case C-585/10 Niels Møller v Haderslev Kommune [15 December 2011] ERC I-13407.
Case T-739/17 Euracoal and Others v Commission ECLI:EU:T:2018:959.
Comitology. https://eur-lex.europa.eu/legal-content/EN/ALL/?uri=LEGISSUM:comitology. Accessed 23 June 2022.
Commission (EC). Towards sustainability, A European Community programme of policy and action in relation to the environment and sustainable development. OJ C 138/5, 17 May 1993.
Commission (EC). Proposal for a Council Directive on Integrated Pollution Prevention and Control. COM(93) 423 final, 14 September 1993.
Commission (EC). (2006). Integrated Pollution Prevention and Control Reference Document on Economics and Cross-Media Effects. Retrieved on July 30, 2006 from https://eippcb.jrc.ec.europa.eu/sites/default/files/2019-11/ecm_bref_0706.pdf. Accessed 3 November 2021.
Commission (EU). Commission Staff Working Document Accompanying document to the proposal for a Directive of the European Parliament and of the Council on industrial emissions (integrated pollution prevention and control) (recast) IMPACT ASSESSMENT. SEC(2007) 1679.
Commission (EU). Proposal for a Directive of the European Parliament and of the Council on industrial emissions (integrated pollution prevention and control). COM(2007) 844 final, 21 December 2007.
Commission (EU). Report from the Commission on the implementation of Directive 2008/1/EC concerning integrated pollution prevention and control and Directive 1999/13/EC on the limitation of emissions of volatile organic compounds due to the use of organic solvents in certain activities and installations. COM(2010) 593 final, p. 25 October 2010.
Commission (EU). Decision of 16 May 2011 establishing a forum for the exchange of information pursuant to Article 13 of the Directive 2010/75/EU on industrial emissions. OJ C 146/3, 17 May 2011.
Commission (EU). Implementing Decision (EU)2012/119 of 10 February 2012 laying down rules concerning guidance on the collection of data, on drawing up BAT reference documents, and on quality assurance referred to in Directive 2010/75/EU of the European Parliament and of the Council on industrial emissions (2012) OJ L 63/1.
Commission (EU). Commission Staff Working Paper Impact Assessment Accompanying the document Proposal for a Directive of the European Parliament and of the Council amending Directive 2011/92/EU on the assessment of the effects of certain public and private projects on the environment SWD(2012) 355 final, 26 October 2012.
Commission (EU). Implementing Decision (EU) 2017/1442 of 31 July 2017 establishing best available techniques (BAT) conclusions, under Directive 2010/75/EU of the European Parliament and of the Council, for large combustion plants. C/2017/5225, OJ L 212/1.
Commission (EU). Fitness Check of the Water Framework Directive and the Floods Directive (2019) SWD(2019) 439 final, 10 December 2019.

Commission (EU). Commission Staff Working Document Evaluation of the Industrial Emissions Directive SWD (2020) 181 final, 23 September 2020.

Commission (EU). EU Action Plan: Towards Zero Pollution for Air, Water and Soil. COM(2021) 400 final, 12 May 2021.

Commission (EU). Proposal for a DIRECTIVE OF THE EUROPEAN PARLIAMENT AND OF THE COUNCIL amending Directive 2010/75/EU of the European Parliament and of the Council of 24 November 2010 on industrial emissions (integrated pollution prevention and control) and Council Directive 1999/31/EC of 26 April 1999 on the landfill of waste. COM(2022)156 final, 5 April 2022.

Council Directive 78/176/EEC of 20 February 1978 on waste from the titanium dioxide industry (1978) OJ L 54/19.

Council Directive 84/360/EEC of 28 June 1984 on the combating of air pollution from industrial plants (1984) OJ L 188/20.

Council Directive 82/501/EEC of 24 June 1982 on the major-accident hazards of certain industrial activities (1982) OJ L 230/1.

Council Directive 82/883/EEC of 3 December 1982 on procedures for the surveillance and monitoring of environments concerned by waste from the titanium dioxide industry (1982) OJ L 378/1.

Council Directive 92/112/EEC of 15 December 1992 on procedures for harmonising the programmes for the reduction and eventual elimination of pollution caused by waste from the titanium dioxide industry (1992) OJ L 409/11.

Council Directive 1999/13/EC of 11 March 1999 on the limitation of emissions of volatile organic compounds due to the use of organic solvents in certain activities and installations (1999) OJ L 85/1.

Council Directive 96/61/EC of 24 September 1996 concerning integrated pollution prevention and control (1996) OJ L 257/26.

Council (EC). Outcome of Proceedings of Working Party on the Environment on 8 December 1993. (10.01) 11508/93, 21 December 1993.

Council (EC). Outcome of Proceedings of Working Party on the Environment on 12 and 13 January 1994. (04.02) 4383/94, 28 January 1994.

Council (EC). Working document ENV/94/22 on Proposal for a Council Directive on integrated pollution prevention and control–Meeting of the Working Party on the Environment on 15 June 1994. (14.06) SN 2860/94, Brussels, 10 June 1994.

Council (EC). Outcome of Proceedings of Working Party on the Environment on 15 June 1994. (11.07) 8019/94, Brussels, 28 June 1994.

Council (EC). Common Position (EC) No 9/96 adopted by the Council on 27 November 1995 with a view to adopting Council Directive 96/.../EC concerning integrated pollution prevention and control, 25 March 1996.

Council (EU). Position (EU) No 1/2010 of the Council at first reading with a view to the adoption of a Directive of the European Parliament and of the Council on industrial emissions (integrated pollution prevention and control) Adopted by the Council on 15 February 2010 (Text with EEA relevance). OJ C 107E/1, 27 April 2010.

Directive 85/337/EEC of 27 June 1985 on the assessment of the effects of certain public and private projects on the environment (1985) OJ L 175/40 (EIA).

Directive 96/82/EC of 9 December 1996 on the control of major-accident hazards involving dangerous substances (1996) OJ L 10/13.

Directive 97/11/EC of 3 March 1997 amending Directive 85/337/EEC on the assessment of the effects of certain public and private projects on the environment (1997) OJ L 73/5.

Directive 2000/60/EC of the European Parliament and of the Council of 23 October 2000 establishing a framework for Community action in the field of water policy (2000) OJ L 327/1.

Directive 2000/76/EC of the European Parliament and of the Council of 4 December 2000 on the incineration of waste (2000) OJ L 332/91.

Directive 2001/80/EC of the European Parliament and of the Council of 23 October 2001 on the limitation of emissions of certain pollutants into the air from large combustion plants (2001) OJ L 309/1.

Directive 2001/81/EC of the European Parliament and of the Council of 23 October 2001 on national emission ceilings for certain atmospheric pollutants (2001) OJ L 309/22.

Directive 2003/35/EC of the European Parliament and of the Council of 26 May 2003 providing for public participation in respect of the drawing up of certain plans and programmes relating to the environment and amending with regard to public participation and access to justice Council Directives 85/337/EEC and 96/61/EC (2003) OJ L 156/17.

Directive 2003/87/EC of the European Parliament and of the Council of 13 October 2003 establishing a scheme for greenhouse gas emission allowance trading within the Community and amending Council Directive 96/61/EC (Text with EEA relevance) (2003) OJ L 275/32.

Directive 2008/1/EC of the European Parliament and of the Council of 15 January 2008 concerning integrated pollution prevention and control (Codified version) (2008) OJ L 24/8.

Directive 2009/31/EC of the European Parliament and of the Council of 23 April 2009 on the geological storage of carbon dioxide and amending Council Directive 85/337/EEC, European Parliament and Council Directives 2000/60/EC, 2001/80/EC, 2004/35/EC, 2006/12/EC, 2008/1/EC and Regulation (EC) No 1013/2006 (2009) OJ L 140/114.

Directive 2010/75/EU of the European Parliament and of the Council of 24 November 2010 on industrial emissions (integrated pollution prevention and control) (2010) OJ L 334/159 (IED).

Directive 2011/92/EU of the European Parliament and of the Council of 13 December 2011 on the assessment of the effects of certain public and private projects on the environment (codification) (2011) OJ L 26/1.

Directive 2012/18/EU of the European Parliament and of the Council of 4 July 2012 on the control of major accident hazards involving dangerous substances, amending and subsequently repealing Council Directive 96/82/EC (2012) OJ L 197/1.

Directive 2014/52/EU of the European Parliament and of the Council of 16 April 2014 amending Directive 2011/92/EU on the assessment of the effects of certain public and private projects on the environment (2014) OJ L 124/1.

Directive (EU) 2016/2284 of the European Parliament and of the Council of 14 December 2016 on the reduction of national emissions of certain atmospheric pollutants, amending Directive 2003/35/EC and repealing Directive 2001/81/EC (Text with EEA relevance) OJ L 344/1.

Doppelhammer, M. (2000). More difficult than finding the way round Chinatown? The IPPC Directive and its implementation. *European Energy and Environmental Law Review, 9*(7), 246–252.

Emmott, N., & Haigh, N. (1996). Integrated pollution prevention and control: UK and EC approaches and possible next steps. *J. Envtl. L., 8*, 301.

European Commission (EC). Amended proposal for a Council Directive concerning Integrated Pollution Prevention and Control. COM (95) 88 final—SYN 526, 15 May 1995.

European Environmental Bureau. New Features under the Industrial Emissions Directive, 14 July 2011.

European IPPC Bureau. https://eippcb.jrc.ec.europa.eu/reference. Accessed 7 August 2020.

European Parliament (EC). Legislative resolution embodying Parliament's opinion on the proposal for a Council Directive on integrated pollution prevention and control (Cooperation procedure: first reading). COM (93)0423 - C3–0363/93 - 00/0526(SYN) OJ C 18/82, 23 January 1995.

Faure, M., & Lefevere, J. G. (1996). The draft directive on integrated pollution pollution prevention and control: An economic perspective. *European Energy and Environmental Law Review, 5*(4), 112–122.

Faure, M. (2000). The harmonization, codification and integration of environmental law: a search for definitions. *European Energy and Environmental Law Review, 9*(6), 174–182.

Fisher, E., Lange, B., & Scotford, E. (2019). *Environmental law: Text, cases and materials*. Oxford University Press.

Giljam, R. A. (2017). Better BAT to bolster ecosystem resilience: Operationalizing ecological governance through the concept of best available techniques. *Review of European, Comparative and International Environmental Law, 26*(1), 5–18.

Groothuijse, F., & Uylenburg, R. (2014). Everything according to plan? Achieving environmental quality standards by a programmatic approach. In *EU Environmental Legislation* (pp. 116–145). Edward Elgar Publishing.

Industrial emissions. https://eur-lex.europa.eu/EN/legal-content/summary/industrial-emissions.html. Accessed 11 April 2022

Industrial Emissions Portal. https://industry.eea.europa.eu/. Accessed 5 May 2024

IPPC Review Process. https://ec.europa.eu/environment/archives/air/stationary/ippc/ippc_review_process.htm. Accessed 3 April 2020.

Irish environmental protection agency, Draft guidance on Article 15 of Industrial Emission Directive (2010/75/EU), at https://www.epa.ie/publications/licensing--permitting/industrial/ied/draft_guidance_art15_IED.pdf. Accessed 15 January 2022.

Joined cases C-165/09 to C-167/09 Stichting Natuur en Milieu and Others v College van Gedeputeerde Staten van Groningen (C-165/09) and College van Gedeputeerde Staten van Zuid-Holland (C-166/09 and C-167/09) [26 May 2011] ECR I-4599.

Kimmel, J. (2018). Assessing the democratic quality of new modes of eu governance: The industrial emissions directive as a test case. *European Political Science, 17*, 240–257.

Koutalakis, C., Buzogany, A., & Börzel, T. A. (2010). When soft regulation is not enough: The integrated pollution prevention and control directive of the European Union. *Regulation and Governance, 4*(3), 329–344.

Krämer, L. (2015). *EU environmental law*. Sweet & Maxwell.

Lange, B. (2008). *Implementing EU pollution control: Law and integration*. Cambridge University Press.

Lee, M. (2014). *EU environmental law, governance and decision-making*. Bloomsbury Publishing.

Misonne, D. (2015). The importance of setting a target: The EU ambition of a high level of protection. *Transnational Environmental Law, 4*(1), 11–36.

Moregera, E. (2020). Environmental law. In C. Barnard & S. Peers (Eds.), *European Union law* (pp. 1–10). Oxford University Press.

Oosterhuis, F., & Peeters, M. (2014). Limits to integration in pollution prevention and control. In: *EU Environmental Legislation* (pp. 91–115). Edward Elgar Publishing.

Organisation for Economic Co-operation and Development (OECD). (1991). Recommendation of the Council on Integrated Pollution Prevention and Control. OECD/LEGAL/0256.

Parliament (EC). Legislative resolution embodying Parliament's opinion on the proposal for a Council Directive on integrated pollution prevention and control (Cooperation procedure: first reading). COM(93)0423 – C3-0363/93 – 00/0526(SYN) OJ C 18/82, 23 January 1995.

Parliament (EU). REPORT on the proposal for a directive of the European Parliament and of the Council on industrial emissions (integrated pollution prevention and control) (recast) (COM (2007)0844 – C6–0002/2008 – 2007/0286(COD) A6–0046/2009, 6 February 2009.

Parliament (EU). ***II RECOMMENDATION FOR SECOND READING on the Council position at first reading for adopting a directive of the European Parliament and of the Council on industrial emissions (integrated pollution prevention and control) (recast) (11962/2009 – C7–0034/2010 – 2007/0286(COD)), A7–0145/2010, 6 May 2010.

Pallemaerts, M. (1996). The proposed IPPC Directive: Re-regulation or de-regulation? *European Energy and Environmental Law Review, 5*(6), 174–179.

Pettersson, M., & Söderholm, P. (2014). Industrial pollution control and efficient licensing processes: The case of Swedish regulatory design. *Sustainability, 6*(8), 5401–5422.

Register of Commission Expert Groups and Other Similar Entities. https://ec.europa.eu/transparency/expert-groups-register/screen/expert-groups/consult?do=groupDetail.groupDetail&groupID=2611&NewSearch=1&NewSearch=1. Accessed 5 May 2024.

Reins, L. (2020). Where eagles dare: How much further may EU member states go under Article 193 TFEU?. In *Research Handbook on EU Environmental Law* (pp. 22–35). Edward Elgar Publishing.

Report of the Commission on the implementation of Directive 96/61/EC concerning integrated pollution prevention and control COM(2005) 540 final, 3 November 2005.

Ricardo. (2020). Support to the evaluation of the Industrial Emissions Directive (Directive 2010/75/EU) Final report

Richard Macrory, report of emissions performance standards published by House of Commons of the United Kingdom 24 November 2010, paras 5–9, https://publications.parliament.uk/pa/cm201011/cmselect/cmenergy/523/523uw.pdf. Accessed 29 March 2022.

Sanden, J. (2012). Coherence in European Environmental Law with particular regard to the Industrial Emissions Directive. *European Energy Environmental Law Review, 21*, 220.

Schoenberger, H. (2009). Integrated pollution prevention and control in large industrial installations on the basis of best available techniques—The Sevilla Process. *Journal of Cleaner Production, 17*(16), 1526–1529.

Sorrell, S. (2002). The meaning of BATNEEC: Interpreting excessive costs in UK industrial pollution regulation. *Journal of Environmental Policy & Planning, 4*(1), 23–40. https://doi.org/10.1002/jepp.102

Squintani, L., Holwerda, M., & de Graaf, K. (2012). Regulating greenhouse gas emissions from EU ETS installations: what room is left for the member states?. In *Climate Law in EU Member States* (pp. 67–88). Edward Elgar Publishing.

Squintani, L. (2019). *Beyond minimum harmonisation: Gold-plating and green-plating of European environmental law*. Cambridge University Press.

The IPPC Directive. https://ec.europa.eu/environment/archives/air/stationary/ippc/legis.htm. Accessed 23 June 2022.

Tolsma, H. D. (2019). Integrated environmental permitting: Towards a coherent system of environmental law in the Netherlands. Europa Law Publishing.

Vajda, P. (2019). Implementation of the IED—most important legal issue. In: *IED Workshop for National Judges, 11–12*, 26–27.

Van Calster, G., & Reins, L. (2017). *EU environmental law*. Edward Elgar.

Chapter 4
China's Regulatory Approach Regarding the Integrated Emissions Permit System

Abstract On the basis of the conceptual framework of an integrated environmental permit as identified in Chap. 2, this chapter examines how the emissions permit system in China has been developed for implementing integrated pollution prevention and control in terms of its regulatory design. The examination is carried out from three perspectives: substantive integration, procedural integration, and organizational integration. In addition, how the interactions between the emissions permit system and the market-based instruments in China affect integrated pollution prevention and control is also analyzed.

4.1 Introduction

4.1.1 Aim of This Chapter

On 9 December 2020, the State Council of People's Republic of China (hereinafter 'State Council') adopted the Administrative Regulation on Emissions Permitting that establishes one permit system to control industrial emissions in different environmental media.[1] Although the aim of an integrated approach is not explicitly mentioned in this Administrative Regulation on Emissions Permitting, the drafting history of this legislation shows the pursuit of an integrated approach by the legislator in China.[2] This chapter aims to provide a legal analysis of the Administrative Regulation on Emissions Permitting, in order to understand *how the emissions permit system in China has been developed for implementing integrated environmental permits in terms of its regulatory design.*

[1] State Council, Administrative Regulation on Emissions Permitting (in Chinese: 排污许可管理条例), 9 December 2020.

[2] See Sect. 4.3 of this chapter.

X. Chen, *Towards an Integrated Environmental Permit in China*,
https://doi.org/10.1007/978-981-97-5188-4_4

4.1.2 Approach and Structure of This Chapter

In order to address this question, the examination of the Administrative Regulation on Emissions Permitting in this chapter is conducted on the basis of the conceptual framework of an integrated environmental permit as identified in Chap. 2. As discussed in Chap. 2, a regulatory framework for establishing an integrated environmental permit system can be analyzed from three perspectives: substantive integration, procedural integration, and organizational integration. In addition, how the interactions between the permit instrument and market-based instruments would affect integrated pollution prevention and control deserves analysis. Thus, the following sub-questions will be explored:

- Regarding the substantive integration,

  Question 1: in view of the scope of integration, what is the scope of environmental issues subject to the emissions permit system as developed by the Administrative Regulation on Emissions Permitting?
  Question 2: in view of the environmental effectiveness of integration, what is the level of environmental protection required by the emissions permit system as developed by the Administrative Regulation on Emissions Permitting?
  Question 3: in view of the incommensurability of environmental goods, what are the options adopted by the Administrative Regulation on Emissions Permitting to make environmental trade-offs?

- Regarding procedural integration,

  Question 4: does the Administrative Regulation on Emissions Permitting require one permit procedure, or does it allow for several permit procedures?
  Question 5: is a coordination mechanism established by the Administrative Regulation on Emissions Permitting?

- Regarding organizational integration,

  Question 6: according to the Administrative Regulation on Emissions Permitting, how many authorities are involved in the decision-making?

- Regarding the interactions between permit instrument and market-based instruments,

  Question 7: according to the Administrative Regulation on Emissions Permitting, how must the emissions permits interact with the market-based instruments for pollution control in view of integration?

Based on the above analytical focus, this chapter is structured as follows:

After this introductory section, Sect. 4.2 gives an introduction of the legislation and the other normative documents in China to provide the legislative context to discuss the emissions permit system in China.

Section 4.3 provides an introduction to the Administrative Regulation on Emissions Permitting. This Administrative Regulation lays down rules on the emissions permits, which will be analyzed from the perspective of substantive integration, procedural integration, organizational integration, and its interaction with market-based instruments.[3] Precisely, Sect. 4.4 examines the objective of the Administrative Regulation on Emissions Permitting, to understand whether or to what extent a certain scope of integration and the environmental effectiveness of integration are pursued by the Administrative Regulation on Emissions Permitting. However, as we will see, the objective as laid down by the Administrative Regulation on Emissions Permitting is too hollow in nature, without giving a precise instruction as to what emissions have to be controlled and how the environment has to be protected and improved. Hence, it is necessary to delve into the detailed rules on the key stages of the permit procedure: the application for the permit (Sect. 4.5), issuing the permit (Sect. 4.6), and setting permit conditions (Sect. 4.7).

Based on the above analysis, Sect. 4.8 provides the answers to the seven sub-questions as listed above to clarify how the emissions permit system in China has been developed for implementing integrated pollution prevention and control in terms of its regulatory design.

4.2 Legislation and Other Normative Documents

4.2.1 Introduction

This section introduces the legislation and the other normative documents in China,[4] to provide the legislative context to discuss the emissions permit system in China.

The Constitution of People's Republic of China (hereinafter 'Constitution')[5] is the highest source of law in China. In addition to the Constitution, according to the Legislation Law of the People's Republic of China (hereinafter 'Legislation Law'), the legislation in China can be divided into three levels, and all the legislation at each different levels should be implemented in accordance with the hierarchy of the legislation,[6] which is discussed in Sects. 4.2.2–4.2.4. It is noted that 'differing from sharp separation of legislative, executive and judicial powers in many western countries, legislative authority in China is allocated among many organs'.[7] As will

---

[3] For the explanation of these perspectives, see Sects. 2.4.3 and 2.4.4 of Chap. 2.

[4] The discussion is mainly based on the literature, including Xi Wang, 'People's Republic of China' in Emma Lees and JORGE E. VIÑUALES (eds), *The Oxford Handbook of Comparative Environmental Law* (Oxford University Press 2019); Xi Wang and Kun Lu, Environmental Law in China (Wolters Kluwer 2017); and Huanhuan Wang, 'The Chinese Legal System' in Tianbao Qin (ed), *Research Handbook on Chinese Environmental Law* (Edward Elgar 2015).

[5] National People's Congress, Constitution of People's Republic of China (in Chinese: 中华人民共和国宪法), 20 September 1954 and its latest amendment adopted on 11 March 2018.

[6] National People's Congress, Legislation Law of the People's Republic of China (in Chinese: 中华人民共和国立法法), 15 March 2000 and its latest amendment adopted on 15 March 2015, art 1.

[7] Huanhuan Wang (2015), 32.

be shown in the following sub-sections, the executive organs, including the State Council and its ministries, and the local people's governments have the power of legislation. In addition to the legislation, the other normative documents that can have a strong practical influence on the development and implementation of legislation are discussed in Sect. 4.2.5, followed in Sect. 4.2.6 by an explanation of the legislative context to discuss the emissions permit system in China.

4.2.2 Laws

According to the Constitution, the National People's Congress and its Standing Committee have the power of legislation.[8] The laws enacted by the National People's Congress and its Standing Committee enjoy the highest legislative authority after the Constitution.[9] The environmental laws in China can be classified into two categories: the laws related to environmental protection and the laws directly on environmental protection.[10] The following sub-sections respectively discuss the laws *related to* environmental protection (Sect. 4.2.2.1) and the laws *directly on* environmental protection (Sect. 4.2.2.2).

4.2.2.1 Laws Related to Environmental Protection

The laws related to environmental protection 'are not environmental law in nature', but '[t]hey provide legal foundations and conditions for the operation or implementation of environmental laws'.[11] With regard to the laws related to the emissions permit system, three important laws must be highlighted. The Organization Law of the People's Republic of China for Local People's Congress and Local People's Governments (Hereinafter 'Organization Law for Local People's Congress and Local People's Governments')[12] is not an environmental law by nature, but it provides

---

[8] Constitution, art 58.

[9] Legislation Law, art 87 and 88.

[10] Xi Wang (2019), 132. It is noted that the laws related to environmental protection mentioned by Wang only refer to the laws that are enacted by the National People's Congress, but do not include the laws that are enacted by the Standing Committee of the National People's Congress. However, as we will see in the following sections of this chapter, there are also laws that are enacted by the Standing Committee of the National People's Congress that are related to environmental protection. Thus, this sub-section refers to 'the laws related to environmental protection' as both the laws enacted by the National People's Congress and its Standing Committee.

[11] Ibid. Wang provides some examples to illustrate this point: 'the trials of environmental crimes must follow the Criminal Procedural Law, and the trials of civil environmental infringement must follow the Civil Procedural Law. Some of those laws even have provisions on environmental protection, such as Section 6 of Chapter 6 of the Criminal Law, which deals with the 'crime of damaging environmental resources''.

[12] National People's Congress, Organization Law of the People's Republic of China for Local People's Congress and Local People's Governments (in Chinese: 中华人民共和国地方各级人

for the obligation of the local people's governments to implement the mandatory emission reduction targets.[13]

The Administrative Permit Law of the People's Republic of China (hereinafter 'Administrative Permit Law') provides for the rules on the establishment and implementation of administrative permitting,[14] which 'is intended to narrow the scope of activities for which a permit is required, the bias has been shifted in favour of self-regulation'.[15] The Administrative Permit Law is not environmental law in nature, but the establishment and implementation of the emissions permit system have to follow the Administrative Permit Law.[16]

The Administrative Litigation Law of the People's Republic of China (hereinafter 'Administrative Litigation Law') is also closely related to environmental protection. The disputes involving misconduct of the governmental administrative agencies at various levels will be heard by the courts based on the Administrative Litigation Law.[17] For example, the court shall accept a complaint against an environmental authority's refusal or failure to respond within a prescribed period to an application for an emissions permit.[18] In terms of the standing to sue against the authorities, according to the Administrative Litigation Law, a citizen, a legal person or any other organization shall have the right to bring a law suit against the authorities, if he or she or it considers that his or her or its lawful rights and interests have been infringed upon by an administrative act.[19] In addition, the Administrative Litigation Law empowers the people's procuratorates to file administrative environmental public-interest litigation cases.[20] Non-governmental organizations do not have standing in administrative environmental public-interest litigation.[21] The concern of NGOs not having standing in administrative environmental public-interest litigation is that 'China does

民代表大会和地方各级人民政府组织法), 4 July 1979 and its latest amendment adopted on 11 March 2022.

[13] Ibid, art 59. For a further discussion, see Sect. 4.3.2.3.2 of this chapter.

[14] Standing Committee of the National People's Congress, Administrative Permit Law of the People's Republic of China (in Chinese: 中华人民共和国行政许可法), 27 August 2003 and its latest amendment adopted on 23 April 2019.

[15] Lester Ross, 'Rethinking Government Approvals: The New Administrative Licensing Law' (2004) 18(5) China & Practice 30, 30.

[16] For a further discussion, see Sect. 4.4 of this chapter.

[17] Standing Committee of the National People's Congress, Administrative Litigation Law of the People's Republic of China (in Chinese: 中华人民共和国行政诉讼法), 4 April 1989 and its latest amendment adopted on 27 August 2017.

[18] Ibid, art 12(3).

[19] Ibid, art 2.

[20] Ibid, art 25(4).

[21] Tiantian Zhai and Yen-Chiang Chang, 'Standing of Environmental Public-Interest Litigants in China: Evolution, Obstacles and Solutions' (2018) 30 Journal of Environmental Law 369, 384.

not have a sufficiently strong civil society to enforce environmental laws through [public-interest litigation] initiated by NGOs'.[22]

4.2.2.2 Laws Directly on Environmental Protection

Among the laws directly on environmental protection,[23] the Environmental Protection Law of the People's Republic of China (hereinafter 'Environmental Protection Law'),[24] serve as the fundamental and all-around law on environmental protection.[25] In addition to the Environmental Protection Law, there are other environmental laws that can be classified into three categories:

(1) laws on pollution control;
(2) laws on natural resources conservation; and
(3) laws on some specific subject matter such as a law on environmental impact assessments.[26]

In summary, the environmental laws that are enacted by the National People's Congress and its Standing Committee can be classified into the laws related to environmental protection and laws directly on environmental protection. These laws serve as the highest source of environmental laws after the Constitution.

---

[22] Qi Gao and Sean Whittaker, 'Standing to Sue Beyond Individual Rights: Who Should Be Eligible to Bring Environmental Public Interest Litigation in China?' (2019) 8(2) Transnational Environmental Law 327, 342.

[23] Xi Wang (2019), 132.

[24] Standing Committee of the National People's Congress, Environmental Protection Law of the People's Republic of China (in Chinese: 中华人民共和国环境保护法), 13 September 1979 and its amendment adopted on 24 April 2014.

[25] Xi Wang (2019), 135. According to Wang, the fundamental and all-round nature of the Environmental Protection Law is reflected by its contents:

> [The Environmental Protection Law] provides a framework relating to the basic building blocks of environmental protection regulations in China. For example, in Chap. 1, the law defines some basic legal concepts, such as "environment", and determines the scope of its application. The law declares national environmental policy. It also confirms principles for environmental protection work; declares the basic rights and duties of all parties or players in the process of environmental governance including governments, business sectors, and citizens; and establishes the regulatory approach for the country, distributing the regulatory powers among all the relevant ministries in the Central Government and between the Central and local governments.

[26] Ibid.

4.2.3 Administrative Regulations

The second level of legislation, which is below the laws enacted by the National People's Congress and its Standing Committee, consists of administrative regulations that are made by the State Council. The State Council, namely the Central People's Government, is the executive body of the National People's Congress and the highest organ of the state administration.[27] The State Council can, in accordance with the Constitution and the laws, establish administrative regulations to implement the laws.[28] The Administrative Regulation on Emissions Permitting established by the State Council belongs to the legislation at the second level. It is established by the State Council in accordance with the Environmental Protection Law and other relevant laws.[29] The relevant laws include the laws related to environmental protection, such as the Administrative Permit Law,[30] and the laws directly on environmental protection, such as the laws on pollution control.[31]

4.2.4 Local Decrees, Local Rules, and Ministerial Rules

The third level of legislation mainly includes, on the one hand, local decrees and local rules and, on the other hand, ministerial rules.[32] To fully understand the legislature for local matters, it is necessary to explain the administrative units in China. According to the Constitution, the administrative units in China are based on a three-tier system: provincial level, county level, and township level.[33] At the provincial level, the administrative units are provinces, autonomous regions, or municipalities directly under the central government.[34] At the county level, there are autonomous prefectures, counties, autonomous counties, and cities.[35] At township level, there are townships, ethnic minority townships, and towns.[36] According to the Legislation Law, the provincial people's congresses or their standing committees, having regard to the local conditions and needs, can enact local decrees, provided that such decrees

---

[27] Constitution, art 85.

[28] Legislation Law, art 65.

[29] Administrative Regulation on Emissions Permitting, art 1.

[30] See Sect. 4.4 of this chapter.

[31] See Sect. 4.4 of this chapter.

[32] The autonomous regulations and separate regulations also belong to this level. However, the autonomous regulations and separate regulations are less related to the topic of this book, and thus they are not explained in detail.

[33] Xi Wang (2019), 130.

[34] Constitution, art 30(1).

[35] Ibid, art 30(2).

[36] Ibid, art 30(3).

do not contradict the Constitution, the laws and administrative regulations.[37] In addition, the people's congresses or their standing committees of the cities with districts at the county level, having regard to the local condition and needs, can enact local decrees, provided that these decrees do not contradict the Constitution, the laws, administrative regulations, and provincial decrees.[38] The decrees at the county level cannot come into force without the approval of the provincial people's congresses.[39] In terms of the local rules, people's governments at the provincial level and people's governments of cities with districts and autonomous prefectures at the county level may enact rules in accordance with laws, administrative regulations, and local decrees formulated by their provincial people's congress.[40] The local peoples' governments at various levels are the executive bodies of the local People's Congresses and the local organs of the State Administration.[41] The legislative authority of these local rules formulated by the local people's governments rank lower than the local decrees formulated by the people's congress at the higher or the same level.[42] The legislative authority of rules formulated by provincial people's governments ranks higher than that of local rules formulated by their lower level of people's governments, including people's governments of cities with districts and autonomous prefectures.[43] There previously existed local legislation on emissions permitting, but most of them are no longer in force since the adoption of the Administrative Regulation on Emissions Permitting.

Ministerial rules, according to the Legislation Law, are made by the ministries and commissions of the State Council, the People's Bank of China, the National Audit Office, and Institutions directly under the State Council.[44] For example, the Administrative Rules on Environmental Standards established by the environmental ministry as will be discussed in this chapter is a ministerial rule.[45] The ministerial rules enjoy the same legislative authority as the local rules.[46]

---

[37] Legislation Law, art 72.

[38] Legislation Law, art 72.

[39] Legislation Law, art 72.

[40] Ibid, art 82.

[41] Constitution, art 105.

[42] Legislation Law, art 89.

[43] Ibid, art 89.

[44] Ibid, art 80.

[45] Ministry of ecology and environment, Administrative Rules on Environmental Standards (in Chinese: 生态环境标准管理办法), 5 November 2020. For a further discussion on this ministerial rule, see Sects. 4.5.2 and 4.7.4 of this chapter.

[46] Legislation Law, art 91.

4.2.5 Other Normative Documents

The terms for naming the legislation and the so-called 'other normative documents' can overlap. The other normative documents fall outside the scope of legislation, adopted by the people's governments and their departments at all levels. They are not legislation, but they can have a strong practical influence. This is because there is a tradition in China that the drafting of legislation follows the principle that 'rough rules are more suitable than detailed rules' and, therefore, implementation largely relies on other normative documents to provide for detailed rules.[47] This can be illustrated by the reform of the permit system for controlling emissions in China. The permit system for controlling emissions had been adopted in China's legislation since 1980s.[48] However, before the adoption of Administrative Regulation on Emissions Permitting, the rules on the emission permits as laid down in the legislation had been relatively vague.[49] The vague rules on emission permits had led to weak implementation. An investigation conducted in 2004 found that the number of emission permits that had been granted compared to the number of emission permits that should have been granted was low.[50] This showed the insufficient effort of the local governments to carry out the permit system for controlling emissions at that time. On 10 November 2016, the State Council issued an other normative document—the *Implementation Plan for the Permit System for Controlling Emissions* in accordance with Environmental Protection Law.[51] In the same year, another other normative document—*Provisional Regulation on the Emissions Permitting*—was formulated by the environmental ministry.[52] The adoption of these other normative documents

[47] Xiangqian Gong, auxiliary legislation and the implementation of Environmental Protection Law (in Chinese: 配套立法与新《环境保护法》的实施) (2016) (04) Social Science in Chinese Higher Education Institutions 114, 114.

[48] For a further discussion on the introduction of the permit instrument for controlling emissions into legislation, see Sect. 4.3.2 of this chapter.

[49] See Sects. 4.3.2 and 4.3.3.1 of this chapter.

[50] According to the investigation report, the emission permits granting rate, which refers to the number of emission permits that have been granted compared to the number of emission permits that should have been granted, in Shanghai, Jiangsu, Jining, Yunan, and Chongqing was lower than 20%. See Guang Xia, Dongfang Feng, et al., 'Report about situation of the permit system of pollutant discharge operation in six provinces and cities' (in Chinese: 六省市排污许可证制度实施情况调研报告) (2005) 06 Environmental Protection 57, 59.

[51] State Council, Implementation Plan for the Permit System for Controlling Emissions (in Chinese: 控制污染物排放许可制实施方案的通知 国办发〔2016〕81号), 10 November 2016.

[52] Ministry of Environmental Protection (abolished on 17 March 2018), Provisional Regulation on Emissions Permitting (in Chinese: 排污许可证管理暂行规定 环水体〔2016〕186号), 23 December 2016. No legislation or governmental document provides the meaning of 'provisional' and this document itself did not provide for how long it will be in effect. Normally, 'provisional' indicates that it would only be in effect for a short period.

'has played a positive role in helping issue permits to companies', at least according to the official of the environmental ministry at that time.[53]

The other normative documents can also facilitate the development of legislation. For example, on 10 January 2018, the environmental ministry adopted legislation for a trial implementation, namely *Administrative Measures on Emissions* Permitting *(for Trial Implementation).*[54] This trial Administrative Measures on Emissions Permitting was an experimental legislation. Experimental legislation is used extensively by the legislature in China and 'resulted from the necessity to incrementally build a legal system by responding to the challenges of reality'.[55] However, there is no legislation that provides for any rules on experimental legislation.[56] In practice, there is no difference between the experimental legislation and other legislation in terms of binding force.[57] According to article 1 of this trial Administrative Measures, the Implementation Plan for the Permit System for Controlling Emissions as published by the State Council serves as part of the basis for adopting this trial Administrative Measures. In addition, the adoption of the Administrative Measures on Emissions Permitting (for Trial Implementation) concerned the experiences derived from the implementation of the Provisional Regulation on the Emissions Permitting.[58]

The environmental standards established by the environmental ministry and the local people's governments at the provincial level[59] are other normative documents,[60] which do not have binding effect independently, but they need to rely on the legislation.[61] For example, according to the Administrative Regulation on Emissions Permitting, the emission standards have to be complied with as a permit condition,[62]

[53] Jinran Zheng, 'China updates pollutant emission permit system' China Daily, updated on 18 January 2018, available at http://www.chinadaily.com.cn/a/201801/18/WS5a5ff4f9a310e4ebf433e707.html, accessed on 6 December 2020.

[54] Ministry of Environmental Protection (abolished on 17 March 2018), Administrative Measures on Emissions Permitting (for Trial Implementation) (in Chinese: 排污许可管理办法(试行)), 10 January 2018 (no longer in force).

[55] Madeleine Martinek, *Experimental Legislation in China between Efficiency and Legality: The Delegated Legislative Power of the Shenzhen Special Economic Zone* (Springer 2018), 109.

[56] Dengfeng Yang, 'The Basis for Experimental Legislation in China—Examination of legislation for trial implementation and interim legislation' (in Chinese: 我国试验立法的本位回归——以试行法和暂行法为考察对象) (2017) 06 Studies in Law and business 31, 31.

[57] Ibid.

[58] Ministry of Environmental Protection (abolished on 18 March 2018), Press briefing by the Ministry of Environmental Protection official on Administrative Rule on Emissions Permitting (for trial implementation) (in Chinese: 环境保护部有关负责人就《排污许可管理办法(试行)》有关问题答记者问), 17 January 2018, available at http://www.mee.gov.cn/gkml/sthjbgw/qt/201801/t20180117_429822.htm, accessed on 14 October 2020.

[59] Environmental Protection Law, art 15 and art 16.

[60] Kezhu Deng, 'Research on Judicial Review of Technical Standards' (in Chinese: 论技术标准的司法审查) (2010) 87(5) Science Technology and Law 82, 82.

[61] Chunlei Wang, 'The Legal Validity of Environmental Criteria: Theory Review and New Trend in Practice' (in Chinese: 环境标准的法律效力:问题梳理及实践动向) (2016) 11 Academic Journal of Zhongzhou 46, 48.

[62] Administrative Regulation on Emissions Permitting, art 11(2).

which results in the binding effect of the emission standards on the entities subject to the emissions permits.

The legality of other normative documents can be challenged before the people's courts. According to the Administrative Litigation Law, where an administrative decision is made on the basis of an other normative document formulated by a ministry of the State Council or by a local people's government or its department, and the other normative document is allegedly illegal, the plaintiff may request the court to review the legality of the other normative document.[63] For example, provided that an emission standard—an other normative document—is used to refuse an application for an emissions permit, the applicant can ask the court to review the legality of the refusal decision together with the legality of the emission standard.

In short, strictly speaking, the other normative documents are not sources of law. Nevertheless, since these documents can play an important role in the implementation and development of legislation, these documents deserve an examination for a better understanding of the legislation.

4.2.6 The Legislative Context for Discussing the Emissions Permit System in China

The Administrative Regulation on Emissions Permitting, which belongs to the legislation at the second level, is established in accordance with the Environmental Protection Law and other relevant laws by the State Council. Therefore, in order to examine the Administrative Regulation on Emissions Permitting, the Environmental Protection Law and the relevant laws need to be investigated. As will be shown in the following sections, the Administrative Regulation on Emissions Permitting also interacts with the other legislation at various levels, including the laws, the administrative regulation, and the ministerial rules.[64] The analysis of these pieces of legislation is also included. In addition, the other relevant normative documents, which fall outside the scope of legislation but have a strong practical influence on the establishment and implementation of the emissions permit system also deserve analysis.

---

63 Administrative Litigation Law, art 53.

64 For a detailed discussion, see Sects. 4.5 and 4.7 of this chapter.

4.3 Introduction to the Administrative Regulation on Emissions Permitting

4.3.1 Introduction

The Administrative Regulation on Emissions Permitting has not caused much discussion by scholars since its adoption in late 2020.[65] In particular, no research on this legislation from the perspective of an integrated approach can be found, which is precisely the gap this chapter aims to fill. First, this section provides an introduction to the Administrative Regulation on Emissions Permitting in the following way.

Section 4.3.2 discusses how the permit instrument for controlling emissions was initially developed in China and, by doing so, the problem of fragmentation embedded in the initial use of the permit instrument for controlling emissions in China will be highlighted. Section 4.3.3 discusses the reform of the use of the permit instrument for controlling emissions by investigating the amended provisions of the permit for controlling emissions in the environmental laws and the adoption of relevant other normative documents before the adoption of the Administrative Regulation on Emissions Permitting. Section 4.3.4 provides the structure of the Administrative Regulation on Emissions Permitting, followed by an interim conclusion in Sect. 4.3.5.

4.3.2 The Initial Use of the Permit Instrument for Controlling Emissions

This sub-section discusses how the permit system for controlling emissions was introduced in China, in which the problem of fragmentation will be identified to explain why a reform of the permit system for controlling emissions is needed. As will be discussed below, the permit instrument for controlling emissions in China was initially adopted in the area of water pollution prevention and control since 1985 (Sect. 4.3.2.1) and then another permit system was introduced in the area of air pollution prevention and control since 1989 (Sect. 4.3.2.2). Section 4.3.2.3 will then investigate the problem of fragmentation embedded in the initial use of the permit instrument for controlling emissions, which will be done based on the literature, followed by an interim conclusion in Sect. 4.3.2.4.

---

[65] Some literature is highlighted in Sect. 1.2 of Chap. 1.

4.3.2.1 The Introduction of the Water Emissions Permit

In 1985, the Shanghai standing committee of the people's congress adopted the decree on the protection of water resources in the upper reaches of Huangpu River,[66] which was the first legislation in China introducing a permit instrument for controlling emissions into water. This decree required that all operators who would cause emissions into the protected area of Huangpu River shall apply for emission permits, and the environmental authorities should decide whether to grant the emission permits in accordance with the requirements of so-called total water emission control for protecting the Huangpu River.[67] The so-called total emission control system[68] 'is one of the [...] command-and-control regulations, in which the overall emissions limits are set up by governments, and then allocated to different areas or sectors, as allowances, so as to fulfill pollution control'.[69] The so-called 'overall emissions limits' refer to the maximum allowable quantities of emissions of certain pollutants that will be allocated to different areas or sectors and then allocated among operators through a permit system.[70] In 1987, pilot projects of water emissions permits were carried out in eighteen cities, such as Beijing, Shanghai, and Tianjin to provide experience regarding the distribution of the allowable quantities of emissions into water among operators.[71]

Based on the experience of the pilot projects, in 2000, the State Council adopted an administrative regulation—Implementation Rules on Water Pollution Prevention and Control Law of the People's Republic of China (hereinafter 'Implementation Rules on Water Pollution Prevention and Control Law (2000)')[72]—which laid down rules for water emissions permits. The rules for the water emissions permits at that time can be summarized in four steps:

> The first step is a water pollutant report and registration. The second step is the establishment of targets for the total pollutant load control in a specific area and the distribution of pollutant reduction quotas among pollutant dischargers in the area. The third step is the issuance of a pollutant discharge permit. The Environmental Protection Bureau, at [local] level, issues

[66] Standing Committee of People's Congress of Shanghai, Decree on the Protection of Water Resources in the Upper Reaches of Huangpu River (in Chinese: 黄浦江上游水资源保护条例), adopted on 1 October 1985 (no longer in force).

[67] Ibid art 6.

[68] In addition to 'total emission control system', there are other terms used to describe the same system in English literature, such as 'emissions cap system' and 'total pollutant load control system'.

[69] Jing Wu and I-Shin Chang, Environmental Management in China: Policies and Institutions (Chemical Industry Press and Springer 2020), 115.

[70] Zhiping Li, 'The Challenges of China's Discharge Permit System and Effective Solutions' (2005) 24 Temp. J. Sci. Tech. & Envtl. L. 375, 376. For a further discussion on the total emission control system, see Sect. 3.2.3.2 of this chapter.

[71] Xingxiang Zhu, Jianming Luo, 'The Introduction, Development and State of the Licence System for the Water Pollutant Discharge in China' (in Chinese: 中国排污许可证制度的产生、发展及现状) (1991) 01 World Environment 26.

[72] State Council, Implementation Rules on Water Pollution Prevention and Control Law of the People's Republic of China (in Chinese: 中华人民共和国水污染防治法实施细则), 20 March 2000 (no longer in force).

> discharge permits to dischargers based on the targets of the total pollutant load control in that area. The last step is the supervision and regulation of the permit. Environmental Protection Bureaus are authorized to inspect the permit holder's facilities, as well as impose punishments upon those who violate their permit conditions.[73]

From this explanation, it can be seen that the water emissions permit system was adopted together with the system of so-called 'total pollutant load control' or 'total emission control' in the national legislation. However, the rules for the water emissions permits as laid down by the Implementation Rules on Water Pollution Prevention and Control Law were quite vague. It was not clear at that time how operators should report and register water pollutants, how targets for the so-called total emission control should be established, or how environmental authorities should decide, based on the targets of the total water emission control, whether to issue water emission permits, etc.

4.3.2.2 The Introduction of the Air Emissions Permit

In 1989, pilot projects of air emissions permits were carried out in twenty-three cities.[74] The aim of the pilot projects of air emissions permitting was to provide experience regarding the distribution of the allowable quantities of emissions into the air among operators.[75] In 2000, the air emissions permit system, combined with the total emission control system, was adopted in the Air Pollution Prevention and Control Law of the People's Republic of China (2000) (hereinafter 'Air Pollution Prevention and Control Law (2000)'):

> With regard to the areas where the air quality standards have not been fulfilled and the areas that are designated as the acid rain controlled areas or sulfur dioxide pollution controlled areas, the State Council and the people's governments at provincial level can apply the total air emission control in these areas. The competent people's governments should allocate the total air emission quota through granting the emission permits.[76]

However, no further concrete rules were adopted on how the competent people's governments should allocate the total allowed quantities of emissions into the air through the granting of the air emission permits.

---

73 Zhiping Li (2005), 378. It is noted that the meaning of the term 'total pollutant load control' in Li's article is the same as the term 'total emission control' in this section. The different use is due to a different translation.

74 Department of Planning and Finance in the Ministry of Ecology and Environment, 'The reform of the emission permit system in China: History, Reality, and the Future' (in Chinese: 中国排污许可制度改革:历史、现实和未来), China Environment News, 12 September 2018, 003.

75 Lei Li, 'The Technical Framework of the Pilot Projects of the Air Emission Permit System' (in Chinese: 试行排放大气污染物许可证制度的技术框架) (1992a) 5 China Environment Management 9, 9–10; Lei Li, 'The Implementation of the System of Total Air Pollutant Load Control' (in Chinese: 推行大气污染物排放总量控制试行大气排污许可证制度) (1992b) 5(6) Research of Environmental Sciences 49, 50.

76 Standing Committee of the National People's Congress, Air Pollution Prevention and Control Law of the People's Republic of China (2000) (in Chinese: 中华人民共和国大气污染防治法(2000修订)), 29 April 2000 (no longer in force), art 15.

4.3.2.3 The Problems of the Initial Use of Permit Instruments for Controlling Emissions

This sub-section delves into the problems of the initial use of the permit instrument for controlling emissions in China by investigating the relevant literature: Sect. 4.3.2.3.1 explains that the initial use of the permit instrument for controlling emissions was sectoral; Sect. 4.3.2.3.2 discusses that the initial use of the permit instrument for controlling emissions was a means to implement the total emission control system, which is a fragmented system.

4.3.2.3.1 Sectoral Emission Permits

The initial use of the permit instrument for controlling emissions was sectoral. As discussed in Sects. 4.3.2.1 and 4.3.2.2, the permit system for controlling emissions in China was developed incrementally, by environmental sector by environmental sector: the emissions permit instrument was initially adopted in the field of water pollution prevention and control since 1985 and then another permit was introduced into the field of air pollution prevention and control since 1989. As a result, there were two separate emissions permit procedures.[77] There were two permitting authorities respectively in charge of the water emissions permitting procedure and the air emissions permitting procedure at that time.[78] According to the Implementation Rules on Water Pollution Prevention and Control Law (2000), the competent authorities in charge of granting water emissions permits were the local environmental authorities,[79] while according to the Air Pollution Prevention and Control Law (2000), the competent authorities in charge of granting air emissions permits were the local people's governments.[80] The local environmental authorities and the local people's governments are two different authorities.[81] In addition, no mechanism was provided for the coordination between the local environmental authorities in charge of water emissions permitting procedure and the local people's governments in charge of the air emissions permitting procedure.[82] Hence, sectoral permits were initially adopted to control emissions into water and to control emissions into air respectively.

[77] Youhai Sun, 'How to Improve and Implement the Pollution Discharge License System' (in Chinese: 如何完善落实排污许可制度) (2014) 42(14) Environmental Protection 17, 19.

[78] Ibid.

[79] Implementation Rules on Water Pollution Prevention and Control Law (no longer in force), art 10.

[80] Air Pollution Prevention and Control Law (2000) (no longer in force), art 15.

[81] The local environmental authorities are the departments of the local people's governments.

[82] Youhai Sun, 'Environmental Permit System: History, Challenges and Proposals' (in Chinese: 排污许可制度:立法回顾、问题分析与方案建议) (2016) 38(2) Environmental Impact Assessment 1, 2.

4.3.2.3.2 The Instrumental Role of the Permit for Implementing the Fragmented Total Emission Control System

The initial use of the permit instrument for controlling emissions was introduced as a means to implement the total emission control, namely to distribute allowable emissions quantities.[83] As already explained in Sect. 4.3.2.1, under the so-called total emission control system, the maximum allowable quantities of emissions of certain pollutants is determined by the governments in each area or sector and is then allocated among operators through a permit system. Considering this, to what extent this total emission control system is aimed at an integrated approach deserves further analysis.

The establishment and implementation of the so-called total emission control system in China has been mostly based on the national five-year plans.[84] On 17 March 1996, the National People's Congress approved the 9th Five-Year Plan of National Economic and Social Development and the Outline of 2010 Long-Term Plan Targets, in which the total emission control was considered an important instrument for environmental protection.[85] Since then, the system of total emission control was adopted together with the emission permit system in the national environmental legislation.[86] On 14 March 2006, the 11th Five-Year Plan of national economic and social development was published, which for the first time specified the mandatory total emission reduction targets.[87] According to the 11th Five-Year Plan, the total emission reduction targets 'have legally binding force' and 'should be allocated to relevant authorities'.[88] The 11th Five-Year Plan was not a piece of legislation. However, according to the Organization Law for Local People's Congress and Local People's Governments, the local people's governments have to implement the national five-year plans.[89] Therefore, the mandatory targets as laid down in the 11th Five-Year Plan could have legally binding force applicable within the people's governments, but they could not be directly extended to individuals (except for state-owned enterprises).[90] In the

---

83 Charles R. McELWEE, *Environmental Law in China: Mitigating Risk and Ensuring Compliance* (Oxford University Press 2010), 178.

84 Five-Year plans have been developed in China by national people's congress since 1953, which includes the plan for national economic and social development and the report on its implementation, and it is examined and approved by the National People's Congress. For a further explanation of the five-year plans, see Charles R. McELWEE (2011), Sect. 5.1 of Chap. 5.

85 National People's Congress, the 9th Five-Year Plan of National Economic and Social Development and the Outline of 2010 Long-Term Plan Targets of the People's Republic of China (in Chinese: 中华人民共和国国民经济和社会发展"九五"计划和2010年远景目标纲要), 17 March 1996, point 9(2).

86 See Sect. 4.3.2 of this chapter.

87 National People's Congress, Outline of the 11th Five-Year Plan of National Economic and Social Development of the People's Republic of China (in Chinese: 中华人民共和国国民经济和社会发展第十一个五年规划纲要), 14 March 2006, special columns 2 and 3 in chapter 3.

88 Ibid.

89 Organization Law for Local People's Congress and Local People's Governments, art 59.

90 Zhen Jin, 'Environmental Management System in China: The Target Achieving Process' in Hideki Kitagawa (eds), *Environmental Policy and Governance in China* (Springer 2017), 76–79

later national five-year plans, a set of mandatory total emission reduction targets have been established. Tian and Huang investigated the total emission reduction targets as laid down in the 9th to 12th Five-Year Plans (covering the period from 1996–2015) and found that the scope of emission reduction targets as laid down in these plans had been narrow.[91] A narrow scope means that a limited set of pollutants were covered by the total emission reduction targets.[92] Research found that, as a consequence of the narrow scope of the total emission control system, local governments attempted to shut down industries with high COD (a measure of organic pollutants concentration in water),[93] while they permitted industries with low COD, such as mining, metallurgical, and building industries, which has likely led to a rising level of heavy metals pollution to the soil since 2000.[94] In other words, while focusing on addressing water emissions, the implementation of the total emission control system caused the transfer of pollution from water to soil. Hence, rather than an integrated approach, the narrow scope of the so-called total emission control system indicated a fragmented approach of pollution control, which encouraged the transfer of pollution from one media to another. In this vein, since the initial permit system for controlling emissions was oriented at the allocation of the allowed emissions quantities, it did not explicitly accommodate the need to prevent the transfer of pollution from one sector to another environmental sector.

4.3.2.4 Interim Conclusion

In China, the permit instrument for controlling emissions was initially adopted in the field of water pollution prevention and control and then another permit was separately introduced into the field of air pollution prevention and control. As a result, two separate emissions permit systems had been established. There were two separate permitting authorities respectively in charge of granting water emissions permits and granting air emissions permits. In addition, the initial use of permit instruments for controlling emissions merely played an instrumental role for implementing the so-called total emission control system in view of distributing allowable emissions

and 84 discussing the legal effect of the mandatory targets or other values as set in the national plans. Also see Haisong Chen, 'The Normative Effectiveness and Legalization Path of 'Eco-Red Line'' (in Chinese: "生态红线"的规范效力与法治化路径 ———解释论与立法论的双重展开) (2014) 36(4) Modern Law Science 85, 90.

[91] Qiyun Tian and Biao Huang, 'Study on the Total Pollutant Control System in China' (in Chinese: 我国污染物总量控制制度探讨) (2014) 20 Environmental Protection 42, 42.

[92] Ibid. For example, the 13th Five-Year Plan set the mandatory emission reduction targets only for four pollutants, including chemical oxygen demand (COD, a measure of organic pollutants concentration in water), sulfur dioxide, ammonium-nitrogen, nitrogen oxides. See National People's Congress, Outline of the 13th Five-Year Plan of National Economic and Social Development of the People's Republic of China (in Chinese: 中华人民共和国国民经济和社会发展第十三个五年规划纲要), 16 March 2016, special column 2 in chapter 3.

[93] Qing Hu, Xiaoliang Li, Aijun Lin, Weikang Qi, Xiujin Li and Xiaojin Yang, 'Total emission control policy in China.' (2018) 25 Environmental Development 126, 127.

[94] Ibid.

quantities among operators. It was found that the total emission control system caused fragmentation, as it only regulated a narrow range of pollutants. In that sense, the initial permit system for controlling emissions oriented at the allocation of the allowable emissions quantities did not explicitly accommodate the need to prevent the transfer of pollution from one environmental sector to another environmental sector.

4.3.3 The Reform of the Emissions Permit System

Since the 13th Five-Year Plan period concerning the years 2016–2020, effort at the central level went into considering how to reform the use of the permit instrument for controlling emissions through the adoption of new provisions or amendments of environmental laws and the adoption of other normative documents.[95] The following sub-sections discuss what provisions related to the permit regulation on controlling emissions were adopted in the environmental laws (Sect. 4.3.3.1); and what other normative documents were developed for the reform of the emissions permit system to make progress towards integration (Sect. 4.3.3.2); followed by an interim conclusion.

4.3.3.1 Provisions of the Permit Regulation on Controlling Emissions Adopted in the Environmental Laws

Several laws on environmental protection have been amended and newly established since 2014. On 24 April 2014, the amendment of Environmental Protection Law was adopted, which explicitly prescribed that no emissions are allowed without an emissions permit, and the operators subject to the permit regulation for controlling emissions shall only emit pollutants in accordance with the requirements of their emission permits.[96] The Environmental Protection Law does not provide for a definition of 'emission'. Therefore, according to the Environmental Protection Law, it is not clear what emissions have to be regulated through the permit instrument.[97] Also, the permit instrument for controlling emissions is no longer prescribed together with the so-called total emission control system. In this vein, in the literature it was considered that, rather than serving as an instrumental tool for implementing the total emission control on just a limited range of pollutants, the permit system for controlling emissions could have a broader scope.[98] However, the Environmental

---

[95] Ministry of Environmental Protection (abolished on 18 March 2018) (2018).

[96] Environmental Protection Law, art 45.

[97] For further insights on the scope of emissions regulated through the permit instrument in China, this book delves into the Administrative Regulation on Emissions Permitting and the other provisions related to the permit regulation on controlling emissions prescribed in sectoral environmental laws and other relevant legislation, see Sect. 4.2 of this chapter.

[98] Xingfeng Li, 'Research on Reforming the Emissions Permit System—from the Perspective of Allocating Environmental Capacity' (in Chinese: 排污许可法律制度重构研究——环境容量资

Protection Law does not provide any further concrete rules on the permit system for controlling emissions, and thus it is not clear how the permits should be applied for by operators, how the permit conditions should be set, and how the permits should be granted by the authorities, etc..

After the amendment of the Environmental Protection Law, sectoral laws on pollution prevention and control were amended sequentially or newly established. This concerns:

- the amendment of the Water Pollution Prevention and Control Law of the People's Republic of China adopted on 27 June 2017 (hereinafter 'Water Pollution Prevention and Control Law (2017)');[99]
- the amendment of the Air Pollution Prevention and Control Law of the People's Republic of China adopted on 26 October 2018 (hereinafter 'Air Pollution Prevention and Control Law (2018)');[100]
- the amendment of the Law of the People's Republic of China on Pollution Prevention and Control caused by the Solid Wastes adopted on 1 September 2020 (hereinafter 'Law on Solid Wastes Pollution Prevention and Control (2020)');[101]
- the establishment of the Soil Pollution Prevention and Control Law of the People's Republic of China adopted on 31 August 2018 (hereinafter 'Soil Pollution Prevention and Control Law');[102]
- the establishment of the Law of the People's Republic of China on Prevention and Control of Pollution from Noise adopted on 24 December 2021 (hereinafter 'Law on Prevention and Control of Pollution from Noise');[103]
- the amendment of Marine Environment Protection Law of the People's Republic of China adopted on 24 October 2023 (hereinafter 'Marine Environment Protection Law (2023)').[104]

源配置视角) (2016) 16(2) Journal of China University of Geosciences (Social Sciences Edition) 32, 38.

[99] Standing Committee of the National People's Congress, Water Pollution Prevention and Control Law of the People's Republic of China (2017) (in Chinese: 中华人民共和国水污染防治法(2017修正)), 27 June 2017.

[100] Standing Committee of the National People's Congress, Air Pollution Prevention and Control Law of the People's Republic of China (2018) (in Chinese: 中华人民共和国大气污染防治法(2018修正)), 26 October 2018.

[101] Standing Committee of the National People's Congress, Law of the People's Republic of China on Pollution Prevention and Control caused by the Solid Wastes (2020) (in Chinese: 中华人民共和国固体废物污染环境防治法(2020修订)), 1 September 2020.

[102] Standing Committee of the National People's Congress, Soil Pollution Prevention and Control Law of the People's Republic of China (in Chinese: 中华人民共和国土壤污染防治法), 31 August 2018.

[103] Standing Committee of the National People's Congress, Law of the People's Republic of China on Prevention and Control of Pollution From Noise (in Chinese: 中华人民共和国噪声污染防治法), 24 December 2021.

[104] Standing Committee of the National People's Congress, Marine Environment Protection Law of the People's Republic of China (in Chinese: 中华人民共和国海洋环境保护法), 23 August 1982 and its latest amendment adopted on 24 October 2023.

Similar to the Environmental Protection Law, these sectoral laws on pollution prevention and control roughly prescribe the permit instrument for controlling emissions covered by those laws,[105] but they do not provide for any further concrete rules on how the permit instrument should be implemented by operators and authorities.[106]

Meanwhile, some of the laws on pollution prevention and control delegate the establishment of concrete rules for the emission permits to the State Council.[107] In this vein, the permit system for controlling various emissions can be established in one legislation in the form of the administrative regulation by the State Council instead of in the various provisions prescribed in sectoral laws. From the perspective of legislative techniques for internal integration, the delegation to the State Council to establish one legislation laying down concrete rules on the permit instrument for controlling emissions indicates a codification, referring to moving the content of sectoral environmental legislation into one code, for implementing integration.[108]

4.3.3.2 The Other Normative Documents Regarding the Reform of the Emission Permit System

Several other normative documents were developed for the reform of the emissions permit system since 2016. On 10 November 2016, the State Council released the Implementation Plan for the Permit System for Controlling Emissions.[109] According to this Implementation Plan, the State Council aimed at establishing one permit system that regulates emissions in various environmental media in an integrated way.[110] However, no clear explanation of 'integrated' was provided by this implementation plan. On 23 December 2016, the environmental ministry published an other normative document—the *Provisional Regulation on Emissions Permitting*.[111] In this other normative document, the term 'integrated permit' was mentioned explicitly. According to article 6 of this provisional regulation on the emissions permits, emissions of water pollutants, air pollutants, and other pollutants arising from stationary sources shall be subject to an integrated permit. However, no definition of 'an integrated permit' was provided by this provisional regulation. According to a special

[105] Water Pollution Prevention and Control Law (2017), art 21; Soil Pollution Prevention and Control Law, art 21; Air Pollution Prevention and Control Law (2018), art 19; Law on Solid Wastes Pollution Prevention and Control (2020), art 38; Law on Prevention and Control of Pollution from Noise, arts 36, 38, and 75.

[106] Jia Pan, Legal Review and Steering of China's Emission Permit Setting (in Chinese: 我国排污许可设定法律审视及转向) (2020) 22(01) Journal of Hohai University (Philosophy and Social Sciences) 99, 99.

[107] Water Pollution Prevention and Control Law (2017), art 21; Soil Pollution Prevention and Control Law (2018), art 21; Air Pollution Prevention and Control Law (2018), art 19; and Law on Solid Wastes Pollution Prevention and Control (2020), art 38.

[108] See Sect. 2.2.2 of Chap. 2.

[109] Implementation Plan for the Permit System for Controlling Emissions6.

[110] Ibid, Sects. 4.2–4.3.

[111] Provisional Regulation on Emissions Permitting.

research group addressing the emissions permits under the environmental ministry, an integrated permit means that ***one*** emissions permit system regulates emissions in various environmental media, which aims at preventing the transfer of pollution from one medium (such as air) to another (such as water) caused by purely reducing one specific emission.[112] In addition, one emission permit system also can reduce administrative burden of compliance with emissions permitting for operators.[113] Furthermore, this special research group also explained that the environmental requirements, as set out in accordance with other environmental regulatory systems, should be specified in the emissions permit.[114] With regard to this, the literature points out that an integrated permit enables coordination between the emissions permit system and other environmental regulatory systems.[115] From the perspective of procedural integration,[116] this shows that full procedural integration, referring to incorporating various regulatory subjects exclusively into one procedure,[117] as well as coordination, meaning that where various separate procedures for each decision subject exist a mechanism is applied aiming to achieve coherence among decisions,[118] were pursued in the reform of the emissions permit system.

Furthermore, according to the provisional regulation on the emissions permits, the environmental authorities at various levels are responsible for the issuing of emissions permits within their jurisdiction.[119] Hence, the provisional regulation on the emissions permits was aimed at establishing one permit procedure where one single authority is responsible for issuing emissions permits. From the perspective of organizational integration, this shows that a high degree of organizational integration, referring to a low number of authorities involved in the process of decision-making and a clear competence structure,[120] was pursued in the reform of the emissions permit system.

[112] Special Research Group regarding Emissions Permitting, 30 Questions and Answers about Implementation Plan for the Permit System for Controlling Emissions (in Chinese: 《控制污染物排放许可制实施方案》30问), 5 January 2017, point 2, available at https://www.mee.gov.cn/zcwj/zcjd/201701/t20170105_394014.shtml, accessed on 12 April 2022.

[113] Ibid.

[114] Ibid.

[115] Hong Mei, 'What are the Reasons for Emissions Permit System Serving as a Core of Environmental Regulation on Stationary Sources?' (in Chinese: 排污许可制度何以成为点源环境治理的核心制度) (2017) 50(05) Journal of Zhengzhou University (Philosophy and Social Sciences Edition) 31, 32.

[116] For a discussion on the concept of procedural integration in theory, see Sect. 2.3.2 of Chap. 2.

[117] See Sect. 2.3.2 of Chap. 2.

[118] Ibid.

[119] Provisional Regulation on Emissions Permitting.

[120] See Sect. 2.3.3 of Chap. 2.

4.3.3.3 Interim Conclusion

From the above analysis, since the adoption of the amendment of the Environmental Protection Law from 24 April 2014, the permit system for controlling emissions is no longer prescribed as a mere means for implementing the so-called total emission control system in view of distributing allowable emissions quantities among operators. After the amendment of the Environmental Protection Law, similar provisions of the permit regulation on emissions were adopted in the sectoral laws on pollution prevention and control, some of which delegate the establishment of concrete rules for the permit regulation on emissions to the State Council. In this vein, the detailed rules on the permit system for controlling emissions in different environmental media can be established in one legislation in the form of the administrative regulation by the State Council, instead of various provisions prescribed in sectoral laws.

According to the other normative documents regarding the reform of the emissions permit system, an integrated approach by establishing one permit procedure that regulates emissions in various environmental media by single authorities—namely the environmental authorities—was pursued in the process of preparing the draft of the Administrative Regulation on Emissions Permitting. From the perspective of an integrated approach, this shows that, in the process of drafting the Administrative Regulation on Emissions Permitting, procedural integration as well as organizational integration were pursued.

4.3.4 The Structure of the Administrative Regulation on Emissions Permitting

On 9 December 2020, the State Council adopted the Administrative Regulation on Emissions Permitting.[121] With the adoption of the Administrative Regulation, the rules for emissions permits for controlling industrial pollution were established in one legislation.

The Administrative Regulation on Emissions Permitting consists of five chapters:

- Chapter 1 provides for general provisions for the emissions permit system, in which the objective of the Administrative Regulation on Emissions Permitting and the organizational arrangement for the issuing of permits are prescribed;
- Chapter 2 provides for a set of rules regarding the stages of permitting—including the application for permits and the conditions for issuing permits;
- Chapter 3 contains the provisions regarding the operators' obligations to comply with the emissions permits;
- Chapter 4 provides for the rules regarding the monitoring and inspection of the compliance with the emissions permits by the competent authorities;
- Chapter 5 contains provisions for penalties.

[121] Administrative Regulation on Emissions Permitting.

On the basis of the conceptual framework of an integrated environmental permit as identified in Chap. 2, the following Sects. 4.4–4.7 focus on examining chapters 1 and 2 of this Administrative Regulation.

4.3.5 Interim Conclusion

China initially introduced a permit instrument for controlling emissions incrementally, in the sense of addressing environmental sector by environmental sector: the permit instrument was first adopted in the area of water pollution prevention and control and then another permit was separately introduced in the area of air pollution prevention and control. As a result, sectoral emissions permit systems had been established. In addition, the previously existing sectoral emissions permit systems merely played an instrumental role for implementing the so-called total emission control system to distribute allowable emissions quantities among operators. It is found that the implementation of this total emission control had a narrow scope of pollution regulation and thus the initial use of permit instrument for controlling emissions oriented at implementing this fragmented total emission control system did not explicitly prevent the transfer of pollution from one sector to another environmental sector.

In order to address the problem of fragmentation under the previously existing permit instrument for controlling emissions, during the 13th Five-Year Plan period concerning the years 2016–2020, efforts at the central level went into considering the reform of the emissions permit system. The provisions of the permit regulation on controlling emissions adopted in the environmental laws no longer consider the permit system for controlling emissions as an instrument to facilitate the implementation of the so-called total emission control system, which may have the advantage of a broader scope of the regulation of emissions rather than only focusing on a limited set of pollutants under the total emissions control. Meanwhile, the environmental laws delegate to the State Council to adopt an administrative regulation laying down concrete rules on the permit instrument for controlling emissions, which creates an opportunity for the adoption of one legislation to implement an integrated approach. The other normative documents published by the State Council and the environmental ministry, which aimed at facilitating the drafting of the Administrative Regulation on Emissions Permitting, called for one permit procedure as well as a coordination mechanism that regulates emissions in various environmental media by single authorities in an integrated way.

On 9 December 2020, the State Council adopted the Administrative Regulation on Emissions Permitting. With its adoption, the rules on the permit instrument for controlling emissions in different environmental media are laid down in one legislation. The following research will further delve into the Administrative Regulation on Emissions Permitting to understand whether and how the emissions permit system has been developed by the Administrative Regulation on Emissions Permitting to implement integrated pollution prevention and control.

4.4 The Objective of the Administrative Regulation on Emissions Permitting

4.4.1 Introduction

This section aims to examine the objective of the Administrative Regulation on Emissions Permitting from the perspective of substantive integration. Article 1 of the Administrative Regulation on Emissions Permitting prescribes that this administrative regulation is established, in accordance with the Environmental Protection Law and other relevant laws, to control emissions, to protect and to improve the environment. The literature criticized that the Administrative Regulation on Emissions Permitting does not provide a clear objective that has to be reached with the emissions permitting.[122] In particular, this provision is too hollow in nature without giving a precise instruction as to what emissions have to be controlled and how the environment has to be protected and improved. The issues of what emissions have to be controlled and how the environment has to be protected and improved can be interpreted as relevant within the two dimensions of substantive integration: the scope of integration and the environmental effectiveness of integration (in the sense of the level of environmental quality to be achieved).[123]

In order to examine the scope and the environmental effectiveness of an integrated approach pursued by the Administrative Regulation on Emissions Permitting, the following sub-sections investigate the laws that provide the legal basis for establishing Administrative Regulation on Emissions Permitting, the drafting history regarding the objective of the Administrative Regulation on Emissions Permitting, and the relevant literature.

4.4.2 The Scope of Integration

The scope of integration refers to which environmental elements and their interrelationships would be integrated in permit decisions.[124] This sub-section aims to examine the scope of an integrated approach pursued by the Administrative Regulation on Emissions Permitting. This examination focuses on identifying what environmental issues are subject to the emissions permits and what environmental issues are not.

122 Zhiping Li, 'Reconstruction of China's Legal System of Eco-environmental Protection from the Perspective of Land and Sea Coordination' (in Chinese: 陆海统筹视阈下我国生态环境保护法律体系重构) (2021) 06 Academic Journal of Zhongzhou 46, 46–48.

123 For an explanation of the concept of the scope of integration and the environmental effectiveness of integration, see Sects. 2.3.1.1 and 2.3.1.2 of Chap. 2.

124 See Sect. 2.3.1.1 of Chap. 2.

The Administrative Regulation on Emissions Permitting establishes criteria for classifying entities subject to emissions permits into two types: entities under key management and entities under simplified management.[125] Entities that produce a relatively substantial quantity of emissions, or have significant environmental impacts, should be subject to key management, while entities that produce a relatively small quantity of emissions or have mild environmental impacts should be subject to simplified management.[126] Concerning the entities that produce a small quantity of emissions, or have very little environmental impacts should be registered with the environmental authorities.[127] There is no further explanation on what accounts for a relatively substantial/small quantity of emissions or significant/mild environmental impacts. Hence, Liu and Wang criticized that the Administrative Regulation on Emissions Permitting does not provide a clear scope of application for the emissions permits.[128]

The Administrative Regulation on Emissions Permitting was established in accordance with the Environmental Protection Law and other relevant laws.[129] Since the Administrative Regulation on Emissions Permitting does not provide a clear scope of emissions permitting, in order to examine the scope of integration as pursued by the Administrative Regulation on Emissions Permitting, the Environmental Protection Law and other relevant laws should be investigated.

4.4.2.1 Environmental Issues Subject to Emissions Permitting

This sub-section discusses, according to the Environmental Protection Law and other relevant laws, what environmental issues are subject to emissions permitting as prescribed by the Administrative Regulation on Emissions Permitting.

The Environmental Protection Law prescribes that no emissions are allowed without an emission permit, and the operators subject to the emission permit regulation shall only emit pollutants in accordance with the requirements of their emission permits.[130] However, the Environmental Protection Law does not provide for concrete rules on which emissions are subject to the permit regulation. The literature has interpreted the provision concerning the permit regulation on emissions as laid

---

[125] Administrative Regulation on Emissions Permitting, art 2. The Administrative Regulation on Emissions Permitting does not provide definitions of 'key management' or 'simplified management'. Nevertheless, a few differences between the 'key management' and 'simplified management' can be identified from the detailed rules on the application for permit and the rules on monitoring and inspection: entities subject to key management may take a longer time to apply emissions permits and take more emissions monitoring measures. See Administrative Regulation on Emissions Permitting, art 8, art 12, and art 20. Since these issues are less relevant in view of integration, they are not discussed in detail in this book.

[126] Administrative Regulation on Emissions Permitting, art 2.

[127] Administrative Regulation on Emissions Permitting, art 24.

[128] Ning Liu and Jin Wang (2021), 15–16.

[129] Administrative Regulation on Emission Permitting, art 1.

[130] Environmental Protection Law, art 45.

down by the Environmental Protection Law as serving as a fundamental starting point in applying the permit instrument to control emissions, and the implementation of the permit instrument to control emissions relies on the other legislation.[131] According to the Administrative Permit Law, where a permit system has been established in any law, such as in this case the Environmental Protection Law, an administrative regulation is allowed to provide for more concrete rules for the purpose of implementation, within the scope of permit system as established by the laws.[132] In other words, the laws may establish a permit system without providing concrete rules and, in this case, the State Council is allowed to lay down concrete rules by enacting an administrative regulation for the purpose of the implementation. In light of this general administrative law approach towards permit systems in China, I will now analyze what this means for the emissions permit.

A first important issue is the fact that several laws have established permit systems to control emissions: in addition to the Environmental Protection Law, there are six laws on pollution prevention and control that explicitly prescribe the permit instrument for controlling emissions. These are:

- the Water Pollution Prevention and Control Law (2017);
- the Soil Pollution Prevention and Control Law (2018);
- the Air Pollution Prevention and Control Law (2018);
- the Law on Solid Waste Pollution Prevention and Control (2020);
- the Law on Prevention and Control of Pollution from Noise;
- the Marine Environment Protection Law (2023).[133]

As already mentioned in Sect. 4.3.3.1 of this chapter, some of these laws explicitly delegate the State Council to lay down concrete rules for the permit regulation on emissions for the purpose of implementation.[134] The Soil Pollution Prevention and Control Law and the Law on Prevention and Control of Pollution from Noise do not explicitly delegate the State Council to lay down concrete rules for the permit regulation on emissions. According to the Administrative Permit Law, while these two laws provide for the permit instrument for controlling pollution, they do not provide for concrete rules; therefore the State Council is allowed to establish an administrative regulation to provide more concrete rules for the purpose of implementation.[135]

---

[131] Legislative Affairs Commission of the Standing Committee of National People's Congress, A Paraphrase on Environmental Protection Law (in Chinese: 中华人民共和国环境保护法释义) (Law Press China 2014), 156.

[132] Administrative Permit Law, art 16.

[133] Water Pollution Prevention and Control Law (2017), art 21; Soil Pollution Prevention and Control Law, art 21; Air Pollution Prevention and Control Law (2018), art 19; Law on Solid Waste Pollution Prevention and Control (2020), art 38; Law on Prevention and Control of Pollution from Noise, arts 36, 38, and 75; Marine Environment Protection Law (2023), art 19.

[134] Also see Water Pollution Prevention and Control Law (2017), art 21; Soil Pollution Prevention and Control Law (2018), art 21; Air Pollution Prevention and Control Law (2018), art 19; and Law on Solid Waste Pollution Prevention and Control (2020), art 38.

[135] Administrative Permit Law, art 16.

In summary, there are the laws on pollution prevention and control and the Environmental Protection Law, together with the Administrative Permit Law, serve as the legal basis for the State Council to establish the Administrative Regulation on Emissions Permitting. According to this legal basis, it is clear that the scope of the emissions permit system, as prescribed by the Administrative Regulation on Emissions Permitting, at least covers emissions into water, soil, air and marine environment, as well as addresses the control of pollution caused by industrial solid waste and industrial noise.

4.4.2.2 Environmental Issues not Subject to Emissions Permitting

This sub-section examines, according to the relevant laws, what environmental issues are certainly not subject to emissions permitting as prescribed by the Administrative Regulation on Emissions Permitting, so as to understand the limits to the scope of integration as pursued by the Administrative Regulation on Emissions Permitting.

4.4.2.2.1 The Use of Water not Subject to Emissions Permitting

In addition to the laws on pollution control, other sectoral environmental laws in China include laws on natural resource conservation.[136] The laws on natural resource conservation have established permit systems on the exploitation and use of natural resources, including minerals, water, grass, and forest, etc.[137] These permit systems have been established separately.[138] Among these permit systems, the water use permits are most relevant for the entities subject to emissions permitting, since water is used for almost all types of production process. The water use permit was established by the Water Law of the People's Republic of China (hereinafter 'Water Law').[139] In particular, the Water Law prescribes the permit instrument for the use of water in a vague sense and delegates the authority to the State Council to lay down more concrete rules for the purpose of implementation.[140] Based on the Water Law,

---

136 Kaijie Wu, 'Legislation on Protected Natural Reserves as a Part of the Environmental Law System' (in Chinese: 环境法系中的自然保护地立法) (2020) 42(03) Chinese Journal of Law 123, 131.

137 Min Jiang, 'The Study on the Institutions of Environmental Administrative License of Our Country' (in Chinese: 我国环境行政许可制度研究) (2013) Dissertation to obtain the degree of Doctor at Southwest University of Political Science & Law, 60–66.

138 EU-China Environment Project, 'China's Regulatory Framework on Pollutant Discharge Permits: An Overview on the Formulation and Implementation of Pollutant Discharge Permits in China and the Sharing of EU experience of Permitting', 2 February 2021, available at: https://www.clientearth.org/latest/documents/china-s-regulatory-framework-on-pollutant-discharge-permits/, accessed on 2 April 2022, 16.

139 Standing Committee of the National People's Congress, Water Law of the People's Republic of China (in Chinese: 中华人民共和国水法), 21 January 1988 and its latest amendment adopted on 2 July 2016, art 7 and art 48.

140 Water Law, art 7 and art 48.

the State Council adopted the Administrative Regulation on Water Use Permitting and Fees, which provides for concrete rules on water use permitting in terms of the applications for permits, the permit conditions, and the granting of permits, etc.[141] Scholars observed that the permit regulation on *the use of* water and the permit regulation on the *emissions into water* have been established separately in different legislation without requiring any coordination mechanism.[142] Wu further argued that the separate permit systems on water use and water emissions could hinder the protection of the water ecosystem as a whole.[143] In this vein, the separate permit systems on the use of water and on the emissions may constitute the limits to the scope of integration as pursued by the Administrative Regulation on Emissions Permitting.

4.4.2.2.2 The Use of Energy not Subject to Emissions Permits

The regulation of energy use in China is addressed separately in legislation[144] concerning:

- Energy Conservation Law of the People's Republic of China (2018);[145]
- Renewable Energy Law of the People's Republic of China (2009);[146]

---

[141] State Council, Administrative Regulation on Water Use Permitting and Fees (in Chinese: 取水许可和水资源费征收管理条例), 21 February 2006 and its latest amendment adopted on 1 March 2017.

[142] Baixin Shen and Zhilin Li, 'Discussion on the Development of Environmental Permit System in China Compared with Germany' (in Chinese: 从中德比较论我国环境许可制度的发展) (2018) 10(04) Chinese Journal of Environmental Management 47, 50–51; Xiaoran Zhou, 'On the Establishment Principles for Basic Systems in General Provisions of Environmental Code' (in Chinese: 论环境法典总则编基本制度的构建理路), 8(04) Journal of Soochow University (Law Edition) 42, 52.

[143] Kaijie Wu, 'Research on the systematic function of General Part of Environmental Code and its formulation' (in Chinese: 论环境法典总则的体系功能与规范配置) (2021) 27(03)) Law and Social Development 167, 184.

[144] Jin Wang, 'Establishment and Innovation of China's Environmental Codification: a Study Based on China's Civil Codification' (in Chinese: 论中国环境法典框架体系的构建和创新——以中国民法典框架体系为鉴) (2021) 35(06) Contemporary Law Review 18, 29.

[145] Standing Committee of the National People's Congress, Energy Conservation Law of the People's Republic of China (in Chinese: 中华人民共和国节约能源法), 1 November 1997 and its latest amendment adopted on 26 October 2018.

[146] Standing Committee of the National People's Congress, Renewable Energy Law of the People's Republic of China (in Chinese: 中华人民共和国可再生能源法), 28 February 2005 and its latest amendment adopted on 26 December 2009.

- Cleaner Production Promotion Law (2012);[147] and
- Circular Economy Promotion Law (2018),[148] etc.[149]

The literature has criticized that the rules on energy use as laid down in these laws are vague.[150] There is no rule in these laws that refers to emissions permits, and thus the use of energy is not subject to emissions permitting.

4.4.2.3 Environmental Issues Unregulated by the Laws

There are some environmental issues that are not regulated by environmental laws in China. The Administrative Permit Law prescribes that the State Council is allowed to establish the permit system by adopting administrative regulations to address the environmental issues that are not regulated by laws.[151] Therefore, there is the possibility that environmental issues not regulated by laws can be subject to emissions permitting if it is explicitly prescribed by the Administrative Regulation on Emissions Permitting. For example, the Green House Gas emissions (hereinafter 'GHG emissions') are not regulated by laws. Based on the Administrative Permit Law, Chen considered that it is possible to subject GHG emissions to emissions permitting, if it is explicitly required by the specific laws and administrative regulations.[152] However, from the objective of the Administrative Regulation on Emissions Permitting, it is not clear whether the GHG emissions or other environmental issues are required in the emissions permitting decisions. Thus, in order to understand whether other environmental issues, such as GHG emissions, can fall within the scope of the permit system as prescribed by the Administrative Regulation on Emissions Permitting, a further analysis of the detailed rules on the key stages of the permitting procedure is conducted in the following sections.

---

[147] Standing Committee of the National People's Congress, Cleaner Production Promotion Law of the People' Republic of China (in Chinese: 中华人民共和国清洁生产促进法), 29 June 2002 and its latest amendment adopted on 29 February 2012.

[148] Standing Committee of the National People's Congress, Circular Economy Promotion Law of the People's Republic of China (in Chinese: 中华人民共和国循环经济促进法), 29 August 2008 and its latest amendment adopted on 26 October 2018.

[149] In addition to the laws, Yang also observed that the regulation on energy use is also prescribed in a set of administrative regulations, ministerial rules, local decrees, and local rules. See Chuntao Yang, 'Deficiency and Improvement of the Energy Legal System in China: from the Perspective of Structure–Function' (in Chinese: 我国能源立法体系的不足与完善——以 "结构-功能"分析方法为视角) (2021) 04 Social Sciences in Guangxi 95, 97.

[150] Jing Song, 'Research on Regulation of Energy Technology from the Perspective of Sustainable Development' (in Chinese: 可持续发展视域下的能源技术规制研究) (2018) 04 Journal of CUPL 25, 32.

[151] Administrative Permit Law, art. 12 and art 14.

[152] Huizhen Chen,'Register System or Permit System: Regulation on the access to the carbon emissions activities' (in Chinese: 许可抑或备案:我国碳排放准入监管的法制进路) (2016) 34(5) Law Review 157, 163.

4.4.3 The Environmental Effectiveness of Integration

The environmental effectiveness of integration refers to a certain level of environmental quality as a whole to be achieved.[153] This sub-section examines whether the environmental effectiveness of an integrated approach in the sense of a certain level of environmental quality is pursued by the Administrative Regulation on Emissions Permitting. In order to do so, the meaning of 'to protect and to improve the environment' as prescribed in the provision on the objective of Administrative Regulation on Emissions Permitting[154] needs to be investigated.

The drafting history can serve as an important source for interpretation. According to the Implementation Plan for the Permit System for Controlling Emissions published by the State Council on 10 November 2016, the reform of the emissions permit system was aimed at improving environmental quality.[155] More specifically, this implementation plan advocated that, in the areas where the environmental quality standards are not achieved, more stringent measures for controlling emissions, such as more stringent emissions limit values, should be included in the permit in order to improve environmental quality.[156] This specific suggestion indicated that the improvement of environmental quality is related to the achievement of the environmental quality standards. As discussed in Sect. 2.3.1.2 of Chap. 2, due to the incommensurability of environmental goods, a certain level of environmental protection can only be quantified in a media-specific way, which is often established as environmental quality standards.[157] This is also the case in China. The existing environmental quality standards established in China are usually a set of values of the concentration of chemicals in a certain environmental media. According to the Environmental Protection Law, the environmental ministry establishes national environmental quality standards; and the people's governments at provincial level are allowed to establish environmental quality standards for items not specified in the national environmental quality standards or they may develop more stringent environmental quality standards with regard to items already specified in the national standards.[158] The literature has pointed out that the environmental quality standards in China can serve to reflect a certain level of environmental protection.[159] In particular, the literature considered that the environmental quality standards can be used to interpret the degree of pollution: where the environmental quality standards are

[153] See Sect. 2.3.1.2 of Chap. 2.

[154] Administrative Regulation on Emissions Permitting, art 1.

[155] Implementation Plan for the Permit System for Controlling Emissions, Sect. 4.1.

[156] Ibid, Sect. 4.4.

[157] See Sect. 2.3.1.2 of Chap. 2.

[158] Environmental Protection Law, art 15. The environmental quality standards are other normative documents. For the explanation of other normative documents, see Sect. 4.2.5 of this chapter.

[159] Xiangmin Xu, 'Environmental Quality Objectives: The Deliberation on Environmental Law Built on Directly Regulating Objective' (in Chinese: 环境质量目标主义:关于环境法直接规制目标的思考) (2015) 06 China Legal Science 116, 128.

exceeded, there a certain degree of pollution exists.[160] There are cases regarding environmental torts where the peoples' courts used the environmental quality standards as an aid to judge whether there was a certain degree of pollution that was harmful to human health or results in damage to property.[161] On 5 November 2018, the environmental ministry released the Draft of Administrative Regulation on Emissions Permitting, which prescribed the improvement of environmental quality as the objective of emissions permitting.[162] Meanwhile, this draft proposed that the permitting authorities should adhere to the improvement of environmental quality as a core in the implementation of integrated emissions permitting; in the areas where the environmental quality standards are exceeded, the permitting authorities should set more stringent emission control measures, and strengthen the inspection of operators, to improve the environmental quality.[163] It can be seen that, similar to the suggestions regarding the improvement of environmental quality as put forward by the State Council in the Implementation Plan for the Permit System for Controlling Emissions, the Draft of the Administrative Regulation on Emissions Permitting proposed by the environmental ministry also laid down the objective of improving environmental quality and prescribed duties for permitting authorities regarding the achievement of environmental quality standards.

From the drafting history, it can be inferred that the objective 'to protect and to improve the environment' as laid down by the Administrative Regulation on Emissions Permitting is relevant to the pursuit of a certain level of environmental quality. Meanwhile, the Administrative Regulation on Emissions Permitting has also laid down a specific provision for environmental quality standards,[164] which requires the achievement of concrete levels of protection for certain environmental media. In this vein, the rule on environmental quality standards as laid down in the Administrative Regulation on Emissions Permitting can provide further insight into the environmental effectiveness of integration, which will be discussed in Sect. 4.7.5.3.

160 Wei Chen, 'Research on the Application of Environmental Quality Standards in the Tort Law' (in Chinese: 环境质量标准的侵权法适用研究) (2017b) 01 China Legal Science 209, 210–213. On the basis of literature review, this paper found that the environmental quality standards are considered as a tool in defining pollution.

161 Xiaoran Zhou, 'Reshaping of Legal Validity of Environmental Standard in Liability for Environmental Pollution - Type Analysis Based on the Laws of Environmental Physics' (in Chinese: 环境标准在环境污染责任中的效力重塑——基于环境物理学定律的类型化分析) (2017) 17(01) Journal of China University of Geosciences(Social Sciences Edition) 46, 53.

162 Ministry of Ecology and Environment, Draft of Administrative Regulation on Emissions Permitting (in Chinese: 排污许可管理条例(草案征求意见稿)), 5 November 2018, art 1.

163 Ibid, art 5.

164 Administrative Regulation on Emissions Permitting, art 11(2).

4.4.4 Interim Conclusion

The objective of the Administrative Regulation on Emissions Permitting—to control emissions to protect and to improve the environment—is formulated in a vague manner without giving a precise instruction as to the scope of integration and the environmental effectiveness of integration. Thus, the objective of the Administrative Regulation on Emissions Permitting should be derived from its legal basis and its drafting history.

From the perspective of the scope of an integrated approach, by investigating the legal basis for establishing the Administrative Regulation on Emissions Permitting, it is clear that the scope of emissions permitting as prescribed by the Administrative Regulation on Emissions Permitting at least covers emissions into water, soil, air and marine environment, as well as pollution caused by industrial solid waste and industrial noise. In terms of the other environmental issues, it was found that the use of water, and the use of energy are not integrated into the emissions permit. Meanwhile, there are other environmental issues that are not regulated by the laws, such as the GHG emissions. It is possible to subject these environmental issues to the emissions permits, if it is explicitly required by the Administrative Regulation on Emissions Permitting. However, from the objective of the Administrative Regulation on Emissions Permitting, it is not clear whether these environmental issues are also subject to the emissions permits.

From the perspective of the environmental effectiveness of integration, while a concrete level of environmental quality as a whole to be achieved cannot be clearly perceived in the objective of Administrative Regulation on Emissions Permitting, the drafting history of the Administrative Regulation on Emissions Permitting shows that the legislator intended to establish an emissions permit system pursuing a certain level of environmental quality. The analysis on the rules on environmental quality standards as laid down by the Administrative Regulation on Emissions Permitting can provide further insight into the meaning of improving environmental quality.[165]

In summary, the concrete meaning of 'to control emissions to protect and to improve the environment' in view of the scope and the environmental effectiveness of integration is clear to a certain extent, since at least emissions into water, soil, air and marine environment, as well as pollution caused by industrial solid waste and industrial noise are covered. However, whether other issues must also be addressed in the emissions permit requires an examination of the detailed regulatory approaches adopted in the Administrative Regulation on Emissions Permitting, which will be undertaken in the following sections.

---

[165] See Sect. 4.7.5.3 of this chapter.

4.5 Rules on the Application for a Permit

As analyzed in Sect. 4.4, the provision prescribing the objective of the Administrative Regulation on Emissions Permitting does not provide sufficiently clear indications as to what extent an integrated approach is pursued by the Administrative Regulation on Emissions Permitting. Hence, it is necessary to delve into the detailed rules on the key stages of the permitting procedure, in order to analyze whether further indications on the scope of the permit can be found. This section examines the rules on the application for a permit as laid down in the Administrative Regulation on Emissions Permitting, which consists of three parts. First, Sect. 4.5.1 analyzes what environmental information must be collected by operators for the application for an emissions permit. Section 4.5.2 explains that the rules on the application for a permit can serve as a coordination tool from the perspective of procedural integration. The last section provides an interim conclusion.

4.5.1 The Obligatory Content of the Permit Application

Article 7 of the Administrative Regulation on Emissions Permitting lists a set of information to be used for the application for the permit, including the sources, nature, and quantities of emissions from the installation, the techniques for preventing and controlling emissions from the installation, the raw and auxiliary materials used in the installation, the products, etc.[166] With this, the Administrative Regulation on Emissions Permitting provides a relatively broad scope of environmental information to be collected by operators applying for an emissions permit: this concerns not just emissions, but also other environmental relevant elements, such as the use of raw materials. A further question arises, however, whether the requirement of a wide scope of environmental information to be submitted to apply for an emissions permit may entail an integrated review by the permitting authorities, which will be discussed in Sect. 4.7 (the section on provisions for setting the conditions of the permit).

4.5.2 The Coordination Tool for Achieving Procedural Integration

The provision regulating the applications for permits in the Administrative Regulation on Emissions Permitting refers to three specific environmental regulatory systems.

First, it prescribes that environmental impact assessment permits (hereinafter 'EIA permits') granted in accordance with the EIA permit system should be submitted in

[166] Administrative Regulation on Emissions Permitting, art 7.

the application for emissions permits.[167] The rules for EIA permitting are mainly laid down in the Environmental Impacts Assessment Law of the People's Republic of China (hereinafter 'EIA Law') and the Administrative Regulation on Environmental Protection for Construction Projects (2017).[168] The EIA law prescribes two kinds of EIA procedures: (1) a procedure on assessing the environmental impacts of planning; (2) a procedure on assessing the environmental impacts of construction projects.[169] The EIA permit system refers to the procedure on assessing the environmental impacts of construction projects.[170] Second, the emission standards that have to be complied with by industry in accordance with the environmental standards system should be submitted in the application for emissions permits.[171] The rules for setting environmental standards are mainly laid down in the Environmental Protection Law and the Administrative Rules on Environmental Standards.[172] Third, the total allowable quantities of emissions distributed to the installations in accordance with the so-called total emission control system should be used in the application for emissions permits.[173]

Therefore, from the perspective of procedural integration, this shows that the Administrative Regulation on Emissions Permitting provides for rules on the coordination between the emissions permit system and the other environmental regulatory systems including EIA permit system, the environmental standards system, and the total emission control system.[174] In practice, it appears that the operators are faced with a shortage of capacity in their process of applying for the emissions permit. For example, Lin observed that in Zhangzhou, Fujian, most applicants of the small-and-medium-sized paper mills are not familiar with the relevant rules and standards and lack sufficient knowledge about the techniques for emissions control, and thus their application materials usually contain a lot of mistakes.[175] In order to address this issue, in practice, some local environmental authorities (e.g. the Provinces of

[167] Administrative Regulation on Emissions Permitting, art 7(2).

[168] Standing Committee of the National People's Congress, Environmental Impacts Assessment Law of the People's Republic of China (in Chinese: 中华人民共和国环境影响评价法), 28 October 2002 and its latest amendment adopted on 29 December 2018, chapter 3; State Council, Administrative Regulation on Environmental Protection for Construction Projects (2017) (in Chinese: 建设项目环境保护管理条例), 16 July 2017. For a detailed discussion on the rules for environmental impact assessment permitting, see Sect. 4.7.3 of this chapter.

[169] Xi Wang and Kun Lu (2017), 64.

[170] For a further discussion on the EIA permit system, see Sect. 4.7.3 of this chapter.

[171] Administrative Regulation on Emissions Permitting, art 7(3).

[172] Environmental Protection Law, art 16; Also see Administrative Rules on Environmental Standards. For a more detailed discussion on the rules for the setting of environmental standards, see Sect. 4.7.4 of this chapter.

[173] Administrative Regulation on Emissions Permitting, art 7(3).

[174] For a discussion on how the authorities must review whether the applicants can comply with the requirements of the EIA permits, the emission standards, and the total allowable quantities of emissions in the decision on whether to grant the emissions permits, see Sect. 4.7 of this chapter.

[175] Ping Lin, 'Research on the Problems of the Application for Emissions Permits for Paper Mills and Suggestions' (in Chinese: 浅析制浆造纸行业排污许可申报常见问题及处理方法) (2021) 08 Straits Science 53, 53.

Guangdong and Guangxi) stepped in at the application stage for emissions permits and undertook a pre-verification of the application to help applicants to submit application materials correctly, but this could result in risks for the environmental authorities.[176] Consider an operator who receives instructions at the application stage and successfully obtains an emissions permit but fails to comply with the permit conditions and thus is faced with penalties, this operator could sue the environmental authorities on the ground that the environmental authorities forced it to apply for a permit against its will.[177]

4.5.3 Interim Conclusion

According to the rules on the application for a permit as laid down in the Administrative Regulation on Emissions Permitting, a relatively broad scope of environmental information must be collected by operators applying for an emissions permit, concerning not just emissions, but also other environmental relevant elements, such as the use of raw materials. In addition, the EIA permit, the emission standards, and the total allowable quantities of emissions distributed to the installations must also be submitted for the application for emissions permits, which indicates the requirement to coordinate the emissions permit system with the EIA permit system, the environmental standards system, and the total emission control system. In practice, the applicants are faced with a lack of knowledge and skills in their process of applying for the emissions permit.

4.6 Rules on Issuing a Permit

Theoretically, procedural integration refers to the idea of integrating procedures where various regulatory subjects are evaluated and decided, and full procedural integration refers to incorporating various regulatory subjects exclusively into one procedure.[178] In addition, from the perspective of organizational integration, an integrated permit system is mainly indicated by a low number of authorities involved and a clear competence structure, while a fragmented permit system is characterized by a high number of authorities involved and an unclear competence structure.[179] This section investigates the rules for issuing emissions permits as provided by the Administrative Regulation on Emissions Permitting from the perspective of procedural integration and organizational integration.

[176] EU-China Environment Project (2021), 32.

[177] Ibid, 32.

[178] See Sect. 2.3.2 of Chap. 2.

[179] See Sect. 2.3.3 of Chap. 2.

According to the Administrative Regulation on Emissions Permitting, the environmental authorities at and above the level of cities with districts are responsible for emissions permitting within their jurisdiction.[180] In addition, the Administrative Regulation on Emissions Permitting does not require separate permitting procedures for different emissions regulations. There is one procedure for issuing emissions permits, and the requirements for controlling various emissions into different environmental media must be documented in one permit.[181]

Therefore, the Administrative Regulation on Emissions Permitting has established one permit procedure that regulates emissions into various environmental media by single authorities. In this vein, from the perspective of procedural integration, one permit procedure covering various emissions into different media indicates that full procedural integration is established by the Administrative Regulation on Emissions Permitting. From the perspective of organizational integration, a single authority responsible for issuing emissions permits as prescribed by the Administrative Regulation on Emissions Permitting indicates a high degree of organizational integration.

4.7 Rules on Setting Permit Conditions

4.7.1 Introduction

As analyzed in Sect. 4.5, according to the rules on the application for a permit as laid down by the Administrative Regulation on Emissions Permitting, a relatively broad scope of environmental information must be collected by operators applying for emissions permits, concerning not just emissions, but also other environmental relevant elements, such as the use of raw materials. In addition, the EIA permits, the emission standards, and the total allowable quantities of emissions also must be submitted for the application for emissions permits.[182] However, it is not clear to what extent the authorities have to review the wide scope of environmental information as well as the EIA permits, the emission standards, and the total allowable quantities of emissions in the decision on whether to issue the emissions permits. Hence, it is necessary to examine the rules on setting permit conditions.

This section consists of six parts. After this introduction, the conditions for issuing permits are investigated. As will be shown in Sect. 4.7.2, the Administrative Regulation on Emissions Permitting incorporates the decisions made through various procedures (including the EIA permitting procedure, the procedure for adopting emission standards, the procedure for adopting the technical specifications for application

[180] Administrative Regulation on Emissions Permitting, art 3.

[181] For detailed information on emissions permits that had been issued, see 'Emissions Permits Portal' (in Chinese: 全国排污许可证管理信息平台), http://permit.mee.gov.cn/permitExt/defaults/default-index!getInformation.action, accessed on 11 January 2022.

[182] See Sect. 4.5 of this chapter.

and issuance of emissions permits, the procedure for distributing the total allowable quantities of emissions and the procedure for adopting local special requirements) into the conditions for issuing emissions permits. Section 4.7.3 delves into the rules on the conditions regarding the EIA permits, in which the rules on EIA permits are analyzed from the perspective of integration. Section 4.7.4 examines rules on the conditions regarding emission standards, in which the rules on setting emission standards are discussed. Section 4.7.5 analyzes other rules on setting permit conditions, followed by an interim conclusion.

4.7.2 Permit Conditions

This section investigates the conditions for issuing emissions permits. Article 11 of the Administrative Regulation on Emissions Permitting provides for the conditions for issuing emissions permits:

The competent authority shall grant an emissions permit if the entity complies with the following conditions:

(1) The entity has obtained the EIA permit or has registered the EIA form;
(2) The emissions comply with emission standards; emissions of key pollutants comply with the technical specifications for application and issuance of emissions permits, the EIA permit and the total allowable quantities of emissions on key pollutants. In the key regions and river basins where the national environmental quality standards are not achieved, emissions also comply with the special requirements for improving environmental quality provided by the local people's governments;
(3) pollution prevention and control techniques applied by the entity can ensure the emission standards to be achieved; or these techniques are in accordance with the guidance on available techniques of pollution prevention and control;
(4) the self-monitoring plan of the entity complies with the national prescription on self-monitoring in terms of the monitoring sites, values, and frequency, etc.[183]

It can be seen that, from article 11(1) and 11(2), the permit conditions consist of the decisions made through various other environmental regulatory instruments, including EIA permitting, emission standards, technical specifications, total emission control, and local instruments for achieving national environmental quality standards. This shows that the coordination mechanism—which is a tool for a situation where the separate decision-making procedures are not harmonized of providing legal rules which force the authorities to take the separate procedures or licences into account[184]—is established by the Administrative Regulation on Emissions Permitting. In addition to the decisions made through other environmental regulatory

[183] Administrative Regulation on Emissions Permitting, art 11(1).

[184] See Sects. 2.2.2 and 2.3.2 of Chap. 2.

systems, the permitting authorities are also required to review the pollution prevention and control techniques in accordance with emission standards or in accordance with the guidance of available techniques of pollution prevention and control. In terms of the self-monitoring plan, the evaluation is less relevant in light of the objective of this research (analyzing to what extent an integrated approach exists), and thus it will not be discussed in detail.

These permit conditions may run counter to one another, since they are determined using different procedures.[185] However, no provision in the Administrative Regulation on Emissions Permitting prescribes how to deal with a conflict between different requirements. In particular, the Administrative Regulation on Emissions Permitting does not have a provision that allows a derogation from these conditions.

4.7.3 Rules on the Conditions Regarding EIA Permits

A permit instrument is established by the legislation on environmental impact assessments for regulating the environmental impacts resulting from construction projects.[186] The system of environmental impact assessments in China adopts the model of 'veto arrangement', which means that a failure to obtain an EIA permit at the pre-construction stage from an environmental authority will definitely lead to the project being terminated.[187] According to article 11(1) of the Administrative Regulation on Emissions Permitting, an EIA permit is a prerequisite to obtain emissions permits. This shows that a coordination mechanism between EIA permits and emissions permits is established by the Administrative Regulation on Emissions Permitting. A question arises here whether or to what extent the coordination between emissions permitting and EIA permitting can facilitate the implementation of integration.

In order to address this question, the following sub-sections will first discuss the rules on EIA permitting. As we will see in Sect. 4.7.3.1, EIA permitting is in fact the first stage to support an integrated approach. Then, it can be asked why and how EIA permitting has to be coordinated with emissions permitting. The rationale for the coordination between EIA permitting and emissions permitting by investigating the drafting history and relevant literature will be addressed in Sect. 4.7.3.2, after which how the EIA permits will be used in setting conditions for issuing emissions permits will be investigated in Sect. 4.7.3.3, followed by an interim conclusion.

---

[185] However, it is not clear whether there is a conflict in view of cross-media effects. No empirical literature on this issue can be found.

[186] EIA Law, chapter 3; and Administrative Regulation on Environmental Protection for Construction Projects (2017).

[187] Yun Ma, 'Dynamics in Central-Local Division of the Authority of EIA Approval in China' (2019) 31(1) Journal of Environmental Law 29, 31–35.

4.7.3.1 Rules on EIA Permitting

This sub-section examines the EIA permit system for construction projects from the perspective of integration. In particular, this sub-section examines what scope of environmental issues have to be considered in EIA permitting; what level of environmental protection has to be required through the EIA permitting; and whether the generic or case-specific options apply to the environmental issues to be considered by the EIA permitting authorities. This examination first analyzes the scope of EIA permitting (Sect. 4.7.3.1.1), and then delves into the rules on the formulation of EIA documents by developers of construction projects when applying for EIA permits (Sect. 4.7.3.1.2). Section 4.7.3.1.3 analyzes the rules on setting EIA permit conditions.

4.7.3.1.1 The Scope of EIA Permits

According to the EIA Law, the scope of construction projects subject to EIA permits is based on the degree of environmental impacts that a construction project may cause.[188] In particular, the EIA law classifies construction projects into three types:

(1) construction projects that may have significant environmental impacts;
(2) construction projects that may have mild environmental impacts;
(3) construction projects that have very little environmental impacts.[189]

Construction projects that may have significant environmental impacts or may have mild environmental impacts are subject to the EIA permitting, while construction projects that have very mild environmental impacts are subject to the EIA registration.[190] The EIA law does not provide a concrete explanation on what accounts for significant environmental impacts or mild environmental impacts, nor does the Administrative Regulation on Environmental Protection for Construction Projects (2017).

The EIA Law delegates the environmental ministry to establish a ministerial rule, namely a Catalogue of Classified Construction Projects subject to EIA, to clarify the scope and the classification of construction projects subject to EIA permitting.[191] The process of establishing and revising the catalogue by the environmental ministry is not transparent and, according to the Administrative Litigation Law, the catalogue,

[188] EIA Law art 16.

[189] Ibid. Xi Wang and Kun Lu (2017), 65.

[190] EIA Law art 16.

[191] EIA Law art 16. For the latest ministerial rule on classified construction projects subject to EIA, see Ministry of Ecology and Environment, Catalogue of Classified Construction Projects subject to EIA (2021) (in Chinese: 建设项目环境影响评价分类管理名录(2021年版)部令 第16号), 30 November 2020.

as a ministerial rule, is exempted from judicial review.[192] In this vein, the environmental ministry has relatively broad discretion in determining the scope and the classification of construction projects subject to EIA permitting. However, the Catalogue of Classified Construction Projects subject to EIA does not explicitly address what environmental impacts must be considered in EIA permitting,[193] but it mainly lists construction projects in each industrial sector that are subject to EIA permitting or EIA registration.

The list of construction projects subject to EIA permitting prescribed in this ministerial catalogue is limited. Given the infinite specific factors (such as technical characteristics, local environmental conditions, etc.), there may be construction projects with significant or mild environmental impacts that are not explicitly listed in the Catalogue of Classified Construction Projects subject to EIA. Whether these construction projects should be regulated by EIA permitting can lead to legal disputes. In addressing these issues, the courts tend to examine whether the contested construction project has similarities with the construction projects explicitly listed in the Catalogue of Classified Construction Projects subject to EIA,[194] helping to insert the contested construction project within the scope of the EIA permit regulation. In other words, it appears that the judicial practice encourages a relatively broad scope of construction projects to be subject to EIA permitting. However, since these cases are more relevant to the scope of construction projects to be regulated under EIA permitting, it is not clear whether the courts would also provide a broad interpretation from the perspective of the scope of integration.

4.7.3.1.2 The Obligatory Content of EIA

The EIA Law prescribes different formats for EIA documents that have to be prepared by developers of construction projects when applying for the EIA permits: an EIA report for construction projects with a significant impact, an EIA statement for construction projects with a mild impact, and an EIA registration form for construction projects with very mild impact.[195] A developer may formulate EIA reports and

---

[192] For a further discussion on how the ministry of ecology and environment exercises its power to establish the catalogue of classified construction projects subject to EIA, see Xiangbai He, 'In the Name of Legitimacy and Efficiency: Evaluating China's Legal Reform on EIA' (2020) 32(3) Journal of Environmental Law 441, 450.

[193] See Ministry of Ecology and Environment, Catalogue of Classified Construction Projects subject to EIA (2021) (in Chinese: 建设项目环境影响评价分类管理名录(2021年版)部令 第16号), 30 November 2020.

[194] Xingchen Liu, 'Judicial Application of Uncertain Legal Concept in Classification of EIA: a Study of 56 Cases of EIA' (in Chinese: 环境影响评价分类中不确定法律概念的司法适用——基于56个环境影响评价案例的实证考察) (2016) Environmental Pollution & Control 38(11) 106, 110.

[195] EIA Law, art 16.

statements by itself if it has the ability to do so, or entrust and pay other entities that it deems appropriate to do so.[196]

The EIA Law further prescribes the obligatory contents of EIA report, including:

(1) an introduction to the construction project;
(2) the surrounding environment of the construction project;
(3) the analysis prediction and assessment of the possible environmental impacts of the construction project;
(4) environmental protection measures and the technological and economic justification;
(5) economic cost/benefit analysis for the environmental impacts of the construction project;
(6) proposals on environmental monitoring of the construction project;
(7) conclusions of the environmental impacts assessment.[197]

Neither the EIA Law nor the Administrative Regulation on Environmental Protection for Construction Projects (2017) provides for a further concrete explanation on what specific 'possible environmental impacts' must be assessed. In addition, the environmental ministry also establishes a set of other normative documents to provide a more detailed instruction on how to formulate EIA reports. These other normative documents consist of the general instruction, media-specific instruction, and industrial-sectoral instruction, which are not mandatory.[198] The media-specific instructions on formulating EIA reports concern various environmental impacts.[199] More specifically, there are media-specific instructions on assessing ecological impact, noise impact, impact on underground water, environmental risks, impact on soil, and impact on air.[200] With regard to the contents of EIA statement, the EIA Law delegates the authority to the ministry of ecology and environment to specify the contents of EIA statement.[201] The specifications provided by the environmental ministry are also other normative documents, which are not legally binding. The contents of EIA

[196] Yun Ma (2019), 33.

[197] EIA Law, art 17. The same provision is also prescribed in the Administrative Regulation on Environmental Protection for Construction Projects (2017) art 8.

[198] Charles R. Mcelwee (2011), 133.

[199] Ibid.

[200] Ministry of Ecology and Environment, Technical Guidelines for Environmental Impact assessment —Ecological Impact (in Chinese: 环境影响评价技术导则 生态影响 HJ 19—2022), 15 January 2022; Ministry of Ecology and Environment, Technical Guidelines for Noise Impact Assessment (in Chinese: 环境影响评价技术导则 声环境 HJ 2.4—2021), 24 December 2021; Ministry of Ecology and Environment, Technical Guidelines for Environmental Impact Assessment Surface Water Environment (in Chinese: 环境影响评价技术导则 地表水环境 HJ 2.3—2018), 30 September 2018; Ministry of Ecology and Environment, Technical Guidelines for Environmental Impact Assessment —Soil Environment (for Trail Implementation) (in Chinese: 环境影响评价技术导则 土壤环境(试行) HJ 964—2018), 13 September 2018; Ministry of Ecology and Environment, Technical Guidelines for Environmental Impact Assessment —Atmospheric Environment (in Chinese: 环境影响评价技术导则 大气环境 HJ 2.2—2018), 31 July 2018.

[201] EIA Law art 17.

statements consist of a relatively brief analysis of the environmental impact of the construction project addressing pollution and ecological issues.[202]

Although these other normative documents on the formulation of EIA reports or statements are not mandatory, it appears that these other normative documents can still have an impact on the formulation of EIA reports or EIA statements in practice. It was observed in the literature that the EIA permitting authorities expect these other normative documents to be followed in preparing EIA reports or statements by the developers or relevant EIA service entities.[203] It is also evident that, in practice, EIA permitting authorities refer to these documents in deciding whether to issue EIA permits or not,[204] although they are not obliged to do so.[205] However, it was also observed in the literature that, in practice, quite often the EIA documents prepared by developers or other entrusted entities failed to correctly identify the environmental impact of the construction project and thus did not put appropriate measures in place to prevent the negative environmental impacts.[206] One reason for the low quality of these environmental impact assessments is that developers or entrusted entities are faced with a lack of knowledge and data and are usually reluctant to spend enough time or resources to compensate for this lack.[207] Hence, the literature suggested that the EIA permitting authorities should review the EIA documents submitted by EIA permit applicants carefully in their decisions on whether to grant EIA permits or not.[208] The following section delves into the rules on the EIA permit conditions, which provides insight into how the EIA permitting authorities have to review the EIA documents and how they have to weigh various environmental impacts.

---

[202] Xiangbai He (2020), 450; Charles R. Mcelwee (2011), 131. Also see the summary on the specification on formulating EIA statements presented on the website of the ministry of ecology and environment: https://www.mee.gov.cn/xxgk2018/xxgk/xxgk05/202101/t20210104_815870.html.

[203] Charles R. Mcelwee (2011), 133.

[204] For example, it can be found on the website of the ministry of ecology and environment that there have been nine cases in which the environmental ministry refused the applications for EIA permits because the EIA reports were not formulated in accordance with the other normative documents on the formulation of EIA reports. For these decisions in Chinese, search 环办环评函〔2016〕285号;环办函〔2015〕1046号;环办函〔2014〕950号;环办环评函〔2016〕1214号;环办函〔2015〕380号;环办函〔2015〕440号 ;环办函〔2014〕1708号;环办函〔2014〕1678号;环办函〔2014〕1465号 at 'Refusal' (in Chinese: 不予审批), see: https://www.mee.gov.cn/searchnew/?searchword=%E4%B8%8D%E4%BA%88%E6%89%B9%E5%87%86, accessed on 8 March 2022.

[205] A further discussion on the rules on EIA permitting is provided in Sect. 4.7.3.1.3.

[206] Ying Hao and Chunxi Hao, 'Problems and Suggestions on the Compilation of Environmental Impact Statements' (in Chinese: 环境影响报告书编制中存在问题与建议) (2015) 37(02) Environmental Impact Assessment 50, 50–51.

[207] Qian Zhu and Yuewen Wu, Deficiency of Low Quality of EIA Documents and the Solution (in Chinese: 建设项目环评文件质量缺陷及其行政治理) (2020) 03 Jiang-huai Tribune 106, 106–108.

[208] Ibid.

4.7.3.1.3 Rules on Setting EIA Permit Conditions

This sub-section delves into the rules on setting EIA permit conditions, to understand how the EIA permitting authorities have to review the EIA documents and how they have to weigh various environmental impacts. The rules on setting EIA permit conditions are mainly laid down by the Administrative Regulation on Environmental Protection for Construction Projects (2017):

> where a construction project falls under any of the following circumstances, the environmental authority shall disapprove the construction project:

(1) the type, site selection, layout, or scale, among others, of the construction project fails to conform to any law or regulation on environmental protection or any relevant statutory plan;
(2) in the areas where the national or local environmental quality standards are not achieved, the proposed measures for environmental protection of the projects cannot satisfy the goal of environmental quality improvement;
(3) the proposed pollution control techniques of the projects cannot ensure the compliance with the national and local emission standards or the applicants do not propose necessary measures for preventing ecological damage;
(4) in the case of reconstruction, expansion, or technological transformation of a project, no effective prevention measure has been put forward with respect to the existing environmental pollution and ecological damage of the project;
(5) the [EIA reports or statements] of the construction project has misrepresented the basic data and there are significant defects and omissions, or the EIA conclusion is unclear and unreasonable.[209]

From the perspective of substantive integration, the provision delineates a certain level of environmental protection in the form of the national or local standards for environmental quality to be achieved through EIA permitting, which indicates the pursuit of environmental effectiveness of integration. However, it is not clear what accounts for measures that can satisfy the goal of environmental quality improvement or not. From the perspective of the scope of integration, in addition to emissions control, ecological issues also have to be considered by permitting authorities in the process of deciding whether to approve a construction project.

In terms of how EIA permitting authorities have to weigh various environmental impacts, a combined use of a generic approach and case-specific approach can be identified. First, the EIA permitting authorities have to review whether the pollution control techniques of the projects can ensure the compliance with the generic national and local emission standards or not, which indicates the generic approach to environmental weighing.[210] Second, the rules on setting EIA permit conditions also prescribe a set of vague concepts. For example, the permitting authorities must

[209] Administrative Regulation on Environmental Protection for Construction Projects (2017), art 11.

[210] A further discussion on the rules on setting emission standards, see Sects. 4.7.4.1 and 4.7.4.2 of this chapter.

review whether the applicants propose necessary measures for preventing ecological damage, but the Administrative Regulation on Environmental Protection for Construction Projects (2017) does not provide a further explanation on what accounts for necessary measures for preventing ecological damage. The ambiguous rules can provide considerable flexibility for the permitting authorities to set the conditions for EIA permits.[211] From the perspective of integration, the flexibility makes case-specific decisions on EIA permitting possible. It is not evident that such flexibility has undergone effective judicial supervision. An empirical analysis on the judicial review of the EIA permitting decisions revealed that the reasoning by the people's courts in their review of the EIA permitting decisions is weak and ambiguous.[212] In this vein, further clarification on the rules on EIA permits can hardly be found in the cases decided by the people's courts.

In summary, the EIA permit system is actually the first stage (the stage of pre-construction) that enables an integrated approach. In view of the scope of integration, the rules on EIA permitting show that EIA permitting addresses a relatively broad scope of environmental issues, at least covering not just emissions, but also ecological issues. In view of the environmental effectiveness of integration, the EIA permit system requires the goal of environmental quality improvement to be considered in setting EIA permit conditions, although the meaning of the criterion of environmental quality improvement is not clear. Since different environmental issues must be weighed by permitting authorities, considering that some of the rules on setting EIA permit conditions are formulated in a relatively vague manner and thus flexibility is afforded to the competent authorities, case-specific decisions on EIA permits are possible. Meanwhile, generic emission standards[213] are also used in setting EIA permit conditions, and thus it can be considered that a generic approach to comparing environmental effects caused by emissions is also adopted by the EIA permit system.

4.7.3.2 Rationale for Coordination Between Emissions Permitting and EIA Permitting

From the above analysis on the rules on EIA permitting, it can be seen that the EIA permit system, addressing the prevention and control of various environmental impacts (at least concerning emissions and ecological issues) at a certain level, is actually the first stage to enable an integrated approach. It can be questioned why another permit system aiming at an integrated approach, namely the emissions permit system, is needed; and why the coordination between the two permit systems is also

[211] Zining Jin, 'Knowledge verse Power: At the Centre of China's EIA Legal System' (in Chinese: 专业知识与行政权力:我国环评审批的制度定位) (2021) 43(3) Modern Law Science 56, 63.

[212] Zining Jin, 'Judicial Review of Administrative Decision Based on Science: Observations on Lawsuits Concerning EIA Approval' (in Chinese: 科技专业性行政行为的司法审查——基于环境影响评价审批诉讼的考察) (2020) 37(03) Studies in Law and Business 154, 168.

[213] A further discussion on the rules on setting emission standards, see Sects. 4.7.4.1 and 4.7.4.2 of this chapter.

needed. In order to address these questions, this sub-section investigates the drafting history of the emissions permit system and relevant literature.

One concern for the coordination between EIA permitting and emissions permitting is that the procedure of EIA permitting is at pre-construction stage. The conditions set at this stage are based on predicted facts, such as production capacity, while in the procedure for emissions permitting, the conditions are set on the basis of the actual facts.[214] In this vein, double-checking is necessary. In addition, the implementation of the EIA permit system in China has shown that non-compliance with the conditions set out in the EIA permits has been a common phenomenon.[215] In order to address the problem of the weak compliance with the EIA permit system, the Implementation Plan for the Permit System for Controlling Emissions called for coordination between emissions permitting and EIA permitting, so as to ensure the 'whole-process' regulation from the pre-construction stage to the operation stage.[216] Specifically, it advocated that the requirements of emissions control as set out in the EIA permits should be incorporated into the emissions permits.[217] The following sub-section will delve into how the EIA permits have to be reviewed in setting conditions for issuing emissions permits.

4.7.3.3 Rules on Setting Permit Conditions Based on EIA Permits

This sub-section examines the rules on how EIA permits have to be used in setting conditions for emissions permits. According to the Administrative Regulation on Emissions Permitting, the competent authorities for issuing emissions permits are not obliged to have a full review of the conditions set out in the EIA permits, but they only focus on the conditions on the control of emissions of key pollutants.[218] As discussed in the above sections, EIA permitting concerns a relatively broad scope of environmental issues, at least covering not only emissions, but also ecological issues. Wang criticized that the failure of incorporating some EIA permit conditions into the emissions permit conditions may lead to weak compliance with these conditions.[219]

---

214 Changman Wu and Feihong Cheng, The interaction and Connection between EIA and Discharge Permit System–From the Perspective of Institutional Logic and Constructive Suggestions (in Chinese: 论环境影响评价与排污许可制度的互动和衔接——从制度逻辑和构造建议的角度) (2020) 22(2) Journal of Beijing Institute of Technology (Social Sciences Edition) 117, 118.

215 Yuanshi Li, Yunhui Du, Xilong Chai and Peng Zhao, 'The Overall Management of Pollution Sources: Promoting the Link of the System of Environmental Impact Assessment and Pollution Permit' (in Chinese: 污染源全面管理的思考——以促进环境影响评价与排污许可制度衔接为核心) (2015) 43(12) Environmental Protection 49, 50.

216 Implementation Plan for the Permit System for Controlling Emissions, point 5.

217 Ibid, point 5.

218 Administrative Regulation on Emissions Permitting, art 11(2).

219 Ya'nan Wang, 'To establish an integrated 'EIA-pollution discharge permit-law enforcement' Eco-environmental Management System: Emphasis, Difficulties and Framework' (in Chinese: 建立 "环评—许可—执法"一体化生态环境管理体系:重点、难点与体系设计) (2021) 46(01) Environment and Sustainable Development 15, 16.

In addition, not all conditions regarding emissions control as set by the EIA permits have to be reviewed in the process of issuing emissions permits, but only the conditions regarding the emissions of key pollutants.[220] However, the Administrative Regulation on Emissions Permitting does not provide a further explanation on what accounts for the emissions of key pollutants. Wang considered that the emissions of key pollutants refer to those that have caused or would cause pollution in certain areas and thus should be strictly controlled, such as the pollutants listed in the national five-year plans with mandatory total emission reduction targets.[221] Related to this, a mandatory target of CO_2 reductions by 18% was prescribed the 14th Five-Year Plan of National Economic and Social Development and the Outline of 2035 Long-Term Plan Targets of the People's Republic of China.[222] In order to fulfill this target, a set of policies was released by the environmental ministry, some of which explicitly state that the GHG emissions have to be subject to the EIA permit system.[223] Subsequently, relevant pilot projects are carried out at the local level, which is expected to provide experiences in view of integrating GHG emissions into the EIA permit system.[224] In this vein, it can be expected that GHG emissions would be considered in emissions permitting through the coordination with the EIA permits. It is noted that GHG emissions are also expected to be subject to the emission trading system. On 14 March 2011, the 12th Five-Year Plan of National Economic and Social Development was adopted, which put forward the aim of establishing a trading system for GHG emissions.[225] Since then, pilot projects were carried out at the local level, including Beijing, Tianjin, Shanghai, Chongqing, Hubei, Guangdong,

[220] Administrative Regulation on Emissions Permitting, art 11(2).

[221] Jin Wang, *Environmental Law (in Chinese: 环境法学)* (Peking University Press 2018), 157.

[222] National People's Congress, the 14th Five-Year Plan of National Economic and Social Development and the Outline of 2035 Long-Term Plan Targets of the People's Republic of China (in Chinese: 中华人民共和国国民经济和社会发展第十四个五年规划和2035年远景目标纲要), 11 March 2021, Sect. 3.2 of Chap. 3.

[223] Ministry of Ecology and Environment, Guidelines on Strengthening Prevention and Control of Ecological Environment Sources for Construction Projects with High Energy Consumption and High Emissions (in Chinese: 关于统筹和加强应对气候变化与生态环境保护相关工作的指导意见 环综合〔2021〕4号), 11 January 2021; Ministry of Ecology and Environment, Guidelines on Coordinating and Strengthening Work related to Climate Change and Ecological and Environmental Protection (in Chinese: 关于加强高耗能、高排放建设项目生态环境源头防控的指导意见 环环评〔2021〕45号), 31 May 2021; and Ministry of Ecology and Environment, Notification of Pilot Carbon Emission Environmental Impact Assessment for Key Industrial Construction Projects (in Chinese: 关于开展重点行业建设项目碳排放环境影响评价试点的通知 环办环评函〔2021〕346号), 27 July 2021.

[224] Shekun Wang, 'On the Construction of China's Carbon Assessment System' (in Chinese: 论我国碳评价制度的构建) (2022) 16(02) Northern Legal Science 27, 30–31.

[225] National People's Congress, Outline of the 12th Five-Year Plan of National Economic and Social Development of the People's Republic of China (in Chinese: 中华人民共和国国民经济和社会发展第十二个五年规划纲要), 14 March 2011, point 22.

Shenzhen, and a set of local decrees, local rules, and local other normative documents were adopted.[226] At the national level, the environmental ministry adopted a ministerial rule—Administrative Rule on Carbon Emission Trading (for Trial Implementation) on 25 December 2020.[227] Therefore, it is expected that GHG emissions would be subject to both permit instruments and market-based instruments. In theory, a combined use of permit instruments and market-based instruments will lead to a sub-optimal outcome.[228] However, neither the Administrative Regulation on Emissions Permitting nor the Administrative Rule on Carbon Emission Trading (for Trial Implementation) clarifies the interaction between the permit instruments and the trading system for controlling the GHG emissions. In this vein, it is not clear how the combined use of permit instruments and market-based instruments for controlling carbon emissions may affect the implementation of integrated pollution prevention and control.

One concern of not requiring all the conditions of emissions control in the EIA permits to be reviewed in the process of emissions permitting is that the conditions for issuing the EIA permits and the conditions for issuing the emissions permits overlap. Specifically, both the Administrative Regulation on Environmental Protection for Construction Projects (2017) and the Administrative Regulation on Emissions Permitting require that the competent authorities should review whether applicants comply with emission standards.[229] The literature has criticized that the overlapping conditions in the EIA permits and the emissions permits can cause a duplicated review and thus lead to inefficiency.[230]

4.7.3.4 Interim Conclusion

From the above analysis, EIA permitting is actually the first stage that enables an integrated approach. It concerns not only emissions, but also other environmental impacts such as the ecological impacts, and it requires the goal of environmental quality improvement to be considered in setting EIA permit conditions, although the meaning of the criterion of environmental quality improvement is not clear. Some of the rules on EIA permitting are formulated in a relatively vague manner, and thus there is flexibility for the competent authorities, which makes case-specific decisions on EIA permitting possible from the perspective of integration. Meanwhile, generic

---

[226] See Jun Yang, Hongming Liu and Jianyu Zhang, 'Thinking on the legislation of the carbon emission trading system' (in Chinese: 关于碳排放权交易制度法治化完善的思考) (2021) 46(03) Environmental and Sustainable Development 26, Sect. 4.2.2.

[227] Ministry of Ecology and Environment, Administrative Rule on Carbon Emission Trading (for Trial Implementation) (in Chinese: 碳排放权交易管理办法(试行)), 25 December 2020.

[228] See Sect. 2.4 of Chap. 2.

[229] Administrative Regulation on Environmental Protection for Construction Projects (2017), art 11(3); Administrative Regulation on Emissions Permitting, art 11(2).

[230] Shekun Wang, 'Linking EIA and Emission Permits: Practice Development and Rule Reconstruction' (in Chinese: 环评与排污许可制度衔接的实践展开与规则重构) (2020) 5 Journal of Political Science and Law 151, 154.

emission standards are used in the EIA permitting, and thus it can be considered that a generic approach to comparing environmental effects caused by emissions is adopted by the EIA permit system.

A coordination mechanism between EIA permitting and emissions permitting has been established by the Administrative Regulation on Emissions Permitting. It can be expected that GHG emissions would be considered in emissions permits through the coordination with the EIA permits. It is also expected that GHG emissions are also subject to the emission trading system. However, no legislation clarifies the interaction between the permit instrument and the trading system for controlling GHG emissions. In this vein, it is not clear how the combined use of permit instruments and market-based instruments for controlling GHG emissions may affect the implementation of integrated pollution prevention and control.

A full coordination between EIA permits and emissions permits is not required. Even though other environmental protection measures concerning ecological issues are explicitly required in EIA permitting, they are not required to be considered in setting emissions permit conditions. A limited scope of coordination only concerning the emissions of key pollutants may lead to a relatively weak compliance with parts of the EIA permit conditions, and thus may weaken the protection for some environmental elements.

4.7.4 Rules on the Conditions Regarding Emission Standards

According to the Administrative Regulation on Emissions Permitting, the compliance with emission standards is one of the permit conditions. In order to understand whether or to what extent the conditions for emission standards can facilitate the implementation of an integrated approach, it is necessary to investigate the rules on setting emission standards.

The rules on setting emission standards are mainly laid down in article 16 of the Environmental Protection Law and chapter 4 of the Administrative Rules on Environmental Standards. According to article 16 of the Environmental Protection Law, emission standards can be classified as national emission standards and provincial emission standards. National emission standards shall be established by the environmental ministry and local emission standards shall be established by the people's governments at the provincial level.[231] According to the Administrative Rules on Environmental Standards, these emission standards include the standards for controlling emissions into the air, standards for controlling emissions into water, standards for controlling solid wastes, and standards for controlling noise, etc.[232] Hence, the establishment of national and provincial emission standards can be considered as the outcomes of the environmental weighing regarding various emissions in a generic

[231] Environmental Protection Law, art 16.

[232] Administrative Rules on Environmental Standards, art 21.

way. As mentioned in Sect. 4.7.2, no derogation clause is provided by the Administrative Regulation on Emissions Permitting. In this vein, it can be questioned whether or to what extent the absolute binding generic emission standards, which have a disadvantage, in theory, that an integrated approach in case-specific situations cannot be reached, would hinder the integration.

The following sub-sections analyze the procedure for adopting national emission standards and the procedure for adopting provincial emission standards to understand how environmental impacts caused by various emissions have to be weighed in a generic way.

4.7.4.1 Rules on Setting National Emission Standards

According to the Environmental Protection Law, national emission standards should be established by the environmental ministry on the basis of national environmental quality standards and the country's economic and technical conditions.[233] However, it is not clear how the national environmental quality standards and the country's economic and technical conditions should be considered by the environmental ministry in setting national emission standards. Zhou and Zhang considered that this provision is too general and thus can have hardly any practical influence.[234] In practice, the setting of national emission standards usually focus on the emissions subject to the mandatory emission reduction targets set in the national five-year plans and may neglect pollutants that are more harmful to the environment and human health.[235] In other words, the scope of national emission standards is relatively narrow. In addition, Shi pointed out that the environmental ministry has been putting economic development in the first place and thus failing to establish stringent emission standards.[236] Bai criticized that technical conditions are not always fully considered by the environmental ministry and, as a result, the development of emission standards usually lags behind the level of advanced techniques, but there are also

233 Environmental Protection Law, art 16.

234 Yangsheng Zhou and Guoning Zhang, 'Study on the Legislative Principles and Procedure of the Air Pollutants Emission Standards' (in Chinese: 大气污染物排放标准制定的法律原则和程序研究) (2015) 7(04) Chinese Journal of Environmental Management 43, 44.

235 Xiaofei Pei et al., 'Thoughts on Several Problems Concerning National Pollutant Emission Standards' (in Chinese: 关于国家污染物排放标准若干问题的思考) (2018) 46(20) Environmental Protection 7, 8. This paper presents an example that some sewage treatment facilities focus on controlling emissions of chemical oxygen demand and ammonia nitrogen, etc., but neglect the emissions of nilines, sulphides, and hexavalent chromium that are more harmful to the environment and human health.

236 Zhiyuan Shi, 'Problems of Environmental Standards and the Improvement of the Legal System' (in Chinese: 环境标准的现实困境) (2016) 01 Studies on Socialism with Chinese Characteristics 95, 96.

emission standards in a few cases that are too stringent to be achieved considering the specific technical conditions.[237]

In addition to the Environmental Protection Law, the Administrative Rules on Environmental Standards provides more rules on the procedure for adopting national emission standards.[238] It prescribes that the environmental ministry should:

(1) formulate a plan for drafting emission standards based on the needs of environmental protection;
(2) organize relevant public institutions, industrial associations, research institutions, or colleges and universities to participate in the drafting;
(3) solicit opinions from relevant national authorities, local people's governments and relevant departments, the industrial associations, relevant enterprises and public institutions, and the public; and
(4) organize experts to examine and review the draft.[239]

However, these rules are also formulated in a relatively vague manner. For example, it is not clear what is referred to by the needs of environmental protection. It is also not clear how the environmental ministry should organize relevant public institutions, industrial associations, research institutions, or colleges and universities, enterprises, the public and experts to participate in the drafting of national emission standards. No further concrete rules on setting national emission standards are provided by the other environmental legislation. In this vein, the environmental ministry is given quite a lot of flexibility in setting national emission standards, since the rules on how to establish national emission standards are too general to entail any binding effects. In practice, Cao criticized that the actual process of establishing national environmental standards is relatively closed, and the environmental ministry plays the main role.[240] Related to this, Zhang also observed that, under the government-centred procedure of adopting emission standards, the roles of industrial associations, research institutions, or colleges and universities in shaping the environmental standards are relatively weak in practice.[241] In addition, no case regarding the legality of national emission standards decided by the people's courts can be found.[242]

[237] Guixiu Bai, 'The Study on the Environmental Standards Based on Perspective of the Science of Law' (in Chinese: 基于法学视角的环境标准问题研究) (2012) 03 Journal of Political Science and Law 82, 84–85.

[238] Ministry of ecology and environment, Administrative Rules on Environmental Standards (in Chinese: 生态环境标准管理办法), 5 November 2020, art 7.

[239] Ibid.

[240] Jingen Cao, 'Deficiency of the Legal System of Environmental Standards and the Solution' (in Chinese: 环境标准制度的困境与出路) (2015) 23(11) Henan Social Sciences 15, 16.

[241] Qingbo Zhang, 'Reflection and Improvement of Environmental Standard System in China' (in Chinese: 行政组织法视角下环境标准制度的反思与完善) (2022) 02 SJTU Law Review 86, 90.

[242] According to article 53 of the Administrative Litigation Law, where an administrative decision is made on the basis of an other normative document formulated by a ministry of the State Council or by a local people's government or its department, and such other normative document is alleged as illegal, the plaintiff may request the court to review the legality of the other normative document. Also see Sect. 4.2.5 of this chapter.

4.7.4.2 Rules for Setting Provincial Emission Standards

This sub-section examines the rules for setting provincial emission standards. According to the Environmental Protection Law, the people's governments at the provincial level are allowed to establish emission standards for items not specified in the national emission standards or develop more stringent emission standards with regard to items already specified in the national emission standards.[243] The provincial emission standards shall be registered with the environmental ministry.[244] In other words, it is an option but not an obligation for the provincial people's governments to establish provincial emission standards. It has been observed in the literature that local environmental standards established by the provincial people's governments has been scarce, and most provincial people's governments even had not exercised their power to establish local environmental standards.[245] One reason is that local governments usually do not have a real incentive to develop more stringent environmental standards, since it may reduce local economic benefits.[246]

In order to address the insufficient development of local emission standards, on 10 April 2014, the environmental ministry published an other normative document—guidance on improving local environmental standards.[247] One of the most important requirements in this guidance is that, under the following circumstances, local emission standards should be established in the regions:

(1) the full implementation of national emission standards cannot ensure the achievement of environmental quality standards;
(2) in the key regions designated in environmental plans approved by the State Council;
(3) in areas with a high density of industries, severe environmental problems, and strong dissatisfaction of local people about the environmental problems;
(4) in the regions with special environmental problems caused by local special industries or special pollutants;

It is noted that the legality of national emission standards and also the legality of other environmental standards are seldom reviewed by the courts. An empirical analysis observed that one reason why the courts seldom review the legality of environmental standards may be that the plaintiffs seldom ask the courts to do so. See Zining Jin (2020), 162.

[243] Environmental Protection Law, art 16.

[244] Ibid.

[245] Xiaofei Pei, 'Current Situation, Problems and Countermeasures of Environmental Standard System in China' (in Chinese: 我国环境标准体系的现状、问题与对策) (2016) 14 Environmental Protection 16, 18.

[246] Jian Chen, Unified Standards: 'Solution to Cross-Province Key Regional Atmospheric Environmental Governance: Based on the NIMBY Expansion' (in Chinese: 统一标准是跨省重点区域大气污染治理的出路——基于邻避扩张的视角) (2017a) 19(2) Journal of Jiangsu University 61, 63–64.

[247] Ministry of Environmental Protection (abolished on 17 March 2018), Guidance of Improving Local Environmental Standards (in Chinese: 加强地方环保标准工作的指导意见 环发〔2014〕49号), 10 April 2014, point 1.

(5) national emission standards cannot adapt to the local environmental governance, and more clarification is needed.[248]

On 10 April 2017, the environmental ministry published the 13th National Five-Year Planning for Environmental Standards.[249] This document gave an assessment on the development of local environmental standards, in which it pointed out that the guidance on improving local environmental standards published on 10 April 2014 had motivated the development of local environmental standards.[250] Some of the requirements in the guidance on improving local environmental standards were incorporated with slight revisions into the Administrative Rules on Environmental Standards. According to the Administrative Rules on Environmental Standards, in the following circumstances, the provincial people's governments have to establish more stringent emission standards than the national standards:

(1) in the regions with a high density of industries and severe environmental problems;
(2) the full implementation of national emission standards cannot meet the local need of improving environmental quality;
(3) the national emission standards are not applicable due to the specific environmental conditions.[251]

In addition, the Administrative Rules on Environmental Standards also prescribes that the provincial people's governments should establish local emission standards for emissions from local specific industries and for emissions of local specific pollutants that are not covered by the national emission standards.[252] Whether the provincial people's governments exercise the duty of developing local emission standards is exempted from judicial review. It is questionable to what extent these rules can continue to encourage the provincial people's governments to establish local emission standards.

4.7.4.3 Interim Conclusion

The rules on setting emission standards are mainly laid down in article 16 of Environmental Protection Law and chapter 4 of the Administrative Rules on Environmental Standards. According to these rules, the national emission standards are set by the environmental ministry and the provincial emission standards are set by the provincial people's governments. Thus, the national and provincial emission standards can

[248] Ibid, point 1(2).

[249] Ministry of environmental protection (abolished on 17 March 2018), the 13th National Five-Year Planning for Environmental Protection Standards (in Chinese: 国家环境保护标准 "十三五" 发展规划 环科技〔2017〕49号), 10 April 2017.

[250] Ibid, 6. It found that until the end of the 12th Five-Year Plan, the number of local environmental standards had reached 148, increased by 85 compared to the number in the end of the 11th Five-Year Plan.

[251] Administrative Rules on Environmental Standards, art 40.

[252] Ibid.

be considered as the outcomes of environmental weighing in a generic way. No derogation from these generic emission standards is allowed by the Administrative Regulation on Emissions Permitting. Thus, these clearly set emission standards serve as the minimum requirements for emissions control. In this vein, it can be questioned whether or to what extent the absolute binding generic emission standards, which have a disadvantage that an integrated approach in case-specific situations cannot be reached, would hinder the implementation of integration in practice.

The rules on setting emission standards are formulated in a relatively vague manner. No evidence in practice has shown that the implementation of these vague rules on the setting of standards for various emissions can facilitate the establishment of emission standards in an integrated way. It is found that the scope of national emission standards is relatively limited, focusing on the emissions subject to the mandatory emission reduction targets set in the national five-year plans. In addition, the national emission standards are usually not stringent enough, although environmental quality standards are considered in setting these standards. This is because the environmental ministry has been placing more emphasis on economic development and does not always fully consider the development of techniques for environmental protection. Meanwhile, in a few cases, there have been emission standards that were too stringent to be technically possible in some specific situations. The procedure for adopting national emission standards is relatively closed, and in which the environmental ministry plays the main role, while the other participants, such as industrial associations, research institutions, or colleges and universities, play a relatively weak role in shaping emission standards.

Provincial emission standards are developed by the provincial people's governments, as they are responsible for establishing local emissions standards in certain circumstances. However, the relevant rules are formulated in a vague manner. In practice, the development of local emission standards has been insufficient. One reason for this is that local governments usually do not have a real incentive to develop more stringent environmental standards than the national ones, particularly given that they could reduce local economic benefits.

4.7.5 Rules on the Other Conditions

According to the Administrative Regulation on Emissions Permitting, the technical specifications for applications for and issuance of emissions permits, the total allowable quantities of emissions, and the special requirements for improving environmental quality provided by the local people's governments also serve as the basis for setting permit conditions.[253] In order to understand whether or to what extent the conditions determined on this basis can facilitate the implementation of an integrated approach, it is necessary to investigate the rules on setting technical specifications

[253] Administrative Regulation on Emissions Permitting, art 11(2).

for the application and issuance of emissions permits, the total allowable quantities of emissions, and the special requirements for improving environmental quality provided by the local people's governments in view of an integrated approach, which are provided in Sects. 4.7.5.1–4.7.5.3.

4.7.5.1 Rules on Setting Technical Specifications for Applications for and Issuance of Emissions Permits

According to the Administrative Regulation on Emissions Permitting, the technical specifications for applications for and issuance of emissions permits are established by the environmental ministry.[254] There are no further concrete rules on how the environmental ministry should establish the technical specifications for applications for and issuance of emissions permits. By 7 January 2022, the environmental ministry established seventy technical specifications for applications for and issuance of emissions permits for defined industries and activities.[255] The establishment of the technical specifications for applications for and issuance of emissions permits for defined industries and activities can be considered as the outcomes of the environmental weighing by the environmental ministry in a generic way.

Nevertheless, by investigating the contents of the technical specifications for applications for and issuance of emissions permits, it was found that, rather than clearly setting a certain emission limit value, these technical specifications provide that the emission levels should be set in the permit on the basis of national or provincial emission standards, water and air emission benchmarks, and the scale of production.[256] In this vein, it seems that the permitting authorities may need to exercise judgment, rather than just mechanically apply the technical specifications for applications for and issuance of emissions permits in deciding the permit conditions. From the perspective of an integrated approach, this issue is relevant with regard to what extent case-specific decisions by the competent authorities are possible in emissions permitting.[257] However, in practice, permitting authorities expressed that it is difficult to understand all of these technical specifications for applications for and issuance of emissions permits.[258] In addition, permitting authorities at the local level are faced with a shortage of resources, such as human resources, and, as a result,

---

[254] Ibid, art 47.

[255] See https://www.mee.gov.cn/ywgz/fgbz/bz/bzwb/pwxk/, assessed on 7 January 2022.

[256] Lu Wang and Ruolin Wang, 'Technical Specifications for Application and Issuance of Emissions Permits' (in Chinese: 排污许可证申请与核发技术规范), in Xiao Zhu and Lizhao Wen et al. (eds), *200 Questions and Answers about the Implementation of Legislation on Emissions Permitting* (in Chinese: 排污许可法律适用200问) (China Environmental Science Press 2017), 117–119. Also see Valerie J Karplus, Junjie Zhang and Jinhua Zhao, 'Navigating and Evaluating the Labyrinth of Environmental Regulation in China' (2021) 15(2) Review of Environmental Economics and Policy 300, 305.

[257] Empirical analysis is needed on this issue, while it is beyond the scope of this research.

[258] EU-China Environment Project (2021), 32.

the quality of most of the emissions permits granted is not high.[259] For example, it was found that in Liuzhou, ‘where the resources were very limited, …the contents of about 70% of the permits issued were wrong’.[260] In this vein, due to the shortage of knowledge, skills and resources, it is unlikely that permitting authorities can make proper case-specific permitting decisions.

4.7.5.2 Rules on Setting Total Allowable Quantities of Emissions

Although the Administrative Regulation on Emissions Permitting requires the total allowable quantities of emissions to be used in setting permit conditions, it does not provide concrete rules on how the total allowable quantities of emissions has to be determined. In addition to the Administrative Regulation on Emissions Permitting, there are vague provisions on the determination of total allowable quantities of emissions provided by Environmental Protection Law: the State Council is responsible for setting the targets of total emission control, and the provincial people’s governments are responsible for allocating the allowable quantities of emissions.[261] The Water Pollution Prevention and Control Law (2017) and the Air Pollution Prevention and Control Law (2018) also lay down similar vague provisions, and delegate the responsibility for the establishment of concrete rules for the total emission control to the State Council.[262] The State Council has not yet adopted legislation providing for concrete rules on total emission control. Since there are only vague provisions on the total emission control, there is no clear legal foundation for implementing the total emission control system in China.[263] In this vein, flexibility is given to permitting authorities, which makes case-specific decision-making possible.

4.7.5.3 Rules on Setting Special Requirements for Improving Environmental Quality

The Administrative Regulation on Emissions Permitting requires that, in the key regions and river basins where the national environmental quality standards are not achieved, the special requirements for improving environmental quality provided by the local people’s governments should be used in setting permit conditions.[264] From the perspective of an integrated approach, this requirement indicates that a certain

---

[259] Chao Yu, ‘Problems and Suggestions in the Current Process of Pollution Permit Application and Issuance’ (in Chinese: 现行排污许可证申请与核发过程中存在的问题及建议) (2020) 38(08) China Resources Comprehensive Utilization 154, 155.

[260] EU-China Environment Project (2021), 32.

[261] See Environmental Protection Law, art 44.

[262] Water Pollution Prevention and Control Law (2017), art 20 and Air Pollution Prevention and Control Law (2018), art 21.

[263] Xiangmin Xu, ‘The system of controlling total outcome of environmental activities’ (in Chinese: 论我国环境法中的总行为控制制度) (2015) 12 Law Science 29, 36–37.

[264] Administrative Regulation on Emissions Permitting, art 11(2).

level of environmental protection is addressed in emissions permitting. However, the Administrative Regulation on Emissions Permitting does not provide an explanation on what is meant by 'key regions and river basins'. It is also not clear what special requirements for improving environmental quality provided by the local people's governments means. Since the Administrative Regulation on Emissions Permitting is established in accordance with the Environmental Protection Law and other relevant laws,[265] the meaning of special requirements for improving environmental quality provided by the local people's governments can be derived from these laws.

According to the Environmental Protection Law, in the key regions and river basins that fail to meet national environmental quality standards, the local people's governments should formulate a plan to reach those environmental quality standards within a prescribed period and take measures to achieve the environmental quality standards within the prescribed period.[266] The Water Pollution Prevention and Control Law (2017), the Air Pollution Prevention and Control Law (2018), and the Law on Prevention and Control of Pollution from Noise also provide similar provisions on the plan for reaching national environmental quality standards within a prescribed period.[267] Therefore, it can be inferred that the special requirements for improving national environmental quality provided by the local people's governments at least include the requirements as set out in the local plan by local people's governments for reaching environmental quality standards. However, no more concrete rules are provided by the legislation in China in terms of how the local people's governments should formulate the local plan for reaching national environmental quality standards. Generally, the literature has criticized that the Administrative Regulation on Emissions Permitting does not provide for clear rules on the relationship between the implementation of emissions permitting and the achievement of environmental quality standards.[268] In this vein, it can be questioned whether the Administrative Regulation on Emissions Permitting truly requires the environmental effectiveness of integration.

4.7.5.4 Rules on Setting Conditions Regarding Pollution Prevention and Control Techniques

According to the Administrative Regulation on Emissions Permitting, the permitting authorities have to review whether the pollution prevention and control techniques applied by the applicants can ensure the achievement of emission standards, or whether the pollution prevention and control techniques are in accordance with the guidance of available techniques for pollution prevention and control.[269] The

---

265 Administrative Regulation on Emissions Permitting, art 1.

266 Environmental Protection Law, art 28.

267 Water Pollution Prevention and Control Law (2017), art 17; Air Pollution Prevention and Control Law (2018), art 14 and Law on Prevention and Control of Pollution from Noise, art 20.

268 Xueying Shi and Bowen Yang (2021), 81.

269 Administrative Regulation on Emissions Permitting, art 11(3).

guidance of available techniques of pollution prevention and control are established by the environmental ministry, which are indicative generic requirements. There is no legislation laying down rules on how this guidance should be established. By now, the environmental ministry has established twenty-four guidance documents of available techniques for pollution prevention and control for defined industries or activities.[270] The literature found that the emission levels associated with the techniques as listed in these guidance documents are more stringent than can be achieved by the national emission standards.[271]

Although the guidance on available techniques of pollution prevention and control are not binding, an empirical analysis on the cement industry found that, with the motivation of the Environmental Protection Tax Law of the People's Republic of China (hereinafter 'Environmental Protection Tax Law'),[272] in practice, cement industries are willing to apply the techniques as listed in the guidance on available techniques for pollution prevention and control to achieve more stringent emission levels than the national emission standards.[273] The environmental tax instrument can be considered a positive outcome of the interaction between the permit instrument and the market-based instruments. Environmental Protection Tax Law requires that the environmental authorities should submit the environmental information as documented in the emission permits to the tax authorities.[274] Except for this procedural requirement, neither the Administrative Regulation on Emissions Permitting nor the Environmental Protection Tax Law provides for substantive rules on how the emissions permit system has to be fine-tuned with the environmental protection tax system, such as sharpening the emissions conditions of the permit since the industry was capable of reducing emissions substantially.

4.7.6 Interim Conclusion

According to the Administrative Regulation on Emissions Permitting, setting permit conditions is based on various other environmental regulatory instruments, including

[270] See the website of environmental ministry: https://www.mee.gov.cn/ywgz/fgbz/bz/bzwb/kxxjszn/.

[271] Yaqiong Wang, Ying Wang et al., 'Permit Items through Negotiation in the Pollutant Discharge Permit System' (in Chinese: 排污许可制度中 "协商式"管理案例研究) (2020) 30(07) China Population, Resources and Environment 93, 95.

[272] Standing Committee of the National People's Congress, Environmental Protection Tax Law of the People's Republic of China (in Chinese: 中华人民共和国环境保护税法), 25 December 2016.

[273] Yaqiong Wang, Ying Wang et al. (2020), 93. In the case study, cement industries can benefit from a tax reduction by 50% if they apply the available techniques that can ensure the emissions of air pollutants 50% lower than the national and provincial emission standards. Also see Environmental Protection Tax Law, art 13.

[274] Environmental Protection Tax Law, art 15.

the EIA permitting, the emission standards, the technical specifications for application and issuance of emissions permits, the total allowable quantities of emissions, and the local instruments for achieving environmental quality standards. This shows a coordination mechanism adopted by the Administrative Regulation on Emissions Permitting. Coordination is relevant for substantive integration in the following aspects.

Regarding the scope of integration, as analyzed in Sect. 4.7.3, EIA permitting is actually the first stage in enabling an integrated approach. It concerns not only emissions, but also other environmental impacts such as ecological impacts. In particular, it can be expected that GHG emissions would be considered in EIA permitting. With a coordination mechanism between EIA permitting and emissions permitting, it can be expected that GHG emissions would be considered in emissions permitting. However, a full coordination between EIA permitting and emissions permitting is not required. Even though other environmental protection measures addressing ecological issues are explicitly required in the EIA permitting, they are not required to be considered in setting emissions permit conditions. A limited scope of coordination only concerning the emissions of key pollutants may lead to relatively weak compliance with parts of EIA permit conditions and thus may weaken the protection of some environmental elements and lead to a relatively narrow scope of integration.

Regarding the environmental effectiveness of integration, it is clear that a certain level of environmental quality must be considered in setting emissions permit conditions, since, as discussed in Sect. 4.7.5.3, in the key regions and river basins where the national environmental quality standards are not achieved, additional measures—special requirements for improving environmental quality as set out in the local planning—must be incorporated in the permit. However, no further concrete rules are provided by the legislation in China in terms of how the local people's governments should formulate the local planning to achieve national environmental quality standards. Meanwhile, Sects. 4.7.3 and 4.7.4 show that a certain level of environmental quality established as environmental quality standards must be considered in setting EIA permit conditions and in setting emission standards. However, the relevant rules on EIA permitting and setting emission standards regarding the achievement of environmental quality standards are also formulated in a vague manner.

Regarding the approaches to environmental trade-offs, the various decisions serving as the basis for setting permit conditions can be classified at least into two ways. First, the emission standards, the technical specifications for applications for and issuance of emissions permits, and the guidance on available techniques are generic requirements. These documents are established at the national level or at the provincial level for defined industries or activities, among which the requirements as set in the guidance on available techniques are indicative, and the others are binding. The rules on setting emissions permit conditions based on these generic requirements indicate that the generic approach for environmental weighing is adopted by the Administrative Regulation on Emissions Permitting. However, the rules on how these generic requirements have to be set by the environmental ministry or the provincial people's governments are too general. In this vein, it is not clear how various environmental impacts have to be weighed in the generic way by the competent authorities.

In practice, it is not evident that the implementation of these generic requirements can effectively facilitate the implementation of an integrated approach. For example, it was found that the national emission standards cover a limited scope of pollutants and are usually not stringent enough, because the environmental ministry has been placing more emphasis on economic development and not always fully considering the development of techniques for environmental protection. The development of local emission standards is also insufficient. On the other hand, it was also found that some emission standards are too stringent to be achieved with regard to the specific technical conditions. However, no derogation from these binding requirements is allowed by the Administrative Regulation on Emissions Permitting. In this vein, such absolute binding generic requirements establish a legal limit to the use of cost-effective approaches in case-specific situations. It can be further questioned to what extent such absolute binding generic requirements would also have a disadvantage that an integrated approach in case-specific situations cannot be reached. Indicative generic requirements are usually more stringent than binding generic requirements. The case of the cement industry shows that the environmental tax reduction can encourage the implementation of these more stringent emissions control measures.

Second, the case-specific approach for environmental weighing is also adopted by the Administrative Regulation on Emissions Permitting. The requirements of emissions control as set out in the EIA permits can be classified as case-specific requirements, since these requirements are set in the specific situations for which a permit is applied for. Most of the rules on setting EIA permit conditions are formulated in a relatively vague manner, and thus flexibility is afforded to the EIA permitting authorities, which makes case-specific decisions on EIA permitting possible. Thus, the rules on incorporating the requirements of emissions control as set out in EIA permits into the emissions permit conditions indicate that a case-specific approach for environmental weighing is adopted by the Administrative Regulation on Emissions Permitting. Nevertheless, the generic emission standards also have an important role in setting EIA permit conditions for controlling emissions, and thus they make the requirements as set out in the EIA permits less case specific. In addition, it was also found that some generic requirements set out in the technical specifications for applications for and issuance of emissions permits contain uncertainties, which require the permitting authorities to make case-specific decisions.[275] Furthermore, since there is no clear legal foundation for implementing the total emission control system in China, flexibility is afforded to permitting authorities in setting the total allowable quantities of emissions, which makes case-specific decisions possible. However, it is questionable whether such flexibility can guarantee case-specific decision-making serving integration, given the fact that, in practice, the permitting authorities usually lack enough knowledge, skills and resources to make effective case-specific decisions.[276]

With regard to the combined use of permit Instrument and market-based instruments for emissions control, it is expected that GHG emissions are subject to both

---

[275] See Sect. 4.7.5.1 of this chapter.

[276] See Sect. 4.7.5.1 of this chapter.

the emissions permit system and emission trading system.[277] However, no legislation clarifies the interaction between the permit instrument and the trading system for controlling GHG emissions.[278] In addition, a positive outcome of the interaction between the permit instrument and the market-based instrument can be found in practice: the environmental tax reduction can encourage the implementation of more stringent emissions control measures.[279] However, neither the Administrative Regulation on Emissions Permitting nor the Environmental Protection Tax Law provides for substantive rules on how the emissions permit system has to be combined with the environmental protection tax system.[280] In this vein, it is not clear how and to what extent the combined use of permit instruments and market-based instruments for controlling emissions may affect the implementation of integrated pollution prevention and control.

4.8 Conclusion on China's Emissions Permit System Towards an Integrated Environmental Permit

This chapter aims to address the question of how the emissions permit system has been developed in China to implement integrated pollution and prevention control. In order to address this question, this chapter provides an in-depth legal examination of the Administrative Regulation on Emissions Permitting and other relevant legislation on the basis of the conceptual framework of an integrated environmental permit as identified in Chap. 2. Below, a conclusion will be provided.

4.8.1 Substantive Integration Under China's Emissions Permit System

This section provides answers to the three questions regarding substantive integration: the scope of integration, the environmental effectiveness of integration, and the options for environmental trade-offs.

4.8.1.1 The Scope of Integration Under China's Emissions Permit System

From the perspective of the scope of integration, what is the scope of environmental issues subject to the emissions permit system as developed by the Administrative

277 See Sect. 4.7.3.3 of this chapter.

278 Ibid.

279 See Sect. 4.7.5.4 of this chapter.

280 Ibid.

Regulation on Emissions Permitting? Section 4.4 shows that the objective of the Administrative Regulation on Emissions Permitting—to control emissions to protect and to improve the environment—is formulated in a vague manner without giving precise instructions as to the scope of integration. Furthermore, the Administrative Regulation on Emissions Permitting establishes criteria for classifying entities subject to emissions permitting into two types: (1) entities that produce a relatively substantial quantity of emissions, or have significant environmental impacts should be subject to key management; (2) entities that produce a relatively small quantity of emissions or have mild environmental impacts should be subject to simplified management.[281] However, there is no further explanation on what accounts for a relatively substantial/small quantity of emissions or significant/mild environmental impacts.[282] Since the objective of the Administrative Regulation on Emissions Permitting does not give precise instructions, the scope of integration as pursued by the Administrative Regulation on Emissions Permitting should be derived from its legal basis—the laws including the Environmental Protection Law, the Administrative Permit Law, and a set of sectoral laws on pollution control that prescribes permit regulation for controlling emissions.[283] By investigating the legal basis for establishing the Administrative Regulation on Emissions Permitting, it was found that the emissions permit system in China at least covers emissions into the water, soil, air and marine environment, as well as pollution caused by industrial solid waste and also industrial noise.[284]

In terms of the other environmental issues, it was found that the use of water, and the use of energy are not integrated into the emissions permit.[285] There are other environmental issues that are not explicitly regulated by the laws, such as GHG emissions, and it is possible to subject these environmental issues to the emissions permitting, if it is explicitly required by the Administrative Regulation on Emissions Permitting.[286] Therefore, the scope of integration as pursued by the Administrative Regulation on Emissions Permitting should also be derived from its detailed rules. The examination of the rules on the application for a permit shows that a relatively broad scope of environmental information has to be collected by operators to apply for an emissions permit, addressing not just emissions, but also other environmental relevant elements, such as the use of raw materials.[287] However, it is questionable whether this requirement could be effectively implemented in practice, given the fact that the applicants are usually faced with the a lack of knowledge and skills in their process of applying for the emissions permit.[288] Although the rules on the application for a permit address a broad scope of environmental issues, the rules on

---

281 See Sect. 4.4.2 of this chapter.

282 Ibid.

283 See Sect. 4.4.2 of this chapter.

284 See Sect. 4.4.2.1 of this chapter.

285 See Sect. 4.4.2.2 of this chapter.

286 See Sect. 4.4.2.3 of this chapter.

287 See Sect. 4.5.2 of this chapter.

288 Ibid.

setting permit conditions only address emissions.[289] Although it is possible to subject GHG emissions to the emissions permitting,[290] the Administrative Regulation on Emissions Permitting does not provide a clear requirement. Nevertheless, it can be expected that GHG emissions would be considered in emissions permitting through coordination with EIA permitting.[291]

Hence, the answer to question 1 is: although the concrete scope of environmental issues subject to the permit system as prescribed by the Administrative Regulation on Emissions Permitting cannot be clearly perceived, it at least concerns emissions into the water, air, soil and marine environment, as well as pollution caused by industrial solid waste and industrial noise. Concerning the other environmental issues, the use of water, and the use of energy are not integrated into the emissions permit. In addition, it can be expected that GHG emissions would be considered in emissions permitting.

4.8.1.2 The Environmental Effectiveness of Integration Under China's Emissions Permit System

In view of the environmental effectiveness of integration, what is the level of environmental quality as a whole required by the emissions permit system as developed by the Administrative Regulation on Emissions Permitting? Section 4.4 shows that, while the objective of the Administrative Regulation on Emissions Permitting—to control emissions to protect and to improve the environment—is hollow, its drafting history indicates that the legislator intended to establish an emissions permit system with the pursuit of a certain level of environmental quality.[292] More specifically, Sect. 4.7.5.3 shows that the Administrative Regulation on Emissions Permitting requires concrete levels of protection for specific environmental media to be achieved by the emissions permit by suggesting that additional measures, namely the special requirements for improving environmental quality provided by the local people's governments, have to be included in the permit. However, no further concrete rules are provided by the legislation in China in terms of how local people's governments should formulate the special requirements for reaching national environmental quality standards.[293] Meanwhile, the EIA permit conditions and the emission standards are required to be considered in setting emissions permit conditions.[294] Sections 4.7.3 and 4.7.4 show that certain levels of environmental quality established as national or provincial environmental quality standards are required to be considered in setting EIA permit conditions and in setting emission standards, but the relevant rules on EIA permitting

[289] See Sect. 4.7 of this chapter.

[290] See Sect. 4.4 of this chapter.

[291] See Sect. 4.7.3 of this chapter. The findings regarding the coordination with EIA permitting will be discussed further in view of procedural integration later in this section.

[292] See Sect. 4.4 of this chapter.

[293] See Sect. 4.7.5.3 of this chapter.

[294] See Sect. 4.7.2 of this chapter.

and setting emission standards regarding the achievement of environmental quality standards are also formulated in a vague manner.

Hence, the answer to question 2 is: according to the Administrative Regulation on Emissions Permitting, concrete levels of environmental quality for specific media (established as the environmental quality standards) are required to be achieved by the emissions permit. However, the rules on how to achieve these environmental quality standards are formulated in a relatively vague manner.

4.8.1.3 The Options for Environmental Trade-Offs Under China's Emissions Permit System

In view of the incommensurability of environmental goods, what are the options adopted by the Administrative Regulation on Emissions Permitting to make environmental trade-offs? Section 4.7 shows that the basis for setting permit conditions can be classified in at least two types. First, the emission standards, the technical specifications for application and issuance of emissions permits, and the guidance of available techniques are generic requirements. These documents are established at the national level or at the provincial level for defined industries or activities, among which the requirements as set in the guidance of available techniques are indicative and the others are binding. The rules for setting emissions permit conditions on the basis of these generic requirements indicate that the generic approach for environmental weighing is adopted by the Administrative Regulation on Emissions Permitting. However, the rules on how these generic requirements have to be set by the environmental ministry or provincial people's governments are too general. In this vein, it is not clear how various environmental impacts have to be weighed in the generic way by the competent authorities. In practice, it is not evident that the implementation of these generic requirements can effectively facilitate the implementation of an integrated approach. For example, it is found that the national emission standards cover a limited scope of pollutants and are usually not stringent enough, because the environmental ministry has been putting more emphasis on economic development and not always fully considering the development of techniques for environmental protection. The development of local emission standards is also insufficient. On the other hand, it was also found that some emission standards are too stringent to be achieved with regard to the specific technical conditions. However, no derogation from these binding requirements is allowed by the Administrative Regulation on Emissions Permitting. In this vein, such absolute binding generic requirements establish a legal limit to the use of cost-effective approaches in case-specific situations. It can be further questioned to what extent such absolute binding generic requirements would also have a disadvantage that an integrated approach in case-specific situations cannot be reached. Indicative generic requirements are usually more stringent than the binding generic requirements. The case of the cement industry shows that the environmental tax reduction can encourage the implementation of these more stringent emissions control measures, which can be considered as an example of a positive outcome of the interaction between the permit instrument and the market-based instrument.

Second, the case-specific approach for environmental weighing is also adopted by the Administrative Regulation on Emissions Permitting. The requirements of emissions control as set out in the EIA permits can be classified as case-specific requirements, since these requirements are set in the specific situations for which a permit is applied for. Most of the rules on setting EIA permit conditions are formulated in a relatively vague manner, and thus flexibility is afforded to the EIA permitting authorities, which makes case-specific decisions on EIA permitting possible. Thus, the rules of incorporating the requirements of emissions control as set out in EIA permits in the emissions permit conditions indicate that a case-specific approach for environmental weighing is adopted by the Administrative Regulation on Emissions Permitting. Nevertheless, the generic emission standards also have an important role in the setting of EIA permit conditions for controlling emissions and thus make the requirements as set in the EIA permits less case specific. In addition, it was also found that some generic requirements set out in the technical specifications for applications for and issuance of emissions permits contain uncertainties, which require the permitting authorities to make case-specific decisions.[295] Moreover, since there is no clear legal foundation for implementing the total emission control system in China, flexibility is afforded to permitting authorities in setting the total allowable quantities of emissions that also have to be used in setting permit conditions, which makes case-specific decisions possible. However, it is questionable whether such flexibility can guarantee case-specific decision-making that serves integration, given the fact that, in practice, the permitting authorities usually lack enough knowledge, skills, and resources to make effective case-specific decisions.[296]

Hence, considering the incommensurability of environmental goods, the answer to question 3 is: a combined use of the generic approach and case-specific approach is adopted by the Administrative Regulation on Emissions Permitting to make environmental trade-offs. The generic approach is indicated by a set of generic requirements established at the national and provincial levels. Some of these generic requirements are binding and no derogation is allowed. It can be questioned to what extent such absolute binding generic requirements would have a disadvantage that an integrated approach in case-specific situations cannot be reached, particularly given the fact that, in practice, some generic requirements are too stringent to be achieved with regard to the specific technical conditions. The case-specific approach is indicated by a set of vaguely formulated rules that give flexibility to the permitting authorities. However, it is questionable whether such flexibility can guarantee case-specific decision-making that serves integration, given the fact that, in practice, the permitting authorities usually lack enough knowledge, skills, and resources to make effective case-specific decisions.

---

[295] See Sect. 4.7.5.1 of this chapter.

[296] See Sect. 4.7.5.1 of this chapter.

4.8.2 *Procedural Integration Under China's Emissions Permit System*

There are two questions regarding procedural integration: does the Administrative Regulation on Emissions Permitting require one permit procedure, or does it allow for several permit procedures; and is there a coordination mechanism imposed by the Administrative Regulation on Emissions Permitting? Section 4.6 shows that one permit procedure covering various emissions was adopted by the Administrative Regulation on Emissions Permitting. Meanwhile, the coordination mechanism is adopted in the Administrative Regulation on Emissions Permitting, which can be illustrated by the rules for the EIA permit, the emission standards, and the total allowable quantities of emissions to be submitted for the application for emissions permits,[297] as well as by the rules on setting permit conditions on the basis of decisions made through various other environmental regulatory instruments, including EIA permitting, emission standards, technical specifications for applications for and issuance of emissions permits, total emission control, and local instruments for achieving environmental quality standards.[298] However, the Administrative Regulation on Emissions Permitting does not require full coordination but addresses emissions only: even though other environmental protection measures addressing ecological issues are explicitly required in EIA permitting, they are not required to be considered in setting permit conditions.[299] Hence, the answers to questions 4 and 5 are: in view of procedural integration, the Administrative Regulation on Emissions Permitting establishes one procedure covering various emissions, but it also requires coordination with other regulatory instruments. However, full coordination is not required addressing emissions only.

4.8.3 *Organizational Integration Under China's Emissions Permit System*

From the perspective of organizational integration, the answer to question 6 is: the Administrative Regulation on Emissions Permitting has established a single authority responsible for issuing emissions permits, which indicates a high degree of organizational integration.[300]

---

[297] See Sect. 4.5 of this chapter.

[298] See Sect. 4.7 of this chapter.

[299] See Sect. 4.7.3.3 of this chapter.

[300] See Sect. 4.6 of this chapter.

4.8.4 The Interaction Between the Emissions Permit System and Market-Based Instruments for Pollution Control in China

Concerning the interaction between emissions permitting and market-based instruments for pollution control, Sect. 4.7.5.4 shows that, although a positive outcome of the interaction between the permit instrument and the market-based instrument in the form of the environmental tax instrument can be found in practice (the environmental tax reduction can encourage the implementation of more stringent emissions control measures), neither the Administrative Regulation on Emissions Permitting nor the Environmental Protection Tax Law provide for substantive rules on how the emissions permit system has to be combined with the environmental protection tax system. In addition, it is expected that GHG emissions would be subject to both the emissions permit system and the emission trading system, but no legislation clarifies the interaction between the permit instrument and the trading system for controlling the GHG emissions.[301] Hence, the answer to question 7 is: it is not clear how the emissions permit system as established by the Administrative Regulation on Emissions Permitting has to be combined with the market-based instruments for pollution control from the perspective of integration.

In summary, the Administrative Regulation on Emissions Permitting establishes an emissions permit system that regulates various emissions into different environmental media through a combined use of a generic approach and a case-specific approach to environmental trade-offs, to achieve certain levels of environmental quality established as environmental quality standards. Meanwhile, the Administrative Regulation on Emissions Permitting establishes one permit procedure that regulates various emissions by single authorities. Thus, it has the features of an integrated environmental permit. The next chapter will bring the findings of this and the previous chapters together by analyzing to what extent this emissions permit system with the features of an integrated environmental permit, considering the EU regulatory experiences towards integration and seen from the perspective of the specific Chinese situation, provides possibilities for or barriers to the implementation of integrated pollution prevention and control.

References

Bai, G. (2012). The study on the environmental standards based on perspective of the science of law (in Chinese: 基于法学视角的环境标准问题研究). *03 Journal of Political Science and Law, 82*, 84–85.

Cao, J. (2015). Deficiency of the legal system of environmental standards and the solution' (in Chinese: 环境标准制度的困境与出路). *Henan Social Sciences, 23*(11).

[301] See Sect. 4.7.3.3 of this chapter.

Chen, H. (2014). The normative effectiveness and legalization path of 'eco-red line" (in Chinese: "生态红线"的规范效力与法治化路径———解释论与立法论的双重展开). *Modern Law Science, 36*(4).

Chen, H. (2016). Register system or permit system: regulation on the access to the carbon emissions activities (in Chinese: 许可抑或备案:我国碳排放准入监管的法制进路). *Law Review, 34*(5).

Chen, J. (2017a). Unified standards: 'solution to cross-province key regional atmospheric environmental governance: Based on the NIMBY expansion' (in Chinese: 统一标准是跨省重点区域大气污染治理的出路——基于邻避扩张的视角). *Journal of Jiangsu University, 19*(2).

Chen, W. (2017b). Research on the application of environmental quality standards in the tort law (in Chinese: 环境质量标准的侵权法适用研究). *China Legal Science, 01*.

Deng, K. (2010). Research on judicial review of technical standards (in Chinese: 论技术标准的司法审查). *Science Technology and Law, 87*(5).

Department of Planning and Finance in the Ministry of Ecology and Environment, The reform of the emission permit system in China: History, Reality, and the Future (in Chinese: 中国排污许可制度改革:历史、现实和未来), China Environment News, 12 September 2018, 003.

'Emissions Permits Portal' (in Chinese: 全国排污许可证管理信息平台). http://permit.mee.gov.cn/permitExt/defaults/default-index!getInformation.action. Accessed 11 Jan 2022

EU-China Environment Project, China's Regulatory Framework on Pollutant Discharge Permits: An Overview on the Formulation and Implementation of Pollutant Discharge Permits in China and the Sharing of EU experience of Permitting, 2 February 2021. https://www.clientearth.org/latest/documents/china-s-regulatory-framework-on-pollutant-discharge-permits/. Accessed 2 April 2022

Gao, Q., & Whittaker, S. (2019). Standing to sue beyond individual rights: Who should Be eligible to bring environmental public interest litigation in China? *Transnational Environmental Law, 8*(2), 327–347.

Gong, X. (2016). Auxiliary legislation and the implementation of Environmental Protection Law (in Chinese: 配套立法与新《环境保护法》的实施). *Social Science in Chinese Higher Education Institutions* (04).

Guidance documents of available techniques for pollution prevention and control. https://www.mee.gov.cn/ywgz/fgbz/bz/bzwb/kxxjszn/. Accessed 3 May 2024.

Hao, Y., & Hao, C. (2015). Problems and Suggestions on the Compilation of Environmental Impact Statements (in Chinese: 环境影响报告书编制中存在问题与建议). *Environmental Impact Assessment 37*(02).

He, X. (2020). In the name of legitimacy and efficiency: Evaluating China's legal reform on EIA. *Journal of Environmental Law, 32*(3), 441–469.

Hu, Q., Li, X., Lin, A., Qi, W., Li, X., & Yang, X. J. (2018). Total emission control policy in China. *Environmental Development, 25*, 126–129.

Jiang, M. (2013). *The study on the institutions of environmental administrative license of our country* (in Chinese: 我国环境行政许可制度研究). Dissertation to obtain the degree of Doctor at Southwest University of Political Science & Law.

Jin, Z. (2017). Environmental management system in China: the target achieving process. In *Environmental policy and governance in China* (pp. 69–88). Springer.

Jin, Z. (2020). Judicial review of administrative decision based on science: Observations on Lawsuits Concerning EIA Approval (in Chinese: 科技专业性行政行为的司法审查——基于环境影响评价审批诉讼的考察). *Studies in Law and Business, 37*(03).

Jin, Z. (2021). Knowledge verse power: At the Centre of China's EIA Legal System (in Chinese: 专业知识与行政权力:我国环评审批的制度定位). *Modern Law Science, 43*(3).

Karplus, V. J., Zhang, J., & Zhao, J. (2021). Navigating and evaluating the labyrinth of environmental regulation in China. *Review of Environmental Economics and Policy, 15*(2), 300–322.

Legislative Affairs Commission of the Standing Committee of National People's Congress. (2014). *A paraphrase on environmental protection law* (in Chinese: 中华人民共和国环境保护法释义). Law Press China.

Li, L. (1992). The technical framework of the pilot projects of the air emission permit system (in Chinese: 试行排放大气污染物许可证制度的技术框架). *China Environment Management, 5*.

Li, L. (1992). The implementation of the system of total air pollutant load control (in Chinese: 推行大气污染物排放总量控制试行大气排污许可证制度). *Research of Environmental Sciences, 5*(6), 49.

Li, Y., Du, Y., Chai, X., Zhao, P. (2015). The overall management of pollution sources: Promoting the link of the system of environmental impact assessment and pollution permit' (in Chinese: 污染源全面管理的思考——以促进环境影响评价与排污许可制度衔接为核心). *Environmental Protection, 43*(12).

Li, X. (2016). Research on reforming the emissions permit system—From the perspective of allocating environmental capacity (in Chinese: 排污许可法律制度重构研究——环境容量资源配置视角). *Journal of China University of Geosciences (Social Sciences Edition), 16*(2).

Li, Z. (2005). The challenges of China's discharge permit system and effective solutions. *Temple Journal of Science, Technology & Environmental Law, 24*, 375.

Li, Z. (2021). Reconstruction of China's legal system of eco-environmental protection from the perspective of land and sea coordination (in Chinese: 陆海统筹视阈下我国生态环境保护法律体系重构). *Academic Journal of Zhongzhou, 06*.

Lin, P. (2021). Research on the problems of the application for emissions permits for paper mills and suggestions (in Chinese: 浅析制浆造纸行业排污许可申报常见问题及处理方法). *Straits Science, 08*.

Liu, X. (2016). Judicial application of uncertain legal concept in classification of EIA: A study of 56 cases of EIA (in Chinese: 环境影响评价分类中不确定法律概念的司法适用——基于56个环境影响评价案例的实证考察). *Environmental Pollution & Control, 38*(11).

Ma, Y. (2019). Dynamics in central–local division of the authority of EIA approval in China. *Journal of Environmental Law, 31*(1), 29–57.

Martinek, M., Martinek, M., & Reschke. (2018). *Experimental legislation in China between efficiency and legality*. Springer International Publishing.

McElwee, C. (2010). *Environmental law in China: Mitigating risk and ensuring compliance*. Oxford University Press.

Mei, H. (2017). What are the reasons for emissions permit system serving as a core of environmental regulation on stationary sources? (in Chinese: 排污许可制度何以成为点源环境治理的核心制度). *Journal of Zhengzhou University (Philosophy and Social Sciences Edition), 50*(05).

Ministry of Environmental Protection. (abolished on 17 March 2018). *Guidance of improving local environmental standards* (in Chinese: 加强地方环保标准工作的指导意见 环发〔2014〕49号), 10 April 2014.

Ministry of Environmental Protection. (abolished on 17 March 2018). *Provisional regulation on emissions permitting* (in Chinese: 排污许可证管理暂行规定 环水体〔2016〕186号), 23 December 2016.

Ministry of environmental protection. (abolished on 17 March 2018). *The 13th national five-year planning for environmental protection standards* (in Chinese: 国家环境保护标准"十三五"发展规划 环科技〔2017〕49号), 10 April 2017.

Ministry of Environmental Protection. (abolished on 17 March 2018). *Administrative measures on emissions permitting (for trial implementation)* (in Chinese: 排污许可管理办法(试行)), 10 January 2018 (no longer in force).

Ministry of Ecology and Environment, Technical Guidelines for Environmental Impact Assessment—Atmospheric Environment (in Chinese: 环境影响评价技术导则 大气环境 HJ 2.2-2018), 31 July 2018.

Ministry of Ecology and Environment, Technical Guidelines for Environmental Impact Assessment—Soil Environment (for Trail Implementation) (in Chinese: 环境影响评价技术导则 土壤环境(试行) HJ 964—2018), 13 September 2018.

Ministry of Ecology and Environment, Technical Guidelines for Environmental Impact Assessment Surface Water Environment (in Chinese: 环境影响评价技术导则 地表水环境 HJ 2.3—2018), 30 September 2018.

Ministry of Ecology and Environment, Draft of Administrative Regulation on Emissions Permitting (in Chinese: 排污许可管理条例(草案征求意见稿)), 5 November 2018.
Ministry of Environmental Protection. (abolished on 18 March 2018). Press briefing by the Ministry of Environmental Protection official on Administrative Rule on Emissions Permitting (for trial implementation) (in Chinese: 环境保护部有关负责人就《排污许可管理办法(试行)》有关问题答记者问), 17 January 2018. http://www.mee.gov.cn/gkml/sthjbgw/qt/201801/t20180117_429822.htm. Accessed 14 Oct 2020.
Ministry of Ecology and Environment, Administrative Rules on Environmental Standards (in Chinese: 生态环境标准管理办法), 5 November 2020.
Ministry of Ecology and Environment, Catalogue of Classified Construction Projects subject to EIA (2021) (in Chinese: 建设项目环境影响评价分类管理名录(2021年版)部令 第16号), 30 November 2020.
Ministry of Ecology and Environment, Administrative Rule on Carbon Emission Trading (for Trial Implementation) (in Chinese: 碳排放权交易管理办法(试行)), 25 December 2020.
Ministry of Ecology and Environment, Guidelines on Strengthening Prevention and Control of Ecological Environment Sources for Construction Projects with High Energy Consumption and High Emissions (in Chinese: 关于统筹和加强应对气候变化与生态环境保护相关工作的指导意见 环综合〔2021〕4号), 11 January 2021.
Ministry of Ecology and Environment, Guidelines on Coordinating and Strengthening Work related to Climate Change and Ecological and Environmental Protection (in Chinese: 关于加强高耗能、高排放建设项目生态环境源头防控的指导意见 环环评〔2021〕45号), 31 May 2021.
Ministry of Ecology and Environment, Notification of Pilot Carbon Emission Environmental Impact Assessment for Key Industrial Construction Projects (in Chinese: 关于开展重点行业建设项目碳排放环境影响评价试点的通知 环办环评函〔2021〕346号), 27 July 2021.
Ministry of Ecology and Environment, Technical Guidelines for Noise Impact Assessment (in Chinese: 环境影响评价技术导则 声环境 HJ 2.4—2021), 24 December 2021.
Ministry of Ecology and Environment, Technical Guidelines for Environmental Impact assessment—Ecological Impact (in Chinese: 环境影响评价技术导则 生态影响 HJ 19—2022), 15 January 2022.
National People's Congress, the 9th Five-Year Plan of National Economic and Social Development and the Outline of 2010 Long-Term Plan Targets of the People's Republic of China (in Chinese: 中华人民共和国国民经济和社会发展"九五"计划和2010年远景目标纲要), 17 March 1996.
National People's Congress, Outline of the 11th Five-Year Plan of National Economic and Social Development of the People's Republic of China (in Chinese: 中华人民共和国国民经济和社会发展第十一个五年规划纲要), 14 March 2006.
National People's Congress, Outline of the 12th Five-Year Plan of National Economic and Social Development of the People's Republic of China (in Chinese: 中华人民共和国国民经济和社会发展第十二个五年规划纲要), 14 March 2011.
National People's Congress, Legislation Law of the People's Republic of China (in Chinese: 中华人民共和国立法法), 15 March 2015.
National People's Congress, Outline of the 13th Five-Year Plan of National Economic and Social Development of the People's Republic of China (in Chinese: 中华人民共和国国民经济和社会发展第十三个五年规划纲要), 16 March 2016.
National People's Congress, Constitution of People's Republic of China (in Chinese: 中华人民共和国宪法), 11 March 2018.
National People's Congress, the 14th Five-Year Plan of National Economic and Social Development and the Outline of 2035 Long-Term Plan Targets of the People's Republic of China (in Chinese: 中华人民共和国国民经济和社会发展第十四个五年规划和2035年远景目标纲要), 11 March 2021.
National People's Congress, Organization Law of the People's Republic of China for Local People's Congress and Local People's Governments (in Chinese: 中华人民共和国地方各级人民代表大会和地方各级人民政府组织法), 11 March 2022.

Pan, J. (2020). Legal review and steering of China's emission permit setting (in Chinese: 我国排污许可设定法律审视及转向). *Journal of Hohai University (Philosophy and Social Sciences), 22*(01).

Pei, X. (2016). Current situation, problems and countermeasures of environmental standard system in China (in Chinese: 我国环境标准体系的现状、问题与对策). *Environmental Protection, 14.*

Pei, X., et al. (2018). Thoughts on several problems concerning national pollutant emission standards (in Chinese: 关于国家污染物排放标准若干问题的思考). *Environmental Protection, 46*(20).

'Refusal'. (in Chinese: 不予审批). https://www.mee.gov.cn/searchnew/?searchword=%E4%B8%8D%E4%BA%88%E6%89%B9%E5%87%86. Accessed 8 March 2022.

Ross, L. (2004). Rethinking government approvals: The new administrative licensing law. *China Law & Practice, 5*, 30.

Shen, B., & Li, Z. (2018). Discussion on the development of environmental permit system in China compared with Germany (in Chinese: 从中德比较论我国环境许可制度的发展). *Chinese Journal of Environmental Management, 10*(04).

Shi, X., & Yang, B. (2021). Research on legislative coordination and normative co-governance structure of China's emission permit management system (in Chinese: 我国排污许可管理制度的立法协同与规范共治结构研究). *Journal of Dalian University of Technology (Social Sciences), 42*(05).

Shi, Z. (2016). Problems of environmental standards and the improvement of the legal system' (in Chinese: 环境标准的现实困境). *Studies on Socialism with Chinese Characteristics, 01.*

Song, J. (2018). Research on regulation of energy technology from the perspective of sustainable development (in Chinese: 可持续发展视域下的能源技术规制研究). *Journal of CUPL, 04.*

Special Research Group regarding Emissions Permitting, 30 Questions and Answers about Implementation Plan for the Permit System for Controlling Emissions (in Chinese: 《控制污染物排放许可制实施方案》30问), 5 January 2017, point 2. https://www.mee.gov.cn/zcwj/zcjd/201701/t20170105_394014.shtml. Accessed 12 April 2022.

Standing Committee of the National People's Congress, Air Pollution Prevention and Control Law of the People's Republic of China. (2000) (in Chinese: 中华人民共和国大气污染防治法(2000修订)), 29 April 2000 (no longer in force).

Standing Committee of the National People's Congress, Renewable Energy Law of the People's Republic of China (in Chinese: 中华人民共和国可再生能源法), 26 December 2009.

Standing Committee of the National People's Congress, Cleaner Production Promotion Law of the People' Republic of China (in Chinese: 中华人民共和国清洁生产促进法), 29 June 2002 and its latest amendment adopted on 29 February 2012.

Standing Committee of the National People's Congress, Environmental Protection Law of the People's Republic of China (in Chinese: 中华人民共和国环境保护法), 24 April 2014.

Standing Committee of the National People's Congress, Water Law of the People's Republic of China (in Chinese: 中华人民共和国水法), 2 July 2016.

Standing Committee of the National People's Congress, Environmental Protection Tax Law of the People's Republic of China (in Chinese: 中华人民共和国环境保护税法), 25 December 2016.

Standing Committee of the National People's Congress, Water Pollution Prevention and Control Law of the People's Republic of China (2017) (in Chinese: 中华人民共和国水污染防治法(2017修正)), 27 June 2017.

Standing Committee of the National People's Congress, Administrative Litigation Law of the People's Republic of China (in Chinese: 中华人民共和国行政诉讼法), 27 August 2017.

Standing Committee of the National People's Congress, Marine Environment Protection Law of the People's Republic of China (in Chinese: 中华人民共和国海洋环境保护法), 23 August 1982 and its latest amendment adopted on 24 October 2023.

Standing Committee of the National People's Congress, Soil Pollution Prevention and Control Law of the People's Republic of China (in Chinese: 中华人民共和国土壤污染防治法), 31 August 2018.

Standing Committee of the National People's Congress, Circular Economy Promotion Law of the People's Republic of China (in Chinese: 中华人民共和国循环经济促进法), 26 October 2018.
Standing Committee of the National People's Congress, Energy Conservation Law of the People's Republic of China (in Chinese: 中华人民共和国节约能源法), 26 October 2018.
Standing Committee of the National People's Congress, Air Pollution Prevention and Control Law of the People's Republic of China (2018) (in Chinese: 中华人民共和国大气污染防治法(2018修正)), 26 October 2018.
Standing Committee of the National People's Congress, Administrative Permit Law of the People's Republic of China (in Chinese: 中华人民共和国行政许可法), 23 April 2019.
Standing Committee of the National People's Congress, Law of the People's Republic of China on Pollution Prevention and Control caused by the Solid Wastes. (2020). (in Chinese: 中华人民共和国固体废物污染环境防治法(2020修订)), 1 September 2020.
Standing Committee of the National People's Congress, Law of the People's Republic of China on Prevention and Control of Pollution From Noise (in Chinese: 中华人民共和国噪声污染防治法), 24 December 2021.
State Council, Implementation Rules on Water Pollution Prevention and Control Law of the People's Republic of China (in Chinese: 中华人民共和国水污染防治法实施细则), 20 March 2000 (no longer in force).
State Council, Implementation Plan for the Permit System for Controlling Emissions (in Chinese: 控制污染物排放许可制实施方案的通知 国办发〔2016〕81号), 10 November 2016.
State Council, Administrative Regulation on Emissions Permitting (in Chinese: 排污许可管理条例), 9 December 2020.
Sun, Y. (2014). How to improve and implement the pollution discharge license system (in Chinese: 如何完善落实排污许可制度). *Environmental Protection, 42*(14), 17.
Sun, Y. (2016). Environmental permit system: history, challenges and proposals (in Chinese: 排污许可制度:立法回顾、问题分析与方案建议). *Environmental Impact Assessment, 38*(2), 1.
Technical specifications for applications for and issuance of emissions permits. https://www.mee.gov.cn/ywgz/fgbz/bz/bzwb/pwxk/. Assessed 7 Jan 2022.
Tian, Q., & Huang, B. (2014). Study on the total pollutant control system in China (in Chinese: 我国污染物总量控制制度探讨). *Environmental Protection, 20*.
Wang, C. (2016). The legal validity of environmental criteria: Theory review and new trend in practice (in Chinese: 环境标准的法律效力:问题梳理及实践动向). *Academic Journal of Zhongzhou, 11*.
Wang, H. (2015). The Chinese legal system. In T. Qin (Eds.), *Research Handbook on Chinese environmental law*. Edward Elgar.
Wang, J. (2018). *Environmental law* (in Chinese: 环境法学). Peking University Press.
Wang, J. (2021). Establishment and innovation of China's environmental codification: A study based on China's civil codification (in Chinese: 论中国环境法典框架体系的构建和创新——以中国民法典框架体系为鉴). *Contemporary Law Review, 35*(06).
Wang, L., & Wang, R. (2017). Technical specifications for application and issuance of emissions permits (in Chinese: 排污许可证申请与核发技术规范). In X. Zhu et al. (Eds.), *200 Questions and answers about the implementation of legislation on emissions permitting* (in Chinese: 排污许可法律适用200问). China Environmental Science Press.
Wang, S. (2020). Linking EIA and emission permits: Practice development and rule reconstruction' (in Chinese: 环评与排污许可制度衔接的实践展开与规则重构). *Journal of Political Science and Law, 5*.
Wang, S. (2022). On the construction of China's carbon assessment system (in Chinese: 论我国碳评价制度的构建). *Northern Legal Science, 16*(02).
Wang, X. (2019). People's Republic of China. In E. Lees & J. E. Viñuales (Eds.), *The Oxford handbook of comparative environmental law*. Oxford University Press.
Wang, X., & Lu, K. (2017). *Environmental law in China*. Wolters Kluwer.
Wang, Y. (2021). To establish an integrated 'EIA-pollution discharge permit-law enforcement' eco-environmental management system: emphasis, difficulties and framework (in Chinese: 建立"

环评—许可—执法"一体化生态环境管理体系:重点、难点与体系设计). *Environment and Sustainable Development, 46*(01).

Wang, Y., Wang, Y., et al. (2020). Permit items through negotiation in the pollutant discharge permit system' (in Chinese: 排污许可制度中"协商式"管理案例研究). *China Population, Resources and Environment, 30*(07).

Wu, C., & Cheng, F. (2020). The interaction and Connection between EIA and discharge permit system–from the perspective of institutional logic and constructive suggestions (in Chinese: 论环境影响评价与排污许可制度的互动和衔接——从制度逻辑和构造建议的角度). *Journal of Beijing Institute of Technology (Social Sciences Edition), 22*(2).

Wu, J., & Chang, I. S. (2020). *Environmental management in China: Policies and institutions*. Springer Nature.

Wu, K. (2020). Legislation on protected natural reserves as a part of the environmental law system (in Chinese: 环境法系中的自然保护地立法). *Chinese Journal of Law, 42*(03).

Wu, K. (2021). Research on the systematic function of General Part of Environmental Code and its formulation (in Chinese: 论环境法典总则的体系功能与规范配置). *Law and Social Development, 27*(03).

Xia, G., Feng, D., et al. (2005). Report about situation of the permit system of pollutant discharge operation in six provinces and cities (in Chinese: 六省市排污许可证制度实施情况调研报告). *Environmental Protection, 06*.

Xu, X. (2015). The system of controlling total outcome of environmental activities (in Chinese: 论我国环境法中的总行为控制制度). *Law Science 12*.

Xu, X. (2015). Environmental quality objectives: The deliberation on environmental law built on directly regulating objective (in Chinese: 环境质量目标主义:关于环境法直接规制目标的思考). *China Legal Science, 06*.

Yang, D. (2017). The basis for experimental legislation in China—Examination of legislation for trial implementation and interim legislation (in Chinese: 我国试验立法的本位回归——以试行法和暂行法为考察对象). *Studies in Law and Business, 06*.

Yang, C. (2021). Deficiency and improvement of the energy legal system in China: from the perspective of structure-function (in Chinese: 我国能源立法体系的不足与完善——以"结构-功能"分析方法为视角). *Social Sciences in Guangxi, 04*.

Yang, J., Liu, H., & Zhang, J. (2021). Thinking on the legislation of the carbon emission trading system' (in Chinese: 关于碳排放权交易制度法治化完善的思考). *Environmental and Sustainable Development, 46*(03).

Yu, C. (2020). Problems and suggestions in the current process of pollution permit application and issuance (in Chinese: 现行排污许可证申请与核发过程中存在的问题及建议). *China Resources Comprehensive Utilization, 38*(08).

Zhai, T., & Chang, Y. C. (2018). Standing of environmental public-interest litigants in China: Evolution, obstacles and solutions. *Journal of Environmental Law, 30*(3), 369–397.

Zhang, Q. (2022). Reflection and improvement of environmental standard system in China (in Chinese: 行政组织法视角下环境标准制度的反思与完善). *02 SJTU Law Review, 86*.

Zheng, J. (2018). China updates pollutant emission permit system' China Daily, updated on 18 January 2018. http://www.chinadaily.com.cn/a/201801/18/WS5a5ff4f9a310e4ebf433e707.html. Accessed 6 Dec 2020.

Zhou, X. (2017). Reshaping of legal validity of environmental standard in liability for environmental pollution—type analysis based on the laws of environmental physics (in Chinese: 环境标准在环境污染责任中的效力重塑——基于环境物理学定律的类型化分析). *Journal of China University of Geosciences (Social Sciences Edition), 17*(01).

Zhou, X. (2021). On the establishment principles for basic systems in general provisions of environmental code (in Chinese: 论环境法典总则编基本制度的构建理路). *Journal of Soochow University (Law Edition), 8*(04).

Zhou, Y., & Zhang, G. (2015). Study on the legislative principles and procedure of the air pollutants emission standards (in Chinese: 大气污染物排放标准制定的法律原则和程序研究). *Chinese Journal of Environmental Management 7*(04).

Zhu, Q., & Wu, Y. (2020). Deficiency of low quality of EIA documents and the solution (in Chinese: 建设项目环评文件质量缺陷及其行政治理). *Jiang-huai Tribune, 03.*

Zhu, X., & Luo, J. (1991). The introduction, development and state of the licence system for the water pollutant discharge in China (in Chinese: 中国排污许可证制度的产生、发展及现状). *World Environment, 01.*

Chapter 5
Comparative Discussion and Conclusions

Abstract This chapter undertakes a comparative analysis aiming to answer the question of to what extent the regulatory design of the emissions permit system in China has similarities and differences with the EU emissions permit system. Based on the comparative analysis, this chapter discusses what sort of regulatory possibilities for or barriers to implementing an integrated permit system appearing in the EU may also be followed in China, after which the conclusion on the whole research is given.

5.1 Introduction

Based on the research presented in the previous chapter, this chapter starts by providing a comparative analysis of the EU and Chinese regulatory approaches towards establishing an integrated environmental permit. This comparative analysis is structured based on the conceptual framework developed in Chap. 2.

After this comparative analysis, the chapter proceeds with discussing what sort of regulatory possibilities for or barriers to implementing an integrated environmental permit system appearing in the EU may also take place in China. The answer to the main question will be given based on that discussion. Section 5.7 concludes with a reflection of the core findings.

The comparative analysis will be conducted in Sects. 5.2–5.5 of this chapter by exploring the following sub-questions:

Section 5.2 examines to what extent substantive integration as developed by the Administrative Regulation on Emissions Permitting shows similarities and differences with that developed by the Industrial Emissions Directive (IED). More precisely, this section addresses the following questions:

> Question 1: in view of the scope of integration, to what extent does the scope of environmental issues subject to the emissions permit system as developed by the Administrative Regulation on Emissions Permitting show similarities and differences with that developed by the IED? (Sect. 2.1).

X. Chen, *Towards an Integrated Environmental Permit in China*,
https://doi.org/10.1007/978-981-97-5188-4_5

Question 2: in view of the environmental effectiveness of integration, to what extent does the level of environmental quality as a whole required by the Administrative Regulation on Emissions Permitting show similarities and differences with that developed by the IED? (Sect. 2.2).

Question 3: in view of the incommensurability of environmental goods, to what extent do the options to make environmental trade-offs adopted by the Administrative Regulation on Emissions Permitting show similarities and differences with those adopted by the IED? (Sect. 2.3).

Sections 5.3, 5.4, and 5.5 then discuss the following questions respectively:

Question 4: to what extent does the procedural integration as developed by the Administrative Regulation on Emissions Permitting show similarities and differences with that developed by the IED? (Sect. 5.3).

Question 5: to what extent does the organizational integration as developed by the Administrative Regulation on Emissions Permitting show similarities and differences with that developed by the IED? (Sect. 5.4).

Question 6: to what extent does the interaction between the emissions permit system and the market-based instruments required by the Administrative Regulation on Emissions Permitting show similarities and differences with that required by the IED? (Sect. 5.5).

On the basis of the insights gained, Sect. 5.6 will provide an in-depth discussion on the regulatory possibilities for or barriers to implementing an integrated environmental permit system that appears in the EU also in China, and then Sect. 5.7 concludes the whole research.

5.2 Comparison of Substantive Integration

Theoretically, there are three focal points of analysis regarding substantive integration, namely the scope of integration, the environmental effectiveness of integration, and the approaches to addressing the incommensurability of environmental goods.[1] This section examines to what extent substantive integration as developed by the Administrative Regulation on Emissions Permitting show similarities and differences with that developed by the IED. Specifically, Sect. 2.1 discusses, in view of the scope of integration, to what extent the scope of environmental issues subject to the emissions permit system as developed by the Administrative Regulation on Emissions Permitting shows similarities and differences with that developed by the IED. Section 2.2 analyzes, in view of the environmental effectiveness of integration, to what extent the level of environmental quality as a whole required by the Administrative Regulation on Emissions Permitting shows similarities and differences with that developed by the IED. In view of the incommensurability of environmental goods,

[1] See Sect. 2.3.1 of Chap. 2.

Sect. 2.3 addresses to what extent the options for environmental trade-offs adopted by the Administrative Regulation on Emissions Permitting shows similarities and differences with those adopted by the IED.

5.2.1 Comparison of the Scope of Integration

The scope of integration refers to what environmental elements and their interrelationships would be integrated in legislation and then permit decisions.[2] Different scopes can be established by the legislators: integration in a narrow sense would seek to find the optimal balance for addressing the emissions into different environmental medias and integration in a broad sense would consider other environmental impacts, such as the use of energy and resources.[3] An ambitious integrated approach, by means of applying a broad scope, may encounter many difficulties when put into practice and thus, for the purpose of implementation, it is necessary to find the right scope of integration in relation to what can be achieved in a particular area at a particular time.[4] This sub-section discusses, from the perspective of the scope of integration, to what extent the scope of environmental issues subject to the emissions permit system as developed by the Administrative Regulation on Emissions Permitting shows similarities and differences with that developed by the IED.

5.2.1.1 The Scope of Integration Under the EU Emissions Permitting

In the EU, the IED is aimed at 'integrated prevention and control of pollution arising from industrial activities', 'in order to achieve a high level of protection of the environment taken as a whole.'[5] This aim, from the perspective of the scope of integration, can be interpreted in a narrow sense and a broad sense.[6] In the narrow sense, the objective of the IED focuses on pollution control, basically covering emissions into the air, water, and land.[7] In the broad sense, the objective of the IED addresses the protection of the environment taken as a whole, which may imply a broader scope of environmental issues to be integrated rather than that just addressing pollution control alone.[8] Meanwhile, the examination of the rules for the application for the permit as laid down by the IED shows that the IED requires a relatively wide scope of environmental issues to be included in the application for the permit, addressing

[2] See Sect. 2.3.1.1 of Chap. 2.

[3] Ibid.

[4] Ibid.

[5] IED art 1.

[6] See Sect. 3.3.1.1 of Chap. 3.

[7] See Sect. 3.3.1.1.1 of Chap. 3.

[8] See Sect. 3.3.1.1.2 of Chap. 3.

not just emissions, but also other environmental elements, such as the use or generation of raw materials and the use of energy.[9] By prescribing a wide scope of the contents of the permit application, the IED aims to encourage operators to consider their environmental performance in an integrated manner in the design of its industrial activities, but whether and to what extent these rules indeed stimulate operators to carry out integrated environmental management is not yet empirically tested.[10] In addition, the IED requires that the contents of permit conditions have to comply with the requirements of general principles governing the basic obligations of the operator, which address a relatively wide scope of environmental issues—not just emissions but also the use of energy.[11] However, the IED does not include the reasonable use of resources in the basic obligations of the operators, and thus it can be questioned to what extent the reasonable use of resources can be integrated into the emissions permit.[12] Moreover, the IED prescribes that the permit conditions have to be set based on the BAT. The rules on the BAT indicate that the scope of an integrated approach as required by the IED does not only address emissions, but also other environmental impacts on the environment as a whole, including consumption of raw materials, water consumption, use of energy, and generation of waste.[13] Hence, given the observations above, it can be concluded that the detailed rules of the IED indicate a broad interpretation of the scope of integration, since they address not just emissions but also other environmental issues.

Nonetheless, specifically for greenhouse gases, legal challenges exist to impose emission limit values for these gases in the emissions permit, thus it is questionable whether and to what extent the reduction of GHGs covered by the ETS market-based instrument can be integrated into the emissions permit instrument as prescribed by the IED.[14]

Hence, the objective of the IED does not clearly define the concrete scope of integration, and the detailed rules need to be interpreted to find out how narrow or broad the scope is. By investigating the detailed rules as laid down by the IED, it can be derived that the scope of environmental issues subject to the IED permit system addresses not just emissions but also other environmental issues, such as the use of energy and resources. Meanwhile, the imposition of emission limit values specifically for GHGs that are covered by the ETS market-based instrument in the IED emissions permit would risk legal challenges, which may hinder these GHGs from being integrated into the emissions permit instrument as prescribed by the IED.

---

[9] See Sect. 3.4.1 of Chap. 3.

[10] Ibid.

[11] See Sect. 3.6 of Chap. 3.

[12] Ibid.

[13] See Sect. 3.7 of Chap. 3.

[14] See Sect. 3.9.1 of Chap. 3.

5.2.1.2 The Scope of Integration Under China's Emissions Permitting

In China, the objective of the Administrative Regulation on Emissions Permitting—to control emissions to protect and to improve the environment—is formulated in a vague manner without giving precise instructions as to the scope of integration.[15] Furthermore, the Administrative Regulation on Emissions Permitting establishes criteria for classifying entities subject to emissions permitting into two types: (1) entities that produce a relatively substantial quantity of emissions, or have significant environmental impacts should be subject to key management; (2) entities that produce a relatively small quantity of emissions or have mild environmental impacts should be subject to simplified management.[16] However, there is no further explanation on what accounts for a relatively substantial or small quantity of emissions, or significant or mild environmental impacts.[17]

Since the objective of the Administrative Regulation on Emissions Permitting does not give precise instructions, the scope of integration as pursued by the Administrative Regulation on Emissions Permitting should be derived from its legal basis: the legislation at the higher level, namely the laws including the Environmental Protection Law, the Administrative Permit Law, and a set of sectoral laws on pollution control that prescribe permit instrument for controlling emissions.[18] By investigating the legal basis for establishing the Administrative Regulation on Emissions Permitting, it is clear that the scope of emissions permitting as prescribed by the Administrative Regulation on Emissions Permitting at least covers emissions into water, soil, air and marine environment, as well as pollution caused by industrial solid waste and industrial noise.[19] In terms of the other environmental issues, it was found that the use of water, and the use of energy are not integrated into the emissions permit.[20] There are other environmental issues that are not regulated explicitly by the laws, such as GHG emissions, and it is possible to subject these environmental issues to emissions permitting if it is explicitly required by the Administrative Regulation on Emissions Permitting.[21] Therefore, the scope of integration as pursued by the Administrative Regulation on Emissions Permitting should also be derived from its detailed rules.

The examination of the rules on the application for a permit in Sect. 4.5 of Chap. 4 shows that a relatively broad scope of environmental information must be collected by operators applying for an emissions permit, addressing not just emissions, but also other environmental relevant elements, such as the use of raw materials. Although the rules on the application for a permit concern a relatively broad scope of environmental issues, the rules on setting permit conditions only address emissions.[22]

---

[15] See Sect. 4.4.2 of Chap. 4.

[16] See Sect. 4.4.2 of Chap. 4.

[17] Ibid.

[18] See Sect. 4.4.2 of Chap. 4.

[19] See Sect. 4.4.2.1 of Chap. 4.

[20] See Sect. 4.4.2.2 of Chap. 4.

[21] See Sect. 4.4.2.3 of Chap. 4.

[22] See Sect. 4.7 of Chap. 4.

Although it is possible to subject GHG emissions to emissions permitting, the Administrative Regulation on Emissions Permitting does not provide such a clear requirement. Nevertheless, it can be expected that GHG emissions would be considered in emissions permitting through the coordination with EIA permitting.[23]

Hence, the objective of the Administrative Regulation on Emissions Permitting does not provide for a concrete scope of integration. By investigating its legal basis and the detailed rules as laid down in this Administrative Regulation, it was found that the scope of environmental issues subject to the emissions permit system is clear to some extent, at least concerning emissions into the air, soil water and marine environment,, as well as pollution caused by industrial solid waste and industrial noise. Concerning the other environmental issues, the use of water, and the use of energy are not integrated into the emissions permit. In addition, it is possible to subject GHG emissions to the emissions permit, but uncertainty remains, since the Administrative Regulation on Emissions Permitting does not provide a clear requirement.

5.2.1.3 Comparative Analysis

From the above analysis, the answer to question 1 is: neither the objective of the IED nor the objective of the Administrative Regulation on Emissions Permitting clearly defines the scope of integration to be achieved, and thus the scope of integration should be derived from the detailed rules and other relevant legislation. Both of the emissions permit systems at least cover the emissions into the air, water, and land, while the IED emissions permit system covers a relatively broad scope of environmental issues, not just emissions, but also other environmental issues, such as the use of energy. The imposition of emission limit values for GHGs that are covered by the ETS market-based instrument in the IED emissions permit would risk legal challenges and thus may hinder these GHGs from being integrated into the IED emissions permitting, while the integration of GHG emissions into the China's emissions permit seems to be more possible, although this is not explicitly regulated.

---

[23] According to the rules on setting emissions permit conditions as prescribed by the Administrative Regulation on Emissions Permitting, emissions permit conditions consist of the decisions made through various other environmental regulatory instruments, such as EIA permitting. This shows the coordination mechanism is established by the Administrative Regulation on Emissions Permitting, which will be further discussed in view of procedural integration in Sect. 5.3 of this chapter.

5.2.2 *Comparison of the Environmental Effectiveness of Integration*

The environmental effectiveness of integration refers to a certain level of environmental quality as a whole to be achieved.[24] Due to the incommensurability of environmental goods, according to the current legal literature, there is no single benchmark or criterion possible to measure the achievement of a certain level of protection of the environment as a whole, and thus only a certain scope of substantive integration can be assessed in terms of the environmental effectiveness through media-specific environmental quality standards.[25] In view of the environmental effectiveness of integration, this sub-section discusses to what extent the level of environmental quality as a whole required by the Administrative Regulation on Emissions Permitting shows similarities and differences with that developed by the IED.

5.2.2.1 The Environmental Effectiveness of Integration Under EU Emissions Permitting

In the EU, the objective of the IED is to 'achieve a high level of protection of the environment taken as a whole'.[26] This objective indicates that the lowest level of protection of the environment taken as a whole is not allowed, while the highest possible level of the environment taken as a whole is not required (in light of the possibility for Member States to adopt stricter measures).[27] Meanwhile, the IED also requires concrete levels of protection for specific environmental media to be achieved with the emissions permit by suggesting that stricter measures have to be included in the permit if this is required in order to achieve environmental quality standards adopted in other EU legislation.[28] However, it is not clear in what case an environmental quality standard requires stricter conditions, nor is clear what additional measures shall be included in the permit to attain the environmental quality standards.[29]

Hence, the IED aims to 'achieve a high level of protection of the environment taken as a whole', which indicates that the lowest level of protection of the environment taken as a whole is not allowed, while the highest possible level of the environment taken as a whole is not required. Meanwhile, concrete levels of environmental quality for specific media (established as environmental quality standards in Union law) are required to be achieved with the emissions permit by the IED. However, the rules on

[24] See Sect. 2.3.1.2 of Chap. 2.

[25] Ibid.

[26] IED art 1.

[27] See Sect. 3.3.1.2 of Chap. 3.

[28] See Sect. 3.8 of Chap. 3.

[29] Ibid.

how to attain these environmental quality standards using emissions permitting are formulated in a relatively vague manner.

5.2.2.2 The Environmental Effectiveness of Integration Under China's Emissions Permitting

In China, while the objective of the Administrative Regulation on Emissions Permitting—to control emissions to protect and to improve the environment—is hollow, its drafting history indicates that the legislator intended to establish an emissions permit system to pursue a certain level of environmental quality.[30] Moreover, the Administrative Regulation on Emissions Permitting requires concrete levels of protection for specific environmental media to be achieved with the emissions permit by suggesting that additional measures, namely the special requirements for improving environmental quality provided by the local people's governments, have to be included in the permit if they are required in order to attain national environmental quality standards.[31] However, no further concrete rules are provided by the legislation in China in terms of how the local people's governments should formulate the special requirements to reach national environmental quality standards.[32] Meanwhile, the EIA permit conditions and the emission standards are required to be considered by permitting authorities in setting emissions permit conditions.[33] By investigating the rules on EIA permitting and the rules on emission standards, the attainment of national or provincial environmental quality standards must be considered in setting EIA permit conditions and in setting emission standards,[34] but these relevant rules are also formulated in a vague manner.[35]

Hence, although the objective of the Administrative Regulation on Emissions Permitting—to control emissions to protect and to improve the environment—is hollow, without giving precise instructions as to the environmental effectiveness of integration, the achievement of concrete levels of environmental quality for specific media (established as environmental quality standards) are required by the Administrative Regulation on Emissions Permitting. However, the rules on how to achieve these environmental quality standards are formulated in a relatively vague manner.

---

[30] See Sect. 4.4 of Chap. 4.

[31] See Sect. 4.7.5.3 of Chap. 4.

[32] Ibid.

[33] See Sect. 4.7.2 of Chap. 4. This shows the coordination mechanism is established by the Administrative Regulation on Emissions Permitting, which will be discussed further in view of procedural integration in Sect. 5.3 of this chapter.

[34] See Sects. 4.7.3 and 4.7.4 of Chap. 4.

[35] Ibid.

5.2.2.3 Comparative Analysis

From the above analysis, the answer to question 2 is: both the IED and the Administrative Regulation on Emissions Permitting require the concrete levels of environmental quality for specific media (established as environmental quality standards) to be achieved using the emissions permit. However, neither the IED nor the Administrative Regulation on Emissions Permitting lays down clear rules on how to attain these environmental quality standards through the emissions permit.

5.2.3 Comparison of the Options for Environmental Trade-Offs

In view of the incommensurability of environmental goods, this sub-section delves into the question to what extent the options for environmental trade-offs adopted by the Administrative Regulation on Emissions Permitting show similarities and differences with those adopted by the IED. Theoretically, there are two options for environmental trade-offs: the generic option, which addresses several decision situations of the same kind and weighs and balances prospective environmental and other effects in a generic and abstract way, resulting in generic trade-offs which apply to all defined cases;[36] and the case-specific option, which is concerned only with the effects of a single case and results in case-specific trade-offs.[37]

5.2.3.1 The Options for Environmental Trade-Offs Under EU Emissions Permitting

In the EU, the rationale for the concept of BAT prescribed by the IED is to deal with the incommensurability of environmental goods by providing a common basis where environmental impacts on different environmental media can be weighed.[38] The rules on the BAT for setting permit conditions indicate that a combined use of a generic approach and a case-specific approach is adopted by the IED. The generic approach is mainly indicated by the mandatory status of the EU generic BAT documents as well as the Union-wide minimum requirements for emission limit values as prescribed in the Annexes to the IED.[39] The EU generic BAT documents include the BREFs and the BAT conclusions.[40] The BREFs need to be developed on the basis of an information exchange between Member States, industries, Environmental NGOs, and

---

[36] See Sect. 2.3.1.3 of Chap. 2.

[37] Ibid.

[38] See Sect. 3.7.2 of Chap. 3.

[39] See Sects. 3.7.4 and 3.7.6 of Chap. 3.

[40] See Sect. 3.7.4 of Chap. 3.

the Commission,[41] and the BREFs serve as the basis for establishing BAT conclusions through the comitology.[42] The BAT conclusions shall be the reference for setting the permit conditions, and particularly, in setting emission limit values in the permit, the permitting authorities have to ensure that emissions levels as described in the BAT conclusions are not exceeded.[43] The minimum emission limit values have to be adopted or amended on the basis of the integrated approach and the BAT through the legislative procedure at the EU level.[44]

Meanwhile, Member States have various degrees of flexibility in the application of generic BAT conclusions in setting permit conditions, which results in some of these generic requirements indicative to some extent and thus leaves room for case-specific decision-making by permitting authorities. Specifically, a small degree of flexibility is given to Member States in the application of BAT conclusions in setting emission limit values in the permits by the relatively wide range of the generic BAT associated emission levels;[45] the provisions allowing emission limit values different from the generic BAT associated emission levels;[46] the provision allowing emission limit values stricter than the generic BAT associated emission levels;[47] and the provisions allowing a derogation from the generic BAT associated emission levels.[48] In addition, a substantial degree of flexibility is available given that there are no clear rules on how to apply BAT conclusions in setting permit conditions for regulating environmental issues other than emissions.[49] In the cases where no generic requirement exists, more flexibility is available.[50]

Hence, in view of the incommensurability of environmental goods, a combined use of a generic approach and a case-specific approach is adopted by the IED to make environmental trade-offs. The generic approach is indicated by the mandatory status of the EU generic BAT documents as well as the Union-wide minimum requirements for emission limit values as prescribed in the Annexes to the IED. The adoption of a case-specific approach is indicated by various degrees of flexibility provided to Member States and, more particularly, the competent authority in setting permit conditions on the basis of the BAT.

---

41 See Sect. 3.7.4.2.1 of Chap. 3.

42 See Sect. 3.7.4.2.2 of Chap. 3.

43 See Sect. 3.7.4 of Chap. 3.

44 See Sect. 3.7.6 of Chap. 3.

45 See Sect. 3.7.4.3.1 of Chap. 3.

46 See Sect. 3.7.4.3.2 of Chap. 3.

47 See Sect. 3.7.5.1 of Chap. 3.

48 See Sect. 3.7.4.3.3 of Chap. 3.

49 See Sect. 3.7.4.4 of Chap. 3.

50 See Sect. 3.7.5.2 of Chap. 3.

5.2.3.2 The Options for Environmental Trade-Offs Under China's Emissions Permitting

In China, the basis for setting permit conditions can be classified into at least two types. First, the emission standards, the technical specifications for applications for and issuance of emissions permits, and the guidance on available techniques are generic requirements.[51] These documents are established at the national level or at the provincial level for defined industries or activities, among which the requirements as set in the guidance on available techniques are indicative and the others are binding. No derogation from the binding generic requirements is allowed by the Administrative Regulation on Emissions Permitting.[52] The rules on setting emissions permit conditions on the basis of these generic requirements indicate that a generic approach to environmental trade-offs is adopted by the Administrative Regulation on Emissions Permitting. However, while the emission standards are clear, serving as minimum requirements for emissions control,[53] the generic technical specifications for applications for and issuance of emissions permits, rather than clearly setting a certain emission limit value, provide that the emission levels should be set in the permit on the basis of national or provincial emission standards, water and air emission benchmarks, and the scale of production.[54] This means that, in the application of these technical specifications, the permitting authorities need to make case-specific decisions.[55] In addition, the rules on how these generic requirements have to be set by the environmental ministry or the provincial people's governments are too general. From this perspective, it is not clear how various environmental impacts have to be weighed in the generic way by the competent authorities.

Second, the requirements of emissions control as set out in the EIA permits can be classified as case-specific requirements, since these requirements are set in the specific situations for which a permit is applied for.[56] Most of the rules on EIA permitting are formulated in a relatively vague manner, and thus there is flexibility for the competent authorities in setting the EIA permit conditions, which makes case-specific decisions possible from the perspective of integration.[57] Meanwhile, generic emission standards are also used in setting EIA permit conditions, which makes the requirements as set out in the EIA permits less case-specific.[58] In addition, as already mentioned above, it was also found that some generic requirements set in the technical specifications for applications for and issuance of emissions permits

[51] The rules on emission standards, the rules on technical specifications for applications for and issuance of emissions permits and the rules on guidance on available techniques for the setting of emissions permit conditions are discussed in Sects. 4.7.4, 4.7.5.1 and 4.7.5.4 of Chap. 4 respectively.

[52] See Sect. 4.7.2 of Chap. 4.

[53] See Sect. 4.7.4 of Chap. 4.

[54] See Sect. 4.7.5.1 of Chap. 4.

[55] Ibid.

[56] Section 4.7.3 of Chap. 4.

[57] Section 4.7.3.1.3 of Chap. 4.

[58] Ibid.

contain uncertainties, which require the permitting authorities to make case-specific decisions. Furthermore, there are only vague rules on setting the total allowable quantities of emissions, and thus there is flexibility for the permitting authorities, which also makes case-specific decisions possible from the perspective of integration.[59] Hence, in view of the incommensurability of environmental goods, a combined use of a generic approach and a case-specific approach is adopted by the Administrative Regulation on Emissions Permitting to make environmental trade-offs.

5.2.3.3 Comparative Analysis

From the above analysis, the answer to question 3 is: in view of the incommensurability of environmental goods, both the IED and the Administrative Regulation on Emissions Permitting adopt a combined use of a generic approach and a case-specific approach to environmental trade-offs. In particular, both the IED and the Administrative Regulation on Emissions Permitting establish the case-specific approach by providing for flexibility, however, this is mainly done based on vague rules[60] addressed to decentralized authorities.

5.3 Comparison of Procedural Integration

Theoretically, there are two approaches to procedural integration: firstly, full procedural integration refers to incorporating various regulatory subjects exclusively into one procedure; and secondly, in the case where various separate procedures for each decision subject exist, a coordination mechanism can be established in order to achieve coherence between decisions that are made in various procedures.[61] This section examines to what extent procedural integration as developed by the Administrative Regulation on Emissions Permitting shows similarities and differences with that developed by the IED.

5.3.1 Procedural Integration Under EU Emissions Permitting

In the EU, according to the rules on granting emissions permits under the IED, Member States are not required to establish one procedure, and where more than one procedure exists, Member States shall establish a full coordination mechanism

[59] Section 4.7.5.2 of Chap. 4.

[60] Giving the flexibility afforded to decentralized authorities for case-specific weighing may also lead to not choosing the best solution for a high level of environmental protection. For a further discussion, see Sect. 5.6.1.3 of this chapter.

[61] See Sect. 2.3.2 of Chap. 2.

to implement an integrated approach.[62] However, the IED does not provide further concrete provisions on how the coordination mechanism should be established, and thus there is flexibility for the Member States.[63]

In addition, the provisions of the IED that allow information produced in response to sectoral Directives, including EIA Directive and Seveso Directive, to be used in the applications for permits also serve as a coordination tool from the perspective of procedural integration.[64] Moreover, the IED prescribes that the relevant information produced in response to the EIA Directive has to be examined and used in the decision on the emissions permit, which can be interpreted as a requirement of coordination between the EIA procedure and the IED permit procedure.[65] However, the IED does not provide a further concrete explanation on what accounts for relevant EIA information, and thus there is flexibility for the Member States.[66] The EIA Directive suggests the so-called 'one-stop-shop' approach to achieve procedural integration: to establish a coordinated procedure and/or joint procedure.[67] However, to adopt the 'one-stop-shop' approach is an option for Member States, not an obligation. Hence, in view of procedural integration, the IED does not require one procedure to be established, but it requires Member States to establish a coordination mechanism for implementing an integrated approach where more than one procedure exists. Meanwhile, the IED establishes coordination with other directives, particularly the EIA Directive. However, since the rules on coordination as laid down by the IED are formulated in a vague manner, it can be questioned how these rules truly require procedural integration through coordination.

5.3.2 Procedural Integration Under China's Emissions Permitting

In China, one permit procedure covering various emissions is adopted by the Administrative Regulation on Emissions Permitting.[68] Meanwhile, the coordination mechanism is adopted in the Administrative Regulation on Emissions Permitting, which can be illustrated by the rules requiring the EIA permits, the emission standards, and the total allowable quantities of emissions to be submitted for the applications for emissions permits,[69] as well as by the rules on setting permit conditions on the basis of decisions made through various other environmental regulatory instruments, including EIA permitting, emission standards, technical specifications for

62 See Sect. 3.5.1 of Chap. 3.

63 Ibid.

64 See Sect. 3.4.2 of Chap. 3.

65 See Sect. 3.5.2 of Chap. 3.

66 Ibid.

67 Ibid.

68 See Sect. 4.6 of Chap. 4.

69 See Sect. 5.5 of this chapter.

applications for and issuance of emissions permits, total emission control, and local instruments for achieving environmental quality standards.[70] However, the Administrative Regulation on Emissions Permitting does not require full coordination but only addresses emissions: even though other environmental protection measures addressing ecological issues are explicitly required in setting EIA permit conditions, they are not required to be considered in setting emissions permit conditions.[71] The Administrative Regulation on Emissions Permitting does not provide further concrete rules on how to coordinate the permit conditions on emissions control derived from the various decisions made through different procedures.[72]

Hence, from the perspective of procedural integration, the Administrative Regulation on Emissions Permitting establishes one procedure covering various emissions, but it also requires coordination with other regulatory instruments. However, full coordination is not required by the Administrative Regulation on Emissions Permitting, since it provides for a limited scope of coordination only addressing emissions.

5.3.3 Comparative Analysis

From the above analysis, the answer to question 4 is: while the IED does not require Member States to establish one procedure for issuing the permit, the Administrative Regulation on Emissions Permitting establishes one permit procedure covering various emissions. In addition, both the IED and the Administrative Regulation on Emissions Permitting prescribe the coordination mechanism for implementing procedural integration. The IED prescribes full coordination where more than one procedure exists, but the relevant rules are formulated vaguely and thus it can be questioned how these rules truly require procedural integration through coordination. In China, the coordination with other regulatory instruments is required by the Administrative Regulation on Emissions Permitting, but the scope of coordination only addresses emissions. Thus, on procedural integration, few similarities can be identified between the EU and China's emissions permit systems. Compared to the IED, since the Administrative Regulation on Emissions Permitting provides for relatively clear rules on procedural integration, at least clearly establishing a single permit procedure that regulates various emissions, a relatively high degree of procedural integration is provided for under China's emissions permit system.[73]

[70] See Sect. 4.7 of Chap. 4.

[71] See Sect. 4.7.3.3 of Chap. 4.

[72] See Sect. 4.7.2 of Chap. 4.

[73] For a further discussion, see Sect. 6.2 of this chapter.

5.4 Comparison of Organizational Integration

Theoretically, a low number of authorities involved in the process of decision-making and a clear competence structure indicate a high degree of organizational integration.[74] This section examines to what extent the organizational integration as developed by the Administrative Regulation on Emissions Permitting shows similarities and differences with that developed by the IED.

The answer to question 5 can be short: while the IED does not provide rules on organizational arrangements given the subsidiarity principle in EU law,[75] the Administrative Regulation on Emissions Permitting has established a single authority responsible for issuing emissions permits.[76] Thus, no similarity can be identified on this issue between the two emissions permit systems in the EU and China. Compared to the EU emissions permit system, a relatively high degree of organizational integration is provided for under China's emissions permit system.[77]

5.5 Comparison of the Interaction Between the Permit System and the Market-Based Instruments from the Perspective of Integration

Theoretically, there may be challenges applying the permit instrument and market-based instruments to pollution control from the perspective of an integrated approach.[78] This section examines to what extent the interaction between the emissions permit system and the market-based instruments required by the Administrative Regulation on Emissions Permitting shows similarities and differences with that required by the IED.

5.5.1 The Interaction Between IED Emissions Permitting and Market-Based Instruments for Pollution Control

In view of the interaction between the IED emissions permit and market-based instruments for pollution control, the IED to some extent overlaps with the ETS Directive and the NEC Directive.[79] While the IED provides for a permit instrument to control emissions, the ETS Directive provides for an emission trading system for a

---

[74] See Sect. 2.3.3 of Chap. 2.

[75] See Sects. 3.1.2 and 3.5.1 of chapter 3.

[76] See Sect. 4.6 of Chap. 4.

[77] For a further discussion, see Sect. 5.6.3 of this chapter.

[78] See Sect. 2.4 of Chap. 2.

[79] See Sect. 3.9 of Chap. 3.

set of GHGs.[80] The ETS Directive requires coordination between the GHGs emission permit and the permit provided in the IED, but it does not provide for any further concrete explanation on how to achieve the coordination.[81] Meanwhile, the imposition of emission limit values for GHGs in the emissions permit would risk legal challenges, and thus it is questionable whether or to what extent the GHGs covered by the ETS market-based instrument can be integrated into the emissions permit instrument as prescribed by the IED.[82]

The NEC Directive leaves it up to Member States to choose instruments to control the emissions of five pollutants, but it does not clearly prescribe how the integrated emissions permit instrument as pursued by the IED would have to interact with the other instruments for emissions control measures taken by Member States, in particular the market-based instruments.[83] Hence, it is not entirely clear how the EU emissions permit system has to interact with the market-based instruments for pollution control from the perspective of integration, but it is at least clear that there are legal challenges of integrating the GHGs covered by the ETS market-based instrument into the emissions permit instrument as prescribed by the IED.

5.5.2 The Interaction Between Emissions Permitting and Market-Based Instruments for Pollution Control in China

In China, the Administrative Regulation on Emissions Permitting does not provide any rules on how the emissions permit system should interact with the market-based instruments (including tax instrument and trading instrument) for pollution control.[84] Hence, it is not clear how the emissions permit system as established by the Administrative Regulation on Emissions Permitting has to interact with the market-based instruments for pollution control from the perspective of integration. In other words, there is no explicit regulatory provision addressing the interaction between the permit instrument and the market-based instrument for pollution control stimulating or hindering an integrated approach.

5.5.3 Comparative Analysis

From the above analysis, the answer to question 6 is: under the IED, it is not entirely clear how emissions permitting has to interact with the market-based instruments

[80] See Sect. 3.9.1 of Chap. 3.

[81] Ibid.

[82] Ibid.

[83] See Sect. 3.9.2 of Chap. 3.

[84] See Sects. 4.7.3.3 and 4.7.5.4 of Chap. 4.

for pollution control from the perspective of integration, but it is at least clear that there are legal challenges of integrating the GHGs covered by the ETS market-based instrument into the emissions permit instrument as prescribed by the IED. In China, there are no rules on how the emissions permit system should interact with the market-based instruments for pollution control provided by the Administrative Regulation on Emissions Permitting. Hence, few similarities between the EU and China's emissions permit systems can be identified in view of the challenges of applying both the permit instrument and market-based instruments to pollution control. Compared to the EU emissions permit system, it seems more possible to integrate GHG emissions into the China's emissions permits, although this is not explicitly regulated.[85]

5.6 Discussion on the Findings

Following the above comparative analysis on the EU and China's emissions permit systems, which in fact also provided a concluding summary of the research undertaken in this book, this section provides an in-depth discussion on what sort of regulatory possibilities for or barriers to implementing an integrated permit system appearing in the EU may also take place in China.

5.6.1 Discussion from the Perspective of Substantive Integration

5.6.1.1 Discussion on the Scope of Integration

From the perspective of substantive integration, neither the IED nor the Administrative Regulation on Emissions Permitting clearly defines the scope of integration to be achieved, but it is at least clear that both emissions permit systems cover emissions into the air, water, and land and thus present possibilities for controlling emissions into the air, water, and land in an integrated way. While the IED emissions permit system covers a relatively broad scope of environmental issues, not just emissions, but also other environmental issues, such as the use of energy, China's emissions permit system does not explicitly address environmental issues other than emissions, and even legally eliminates the scope of an integrated approach to addressing some environmental issues, such as the use of water and energy.[86] While the imposition of emission limit values for the GHGs that are covered by the ETS market-based instrument in the IED emissions permit would risk legal challenges, and thus may hinder these GHGs from being integrated into the IED emissions permitting, no

[85] Also see Sect. 5.2.1 of this chapter.

[86] See Sect. 5.2.1 of this chapter.

similar legal risk can be found in China's emissions permit system.[87] Thus, the integration of GHG emissions in China's emissions permits seems more possible, but uncertainty remains, since this is not explicitly regulated.[88]

5.6.1.2 Discussion on the Environmental Effectiveness of Integration

Both the IED and the Administrative Regulation on Emissions Permitting require concrete levels of environmental quality to be attained for specific media (established as the environmental quality standards) to be considered in setting permit conditions, which present regulatory opportunities towards the environmental effectiveness of integration. However, neither the IED nor the Administrative Regulation on Emissions Permitting lay down clear rules on how to achieve these environmental quality standards with the emissions permit instrument. From this perspective, it can be questioned whether these vague provisions regarding environmental quality standards truly require the environmental effectiveness of integration in the sense of concrete levels of environmental quality for specific media to be achieved. In other words, these rules are too general to ensure environmental effectiveness of integration will be realized. The implementation of the IED shows that, in practice, although the emission levels associated with the generic best available technique are not always sufficient to achieve environmental quality standards, few cases of applying stricter permit conditions on the basis of the IED rules on environmental quality standards have been reported.[89] Thus, it is not evident that the EU emissions permit system, on the basis of the vague rules regarding environmental quality standards, can ensure that the environmental effectiveness of integration will be realized. In this vein, since the rules on environmental quality standards under the China's emissions permit system are also vague, whether or to what extent the environmental effectiveness of integration will be achieved by China's emissions permit system is also questionable.

5.6.1.3 Discussion on the Options for Environmental Trade-Offs

The way in which various environmental issues must be weighed in the permit decision can also define the scope and the environmental effectiveness of integration. Both the IED and the Administrative Regulation on Emissions Permitting adopt a set of generic binding requirements that indicate a generic approach to environmental trade-offs. Both of the systems also provide the flexibility for the permitting authorities, which allows for case-specific environmental trade-offs. With the EU regulatory experiences in practice, it seems that the implementation of generic requirements

[87] Ibid. Also see Sect. 5.3 of this chapter.

[88] Ibid.

[89] See Sect. 3.8 of Chap. 3.

provides for more possibilities for the environmental effectiveness of integration—hence a high level of environmental protection—than flexibility. The implementation of the IED shows that, with regard to emissions control, where Member States enjoy less flexibility due to the relatively clear binding generic requirements, it is obvious that the implementation of the IED has resulted in effective outcomes,[90] while for the non-emissions aspect, where Member States enjoy more flexibility, there is very little information available on what impact the IED may have had in relation to, for example, energy, water, and material use, as well as waste generation.[91] In particular, in some Member States, the requirements of BAT conclusions other than emission levels are even interpreted as being non-binding and thus they are not included in the permit.[92] This shows that, compared to the BAT-associated emission levels, other environmental conditions as specified in BAT conclusions are given a relatively weak legal weight in national practice, thus indicating a relatively narrow scope of integration in practice. While there is flexibility in setting emission limit values in the permits, the implementation of the IED shows that instead of varied emission limit values across Member States, emission limit values are largely set towards the least stringent end of the ranges of emission levels associated with BAT as described in BAT conclusions. This is considered an under-delivery of emissions reductions.[93] In addition, few cases of applying stricter permit conditions based on the IED provision of allowing stricter emission limit values than the generic BAT associated emission levels can be found in practice.[94] It was found that permitting authorities may not have enough capacity to develop case-specific BAT in practice and, as a result, they tend to make use of generic BAT conclusions as 'a tempting refuge' from applying BAT locally.[95] Hence, according to the EU regulatory experiences in practice, allowing for flexibility on the basis of vague rules for case-specific trade-offs may also lead to permitting authorities not choosing the best environmental protection. In this vein, it can be questioned whether or to what extent the vague rules in the Administrative Regulation on Emissions Permitting, that also imply a lot of flexibility for the Chinese emissions permitting authorities, can provide for possibilities of case-specific decision-making that can serve optimal decisions for a high level of environmental protection. In practice, it was found that the Chinese permitting authorities usually lack sufficient cognitive capabilities and resources to make effective case-specific decisions.[96] This shows that the emissions permitting authorities in China are faced with similar regulatory challenges as those in the EU. Hence, it can be inferred that the flexibility afforded because of the vague rules available for emissions permitting authorities in China would not necessarily guarantee case-specific decision applying the best solution for a high level of environmental protection.

---

[90] See Sect. 3.7.4.4 of Chap. 3.

[91] Ibid. Also see Sect. 3.7.5.2 of Chap. 3.

[92] See Sect. 3.7.4.4 of Chap. 3.

[93] See Sect. 3.7.4.3.1 of Chap. 3.

[94] See Sect. 3.7.5.1 of Chap. 3.

[95] Ibid. The wording of 'a tempting refuge' is borrowed from Maria Lee (2014), 120.

[96] See Sect. 4.7.5.1 of Chap. 4.

Nevertheless, the implementation of the IED in practice also shows that an absolute binding generic option is not favourable, since some cases have shown that flexibility is used for case-specific decision-making, considering cross-media effects.[97] In other words, abandoning the flexible approach—the discretion to adopt a case-specific decision—would obviously have a disadvantage that an integrated approach for individual industries situated at a specific location cannot be reached. In this vein, since no derogation from the binding generic requirements is allowed by the Administrative Regulation on Emissions Permitting,[98] the binding generic requirements, particularly the emission standards serving as the minimum requirements for emissions control, as provided by the Administrative Regulation on Emissions Permitting, would legally eliminate the choice of an integrated approach in case-specific situations, particularly given the fact that, in practice, there are generic emission standards that are too stringent to be achieved with regard to the specific technical conditions.[99]

In this regard, a better manner to combine the use of a generic approach and a flexible approach for case-specific decision-making needs to be explored without compromising the level of environmental protection. With the regulatory experience in the EU, it seems that the manner of prescribing relatively concrete mandatory generic requirements but allowing derogation on the basis of specific conditions provides for more possibilities for the environmental effectiveness of integration than the manner of only prescribing vague rules.[100] Therefore, rather than formulating vague rules that can be risky for achieving sufficient level of environmental protection, other regulatory approaches, such as prescribing concrete mandatory generic requirements with a derogation clause, should also be explored by the Chinese legislator. Nevertheless, it is also noted that to adopt concrete rules may also be faced with great obstacles. One concern is that in the legislative process of the IED, it can usually be seen that even though more concrete provisions were proposed, they were finally rejected.[101] There is also a tradition in China that 'rough rules are more suitable than detailed rules'.[102]

5.6.2 *Discussion from the Perspective of Procedural Integration*

From the perspective of procedural integration, few similarities between the EU and China's emissions permit systems can be identified.[103] Compared to the IED that provides for vague rules on procedural integration, the Administrative Regulation

[97] See Sect. 3.7.4.3.3 of Chap. 3.

[98] See Sect. 4.7.2 of Chap. 4.

[99] See Sect. 4.7.4.1 of Chap. 4.

[100] See Sects. 3.7.4.4 and 3.7.5.2 of Chap. 3.

[101] See Sects. 3.5.1 and 3.7.6 of Chap. 3.

[102] See Sect. 4.2.5 of Chap. 4 and also see Gong (2016), 114.

[103] See Sect. 5.3.3 of this chapter.

on Emissions Permitting provides for relatively clear rules on procedural integration—at least it clearly establishes a single permit procedure that regulates various emissions.[104] Theoretically, effective procedural integration of the permit system is a prerequisite for the substantive integration of permit decisions.[105] In this vein, compared to the EU emissions permit system, China's emissions permit system may provide a better prerequisite for the substantive integration of permit decisions. Nevertheless, it is noted that the procedural integration, concerning the form of permit decisions, does not necessarily indicate that substantive integration will be achieved.[106]

5.6.3 Discussion from the Perspective of Organizational Integration

From the perspective of organizational integration, there is no similarity between the two emissions permit systems in the EU and China.[107] While the IED does not provide rules for an organizational arrangement, given the subsidiarity principle in EU law, the Administrative Regulation on Emissions Permitting has established a single authority responsible for issuing emissions permits.[108] Thus, compared to the EU emissions permit system, a relatively high degree of organizational integration is required in China's emissions permit system.[109]

Similar to procedural integration, theoretically, effective organizational integration of the permit system is a prerequisite for the substantive integration of permit decisions, but it does not necessarily guarantee that substantive integration will be achieved. For example, even with a relatively high degree of organizational integration, the Chinese permitting authorities would still be faced with the legal barrier caused by the generic binding emission standards that hinder their choice for an integrated approach in case-specific situations.[110]

[104] See Sects. 5.3 and 5.4 of this chapter.

[105] See Sect. 2.5.3 of Chap. 2.

[106] See Sect. 2.3.2 of Chap. 2.

[107] See Sect. 5.4 of this chapter.

[108] Ibid.

[109] Ibid.

[110] See Sect. 5.6.1.3 of this chapter.

5.6.4 *Discussion in View of the Interaction Between the Permit Instrument and Market-Based Instruments for Pollution Control*

There are challenges of applying both the permit instrument and market-based instruments to pollution control. The IED prohibits the imposition of emission limit values for GHGs, which poses a legal barrier, or at the least a legal risk, if GHG emissions covered by the ETS market-based instrument will be integrated into the emissions permit instrument at the national level.[111] No such prohibition for imposing emission limit values for GHGs is prescribed by the Administrative Regulation on Emissions Permitting,[112] and therefore the integration of GHG emissions in China's emissions permit seems more possible, but uncertainty remains, since this is not explicitly regulated.[113]

5.7 Conclusion Regarding the Main Research Question

In order to combat the hydra-headed ogre of pollution, the legal framework that attempts to implement integrated pollution prevention and control using the permit instrument was adopted in 1996 at EU level and in 2020 in China, twenty-four years later. Based on the above analysis, this section provides a conclusion regarding the main research question: to what extent the regulatory design of the emissions permit system in China, considering the EU regulatory experiences towards integration and seen from the perspective of the specific Chinese situation, provides possibilities for or barriers to the implementation of integrated pollution prevention and control.

From the perspective of substantive integration, the emissions permit system in China presents regulatory possibilities for controlling emissions into the air, water, and land in an integrated manner. Furthermore, the integration of GHG emissions in China's emissions permit also seems possible, but uncertainty remains, since this is not explicitly regulated. With regard to the environmental effectiveness of integration, the Administrative Regulation on Emissions Permitting requires the achievement of concrete levels of environmental quality for specific media (established as environmental quality standards) to be considered in setting permit conditions, which presents regulatory possibilities for the environmental effectiveness of integration. However, these rules that require environmental quality standards to be achieved are formulated in a vague manner. Considering the regulatory experiences with the emissions permit system established in the EU (it is not evident that this EU emissions permit system, given the vague rules regarding environmental quality standards,

[111] See Sect. 5.1 of this chapter.

[112] As already mentioned in Sect. 5.2 of this chapter, the Administrative Regulation on Emissions Permitting does not provide for a rule on how the emissions permit system has to interact with market-based instruments for pollution control.

[113] Also see Sect. 5.6.1.1 of this Chapter.

guarantees the environmental effectiveness of integration to be achieved), it is questionable whether or to what extent the vague rules under the China's emissions permit system will ensure the environmental effectiveness of integration.

Regarding options for environmental trade-offs, China's emissions permit system provides for a set of generic binding requirements at the national and provincial levels that establish a generic approach to environmental trade-offs. It also affords flexibility for the permitting authorities that allows case-specific environmental trade-offs. With the EU regulatory experiences, allowing for flexibility on the basis of the vague rules for case-specific trade-offs may also lead to the permitting authorities not choosing the best solution for a high level of environmental protection. In addition, given the fact that the emissions permitting authorities in China are faced with insufficient knowledge, skills, and resources, it can be inferred that the flexibility given to emissions permitting authorities on the basis of the vague rules in China would not necessarily guarantee case-specific integrated decision-making. Nevertheless, the EU regulatory experiences also show that an absolute binding generic option is not favourable, since it would obviously have a disadvantage that an integrated approach for individual industries situated at a specific location cannot be reached. Since no derogation from the binding generic requirements is allowed by the Administrative Regulation on Emissions Permitting, these binding generic requirements, particularly the emission standards, would legally eliminate the choice for an integrated approach in case-specific situations. This is hence an important barrier to an integrated approach being achieved using the emissions permit instrument. In this regard, a better manner for combining mandatory generic requirements and the flexibility for case-specific permitting decisions should be further explored in China.

From the perspective of procedural and organizational integration, compared to the EU emissions permit system established by the IED, since the Administrative Regulation on Emissions Permitting provides for relatively clear rules that establish a single permit procedure regulating various emissions by a single authority, a relatively high degree of procedural integration and organizational integration is provided for under China's emissions permit system. Thus, China's emissions permit system may provide for a better prerequisite for the substantive integration of permit decisions, but the absolute generic approach (particularly indicated by the generic emission standards) that hinders case-specific decision-making is an important barrier. Indeed, procedural integration and organizational integration do not necessarily indicate that substantive integration will be achieved. The introduction of more opportunities for case-specific decision-making in a proper way[114] would enhance the possibilities for an integrated approach.

Finally, there is no rule on how the emissions permit system should interact with market-based instruments for pollution control in the Administrative Regulation on Emissions Permitting in China. In other words, there is no explicit regulatory provision addressing the interaction between the permit instrument and the market-based instrument for pollution control stimulating or hindering an integrated approach

[114] As already mentioned above, flexibility for emissions permitting authorities based on the vague rules is not a perfect way to provide opportunities for case-specific trade-offs.

under the China's emissions permit system. In this sense, there is formally no barrier to integrating GHG emissions in the emissions permit, but the possibility for a broader scope of integration that covers GHG emissions in the emissions permit should be further clarified by the Chinese legislator.

In summary, China's emissions permit system, which establishes a single permit procedure regulating emissions into the air, water, and land by a single authority in the manner of a combined use of a generic approach and a case-specific approach to environmental trade-offs, has taken a major step towards an integrated approach, but some challenges still exist. The rules that require concrete levels of environmental quality to be achieved for specific media with the emissions permit system are vague and thus will not necessarily ensure the environmental effectiveness of integration. Furthermore, the vague rules that give flexibility for case-specific trade-offs may also lead to permitting authorities not choosing the best solution for a high level of environmental protection. Binding generic requirements, particularly the emission standards serving as the minimum requirements for emissions control under China's emissions permit system, would legally eliminate the choice of an integrated approach in case-specific situations. In this regard, more opportunities for case-specific decision-making need to be explored without compromising the level of environmental protection. It will be important to follow up on these challenges by examining how the implementation of the current emissions permit system will be undertaken in practice and to what extent an improvement of the regulatory framework is necessary.

SPRINGER NATURE

GPSR Compliance

The European Union's (EU) General Product Safety Regulation (GPSR) is a set of rules that requires consumer products to be safe and our obligations to ensure this.

If you have any concerns about our products, you can contact us on ProductSafety@springernature.com

In case Publisher is established outside the EU, the EU authorized representative is:

Springer Nature Customer Service Center GmbH
Europaplatz 3
69115 Heidelberg, Germany

The manufacturer's authorised representative in the EU is Springer Nature Customer Service Centre GmbH, Europaplatz 3, 69115 Heidelberg, Germany. If you have any concerns regarding our products, please contact ProductSafety@springernature.com

Printed and bound by CPI Group (UK) Ltd, Croydon, CR0 4YY
01/10/2026
02225849-0003